CHOCOLATE AND CUCKOO CLOCKS

CHOCOLATE AND CUCKOO CLOCKS

THE ESSENTIAL
ALAN COREN

EDITED AND INTRODUCED BY
GILES COREN AND VICTORIA COREN

CANONGATE
Edinburgh · London · New York · Melbourne

First published in Great Britain in 2008 by
Canongate Books Ltd, 14 High Street,
Edinburgh EH1 1TE

1

British Library Cataloguing-in-Publication Data
A catalogue record for this book is available on request from the British Library

ISBN 978 1 84767 320 6

Typeset by Palimpsest Book Production Ltd, Grangemouth, Stirlingshire

Printed and bound in the UK by CPI Mackays, Chatham ME5 8TD

This book is printed on FSC certified paper

www.meetatthegate.com

'Since both Switzerland's national products, snow and chocolate, melt, the cuckoo clock was invented solely in order to give tourists something solid to remember it by.'

Alan Coren

Contents

The Cricklewood Years: 1990–1999

The Last Decade: 2000–2007

Foreword

by Giles and Victoria Coren

Giles: So who's going to write the introduction?

Victoria: I thought we were doing it together.

G: I don't know. I've never written with anyone else. He never wrote with anyone else.

V: It's not that hard. One person types, the other one paces . . .

G: And how do we refer to him? If it's a serious essay, making a case for his inclusion in the canon, he ought to be referred to as 'Coren'. But that would be weird, coming from us.

V: Well, we can't write 'Our father'. That sounds like God. 'Daddy?' We can't call him Daddy. That's just embarrassing.

G: Maybe it would be better if someone else wrote it. If we do it, it looks like vanity publishing. Any old twonk can die and have his children bind up his writing and say it's great. Maybe we should ask an academic to do the introduction, to give it some gravitas.

V: He'd like an academic. For a long time he thought he was going to be one, after all. He spent those two years at Yale and Berkeley on the Commonwealth Fellowship.

G: And there was post-grad at Oxford before he went. And his First was a serious First. I think maybe even the top one in the year. He got the Violet Vaughan Morgan scholarship.

V: I always confused that with his medal for ballroom dancing.

G: No no, that was just called 'the junior bronze'.

V: Do you think he'd have enjoyed being an academic?

G: Probably, but I don't think his students would have enjoyed failing their exams because all they had at the end of term was a lot of jokes about Flaubert's haemorrhoids, and an ability to write parodies of Trollope as spoken by two dustmen from Croydon.

V: He was brilliant, though. It's a rare man who can go on a panel game and work an argument about the exact dates of the Augustan period in English literature into the middle of a John Wayne impression.

G: He was happier doing it in the middle of a John Wayne impression. Remember how he used the phrase '*homme sérieux*', with a little flounce of the heel? He thought the very idea of a serious person was somehow preposterous.

V: He could have made a wonderful tutor in the 1960s, when it was about infusing students with a love of literature, rather than the rigours of critical theory.

G: But he had a short attention span. That's also why he never wrote a novel. He had ideas for novels, but they were always flashy ideas with a great first sentence. He could never quite be bothered to sit down and write them.

V: Let's not get an academic to write the introduction. We've got serious people introducing each decade anyway.

G: Serious like Victoria Wood, do you mean? Or serious like Stephen Fry?

V: They're serious comedians. And Clive James is a heavyweight.

G: And A.A. Gill spells his name with initials, which is the *sine qua non* of academia. That's better than being a Regius professor. T.S. Eliot, A.J.P. Taylor, F.R. Leavis, A.C. Bradley . . .

V: P.T. Barnum.

G: We still need someone for the 1960s.

V: The four people doing the later decades have written 'appreciations' of someone who was already quite established by then. They're brilliant pieces. But for the 60s, it would be nice to have someone who knew him really well personally, when he was young.

G: Uncle Gus?

V: I was thinking more of Melvyn Bragg. They were at Wadham together, they've been friends ever since – and if you asked most British people to name an academic, they'd probably say Melvyn Bragg anyway. Or Peter Ustinov.

G: Melvyn is a big name. And he does carry intellectual weight. But he won't get the bums on seats at readings in Borehamwood and Elstree like Uncle Gus would.

V: I'm asking Melvyn. And I think we should do the main introduction ourselves. So what shall we write in it?

G: Well, if we were going to treat him as a serious writer, we'd start with the Saul Bellow stuff. The lower-middle-class Jewish home in Southgate. Osidge Primary. East Barnet Grammar. The inspirational English teacher, Ann Brooks, who encouraged him to join the library and start reading. Growing up in the war. The mother who was a hairdresser. The father who was a . . . what was Grandpa Sam exactly? A plumber?

V: That's what they said. I think it's just that he had a spanner. He was an odd job man really. I also heard he was a debt collector.

G: And I heard Great Grandpa Harry was a circus strongman, but I doubt it was true. Harry was born in Poland in 1885 and left in 1903 before the pogroms started. A smart man is what he was.

V: Sam and Martha dreamed of Daddy being articled to a solicitor, didn't they? That's the other reason he loved Miss Brooks, because she went round to the house and persuaded them that he should apply to Oxford instead.

G: God, a solicitor. He'd have been so miserable. And, of course, nepotism being what it is, we'd have ended up solicitors as well. And then we'd have been really miserable too.

V: You *are* really miserable.

G: So then he went off to Oxford. And there was that first morning when he came downstairs in his digs and the landlady had cooked bacon and eggs . . .

V: He always called it 'egg and bacon' . . .

G: . . . she says with Talmudic precision, of the kind which crumbled in 1957 when he took the first forkful. And that was the beginning of the end, really, for all things Jewish.

V: He was always sentimental about Jews though.

G: He was always sentimental about everything. Like America.

V: He loved Yale and Berkeley . . . Do you think he ever actually wanted to be a don, or was he just so happy as a student that he wanted it to go on longer? Going to Oxford transformed his life.

G: Yes, but people know about all that. Not necessarily about him, but about that generation of 1950s grammar-school boys – the Alan Bennetts, the Melvyn Braggs, the Dennis Potters – that brief window between two educational Dark Ages, when a certain kind of lower-middle-class boy got a chance, went to Oxford and had a crack at the Establishment. That's the irony of the antagonism between *Punch* and *Private Eye* later in the '60s . . .

V: Exactly. *Private Eye* tried to mock *Punch* for being fuddy-duddy and Establishment, but *Punch* was run by the working-class boys, the grammar-school boys, the revolutionaries, while *Private Eye* was a bunch of right-wing, privileged public-school boys, sons of diplomats, who looked down on the staff of *Punch* because they thought they were common. And, in Daddy's case, Jewish. In public, *Private Eye* pilloried them for being Establishment, in private Barry Fantoni was telling everyone: 'Alan Coren looks and sounds like a cab driver.'

G: Which is why cab drivers liked him so much.

V: The Establishment is one of the things Daddy was sentimental about. He was so proud to feel part of it. And of Englishness – Keats, Shakespeare, churches, rolling hills, striding through the New Forest in a tweed cap, slashing at the ferns with a shooting stick. He actually enjoyed horseriding. And he was strangely good at it. Despite his grandfather having come over from Poland, he really did feel part of all that.

G: His proudest moment was meeting the Queen. Closely followed by meeting Princess Margaret. Closely followed by meeting Andrew and Fergie. He loved a royal. Almost as much as he loved a punctual postman.

V: But we were talking about America. He was so dazzled by it. All those hamburgers and giant steaks after the austerity of '50s Britain. And better cars. And the literature, all those garish 1960s paperbacks of *Augie March* and *On The Road*. He started sending pieces to *Punch* from there, and they offered him a job so he chucked in the academic plans, came home and went to work in Fleet Street. El Vino's, *Punch* lunches, Toby Club dinners, fellow writers, the old *Punch* table, the line of editors going back to 1841, he loved it all.

G: It was strange reading back through those first pieces from the 1960s. The fledgling him. You can see what was coming in a piece like 'It Tolls For Thee', a domestic comedy about trying to get a phone installed. But the writing is politically engaged, he was still taking things seriously – like racism in 'Through A Glass, Darkly' and the bombing of North Vietnam in 'The House That Jack Built'. He flips them around and makes his own sorts of jokes, but they developed out of a genuine concern for civil rights and social issues of the time – in a way that he left behind by the 1970s, when it started to be all about the jokes.

V: He hadn't decided not to be a novelist yet. If he ever decided that. But he hadn't even decided not to be a serious writer. He wasn't completely a humorist, in the '60s.

G: He was already doing the Hemingway parodies though. 'This Thing With The Lions', that was his first one.

V: How many Hemingway parodies are we going to put in the book, by the way?

G: Any fewer than thirty would be unrepresentative. But it might skew things a bit.

V: He must have written a Hemingway parody a year.

G: Let's have a couple. The book will be full of parodies anyway – Chaucer, Coleridge, Kafka, Conan Doyle, Melville, a lot of Melville – they're some of the most enduring pieces. They work in an anthology. All jokes need a context, and the context of the parodies is, to some extent, eternal. They're not dependent on immediate social or political or cultural context. Humorous writing doesn't last as long as serious – look at Shakespeare's comedies compared to the tragedies. Or *Carry On* films compared to . . . well, almost anything. Lots of Daddy's pieces are still very funny, but the parodies all are. The passage of time doesn't do the same damage to a literary pastiche as it does to a joke about the 1964 general election. We need to use the stuff which still works. He was so proud to be compared to James Thurber and S.J. Perelman – but who reads Thurber and Perelman now?

V: That's all very well, but I see you've put two *Winnie the Pooh* parodies on the list. Do we need two?

G: But which would you remove – 'The Hell At Pooh Corner', or 'The Pooh Also Rises'?

V: Isn't 'The Pooh Also Rises' a double parody of Pooh *and* Hemingway? We don't want to make his frame of reference seem limited.

G: But we must include it! That one's part of a complex triptych of adult/child fictional parodies. Lose 'The Pooh Also Rises' and we lose 'Five Go Off To Elsinore'. We lose 'The Gollies Karamazov'.

V: Speaking of political relevance, what are we going to do about Idi Amin?

G: Yes. Idi Amin. That was always going to be a problem for so many reasons. The Idi Amin parodies don't operate in a timeless context like the literary ones. The Idi Amin of now isn't the one he was writing about. Daddy said himself that he wouldn't have written those pieces later, once it turned out that Amin was such a monster. In 1974, he just thought he was writing about someone funny.

V: In a funny African voice. That's the bigger problem. Even if Amin hadn't turned out to be a monster, those pieces wouldn't read the same now. 'Wot a great boom de telegram are!' 'Dis international dipperlomacy sho' payin' off!' Monster or not, if you were writing a column about Robert Mugabe, you wouldn't do him like that.

G: Tempting though it would be.

V: But I don't want anyone to think he was racist. He wasn't racist. He went on civil rights marches in America in 1961.

And his Idi Amin . . . he's not a 'generic African', he's a fully fledged character: childish, megalomaniac, charming, violent, funny. With this comedy voice – 'Ugandan' sent up no more squeamishly than if it were Cockney – but people might not read it like that.

G: Maybe we shouldn't put it in.

V: It would definitely be safer not to. But *The Bulletins Of Idi Amin* was his best-selling book ever. It sold a million copies. They made a record of it. It made him famous. It's because of the Amin books that *The Sunday Times* called him 'The funniest writer in Britain today.' Richard Ingrams ran a spoof in *Private Eye* with Daddy's picture at the top. Do you remember what that was called? 'The Bulletins of Yiddy Amin', of course. They must have cracked open the champagne when they thought of that. Anyway, the point is, those pieces make us nervous and they might give people the wrong impression of him, but I don't think we can just censor them out.

G: Hang on. Think about *Team America*, one of the best adult comedy films of modern times; a serious, anarchic, liberal and right-thinking movie. And think of the hilarious pastiche of Kim Jong-Il. He is a very decent parallel with Idi Amin, except even more powerful and even more sinister – and when Trey Parker and Matt Stone make an entire film based on his dictatorship, the centrepiece of it is his hilarious Korean accent. When Jong-Il bursts into tears and sings 'I'm So Ronery', it's pure Alan Coren. People might have been a bit squeamish about Idi Amin in the 1980s and '90s, but you only have to look at *South Park* – also created by Parker and Stone – to see that we have come back into a world where everything's fair game, and exaggerated ethnic mimicry doesn't make you a racist. I'd hate to think that future generations of *South Park* viewers would have to watch edited versions, from which Chef has been removed because not all black men sound like Isaac Hayes.

V: Maybe we could put Idi Amin in an appendix?

G: Okay, put those pieces in an appendix, at the end of the 1970s. With a perforated line down the page so people can tear them out if they want, and leave them in the shop.

V: Are we going to put anything in from the Arthur Westerns? I know they were children's books, but I think I might love them more than anything else he ever wrote.

G: I love them too. Originally Arthur was called Giles. Daddy told me the stories at bedtime and then wrote them down, and it was massively exciting, like my own version of the *Alice in Wonderland* creation myth.

V: Except without the naughty photographs.

G: But we shouldn't put them in. The books are brilliant, but they're for children. If you're compiling The Essential T.S. Eliot, you don't include *Old Possum's Book of Practical Cats*.

V: Okay, no Arthur the Kid. No Luke P. Lazarus, no cricket-playing pigs, no Seminole Gap. So will the book just have the magazine and newspaper pieces?

G: Just? What do you mean 'just'? He published twenty-six books of them. Collectively, they're twice the length of Proust. And that's only the pieces he put in books.

V: But would there be room for something that wasn't written at all? Extracts from *The News Quiz*, maybe? He became the twelfth editor of *Punch* in 1977 and that was the start of his golden age. By the 1980s he had a TV career, he was doing chat shows. Maybe we should include some transcripts of those?

G: And the commentaries from *Television Scrabble*? His *Through the Keyhole* work? Look, he was a famous person, he was a sort of celebrity, plenty of people will know him only from *Call My Bluff*. But that's not what this book is about. It's about what will endure of his writing. Let's just have the writing.

V: I wish he had written a novel. Actually, what I really wish is that he had written an autobiography. He had that great idea for writing one based on all the cars he ever drove . . . it would have been so good.

G: The 1990s would have been the time for that sort of writing. He left *Punch* in '88 and all of that Fleet Street romance – cricket in the corridor, drunken lunches, contributors carving their names in the *Punch* table, Sheridan Morley, Miles Kington, Basil Boothroyd, Bill Tidy, Bywater, royal visitors – it all came to an end. It had got too businesslike, he was summoned to too many meetings with people who wore grey suits and talked about revenue streams. He edited *The Listener* for a year and then he came home to write.

V: He wrote the *Times* column twice a week, and talked a lot about novels and the autobiography without actually doing them.

G: I tried to persuade him. If he was that good at writing sentences, I thought he would write a very good novel. But he didn't think the two things necessarily went together – he always said that his old pal Jeffrey Archer could write novels but he couldn't write sentences.

V: I think that was just an excuse. He was never going to get much work done once he came home. Part of the problem was that he had such a happy marriage. He famously never went out for drinks after *The News Quiz* because he was always in such a hurry to get back home to her and eat veal schnitzel together in front of the TV. Once he was working from home, he got all involved with the domestic routine. He always had an ear cocked for Mummy's key in the door. He was much happier helping her unload Waitrose bags than sitting at the computer trying to write.

G: And the writing was all about Cricklewood. That strange Cricklewood of his own invention, which didn't really exist. Except for the domestic frustrations – gas men turning up late, junk mail, plants dying when he went on holiday, tiles falling off the roof, 'narmean' – that was all a comic version of his very genuine obsessions.

V: And he did it brilliantly. The American influence, the youthful inspiration he took from civil rights and political stories, disappeared from the writing, and it became a very British sort of comedy – small things, silly things. Herons, hearing aids, hosepipe bans, talking parrots, QPR fans arguing at cheese counters. He was a master of all that.

G: It's funny to use a word like 'master' in the context of a writer whose work was so ostensibly superficial, so entirely motivated by humour. It's usually the boring ones who get called that. As a writer you want to move people, or at best 'affect' them in some way, and for him the easiest way, the only way, was to make them laugh. He got hundreds and hundreds of letters from *Times* readers, far more, I'm sure, than any of the 'serious' writers. They loved him, and they needed to tell him that.

V: I think they loved him because his comedy was so warm, it reflected a charming and optimistic and kindly vision of the world. And it was ambitious, even if it was only a thousand words long, or half an hour on the radio. It's easy to get a laugh from being nasty or from being philistine, but he didn't do that. He never hid the fact that he was clever, and he never got a cheap laugh at someone's expense – if it was at someone's expense, it was a fair target and cleverly done – but he was always funny, and that's really hard for twenty minutes, never mind a lifetime.

G: I read one obituary of him, a not especially kind one by a man who always bore a grudge, that suggested the old man's prose did not achieve the rank of 'greatness' because he put nothing of himself into his writing – and, at the same time as being annoyed at something negative being said about him, I had to sort of agree with that, at least partly. He was not a seeker after truth in his writing, he was a seeker after laughs. He would also never have dreamed of suggesting he was a major literary figure – the idea would have struck him as laughable. He found the truth a bore, he hated opinions, he distrusted earnestness. His pieces were a flag-wave designed to distract people from the horrors and the tedium of real life and also, in a way, to distract them from looking too closely at him. So you wouldn't really expect him to lay himself bare in there. But then again, reading all his stuff again for this book, I was struck by how much of himself he was including subconsciously: so much of the humour, for example, derives from a sense of impending domestic disaster: something being spilled, a great mess everywhere, things being lost, maps being misread, planes being missed, pipes freezing, children screaming, people being bitten by dogs . . . and you and I both know what a stickler for order and tidiness and planning he was – and how all these sorts of little domestic mishaps in fact drove him round the bend so that he wasted a lot of energy worrying about them. But then in his pieces, for forty-odd years, he was making out like he found it all terribly funny. That's a man's soul informing his writing if ever anything was.

V: He would have written a great piece about his funeral. It was rich with potential catastrophe – if he'd been there to plan it, the worry would have killed him. But the various strange details all fell into place, and they were perfect. The Cricklewood churchyard that he loved because a ventriloquist is buried there with his puppet. And so is Marie Lloyd – we've got his piece about it somewhere in the 1990s section. The rabbi who didn't mind coming to a churchyard – who advised us, in fact, to 'drop this prayer, it's a bit God-heavy'. The cantor who sang a mournful Hebrew song, and then came out to Sandi Toksvig. The moment when Uncle Andrew misread the map, looked in the wrong part of the cemetery and said: 'We've got a disaster on our hands – *they've forgotten to dig a hole.*' It was like an Alan Coren piece being acted out by accident. And it worked: it reflected everything. The sentimentality about Judaism with its gefilte fish balls and anxious tailors . . . and the sentimentality about England's green slopes and church spires . . . with some lovable, fallible, funny human characters in the middle. If we'd only had an Austin Healy with a copy of *Gatsby* and a hamburger on the front seat, it would have ticked every box.

G: Speaking of ticking boxes, we still have to write the introduction.

V: We haven't decided which one of us will type and which will pace . . .

G: We could just leave it as dialogue.

V: Mightn't that look a bit lazy?

G: No, no, people will think it was our plan right from the beginning.

V: But then mightn't it look a bit gimmicky?

G: And thus in some way unsuitable for the introduction to an anthology of writing by Alan Coren . . .?

V: True, true.

G: Remember the introduction he wrote to that anthology of humour in the '80s? It looks like a piece of autobiography – except of course it's all nonsense, not autobiographical at all.

V: And yet at the same time, in a way, it is. Okay, it's a daft story about a man who dreams of compiling anthologies of Boer operetta lyrics. And who has a preposterous soldier father with a giant tattooed arm. But the basic narrative . . . a young man who yearns to get into publishing . . . whose physical, practical, sceptical father thinks he won't make money from it . . . the son pressing on regardless, travelling abroad . . . returning to England at twenty-two, publishing his books and working on a humorous magazine . . . It is actually Daddy's mini-life story, but with everything transformed into cartoon, like the farm hands becoming scarecrows in *The Wizard Of Oz*.

G: Do you think perhaps you're over-reading it?

V: That was a short story which he thought counted as an 'introduction' – but at least he wrote it out in paragraphs.

G: We could call ours a 'foreword'.

V: Fine. Dialogue it is, and a foreword it shall be.

G: It's not as if people have forked out twenty pounds to read a piece by us anyway, is it? It's him they want to read.

1

Present Laughter

*The introduction to an anthology of modern humour,
by Alan Coren (1982)*

Nobody who met my old man ever forgot him. The first thing you saw was the sabre scar across his head. The wound had been stitched up by a *chanteuse* who went in with the first ENSA wave at Salerno, and the only way she could work the needle without passing out was to stay drunk.

His left arm was the size of anyone else's thigh, and it was tattooed in the shape of a cabriole leg. One of his favourite party pieces was where he went out of the room and came back a couple of minutes later as a Regency card table. People still talk about that. His right arm stopped at the elbow: the rest had been left inside the turret of a Tiger tank after the lid came down, somewhere in the Ardennes Forest.

When he came back from the War, he just laughed about it, at first. But then, one night in the winter of 1945, he suddenly said:

'You're going to have to help me at the brewery, son.'

I said: 'I'm only seven, Dad.'

It was the first and only time my old man hit me. If he had hit me with the left, I should not be here now; but it was the right he threw, and being short it had neither the range nor the trajectory, but it hurt just the same when the elbow connected.

Later on, he quietened down and asked me what I intended to do with my life if I didn't want to hump barrels.

'I want to do anthologies, Dad,' I said.

He looked at me hard, with his good eye; the other one is still rolling around near El Alamein, for all I know.

'What kind of job is that for a man?' he said.

'I don't think I'm cut out for humping barrels, Dad,' I said.

He spread his arms wide; or, more accurately, one wide, one narrow.

'It doesn't have to be barrels. There'll be other wars, you could go and leave limbs about.'

I nodded.

'I thought about that, Dad. I could be a war anthologiser. A war provides wonderful opportunities, collected verses, collected letters, collected journalism, things called *A Soldier's Garland* with little bits of Shakespeare in. Did you know that Rupert Brooke's "The Soldier" has appeared in no less than one hundred and thirty-eight anthologies, Dad, nearly as often as James Thurber's "The Secret Life Of Walter Mitty"?'

He thought about this for a while.

'Is there money in it?' he said at last.

'Dear old Dad!' I said. 'An anthologiser doesn't think about money. He is pursued by a dream. He dreams of making a major contribution to gumming things together. He dreams of becoming a great literary figure like Palgrave or Quiller-Couch.'

'And how do you go about learning to anthologise, son?'

I smiled, but tolerantly.

'You can't learn it, Dad. It comes from the heart and the soul. Fifty pounds would help.'

People have asked me, three decades on, in colour supplements, on chat shows, what the major influence on my work has been. I tell them that it wasn't Frank Muir, it wasn't Philip Larkin, it wasn't even Nigel Rees or Gyles Brandreth, important though these have undeniably been: it was the day my old man took his last fifty pounds out of his wooden leg, and set me on my path.

I left school soon after that. There was nothing they could teach me that would not be better learned in the real world: the experience of felt life is what lies at the still centre of all the great anthologies. I shipped aboard a coaler on the Maracaibo rum, and I discovered what a Laskar likes to read in the still watches of the equatorial night. My first anthology, a slim volume and privately circulated, consisted of buttocks snipped from *Health and Efficiency* interlarded with Gujurati limericks and reliable Portsmouth telephone numbers. Juvenilia, perhaps, and afflicted with the sort of critical introduction that I have long since learned always goes unread, but no worse than, say, the annual *Bedside Guardian*.

Two years later, I jumped ship at Dakar, and took up with a Senegalese novelty dancer who had a tin-roofed shack down by the harbour and a brother who worked three days a week as a roach exterminator in the British Council Library. It was perhaps the most idyllic and fruitful period of my life: it was mornings of grilled breadfruit and novelty dancing on the roof overlooking the incredible azure of the Indian Ocean, and afternoons of studying the anthologies her brother would steal from the library, the absence of which, when noticed, he would attribute to the kao-kao beetle which subsisted, he said, entirely upon half-morocco.

I read everything, voraciously: I learned how anthologies worked. I divined the trick of bibliographical attribution whereby the skilled anthologiser credited the original source, rather than the previous anthology from which he himself had worked. I noticed how an expensive thin volume could be turned into a cheap fat volume by amplifying it with long sections of junk that happened to be out of copyright. I made out an invaluable list of titled paupers who could be called upon to endorse the anthologiser's choice with tiny masterpieces of prefatorial cliché, usually beginning: 'Here, indeed, are infinite riches in a little room,' and ending with a holograph signature.

The idyll could not last: there was a waterfront bar where expatriate anthologisers – they called themselves that, though few among them had ever collated anything more remarkable than privately printed regimental drinking songs, or limited-circulation pamphlets called things like *The Best of the Old Eastbournian, 1932–1938* – gathered of an evening to drink and argue recondite theories of anthological technique, and one night I had the misfortune to fall foul of a gigantic ex-Harvard quarterback who claimed to be on the point of closing a two-figure deal for his *Treasury of Mormon Prose*.

I shall not distress you with the details. When I woke up the following morning, my youthful good looks were gone, to be rapidly followed by my Senegalese paramour. Two weeks later, I left the infirmary and returned, far older than my twenty-two years, to England.

Britain, in 1960, was not at all as it had been a few scant years before. A new spirit was abroad, a harsher, grittier, more realistic spirit. It was the Age of Anger, and the whole face of English anthology had changed overnight.

Gone were the elegantly produced collections of ethereal lyrics and robust nineteenth-century narrative verse. Gone were the leatherbound volumes of India paper bearing the jewelled fragments of English prose from *A Treatise on the Astrolabe* to Hillaire Belloc on mowing.

In their place, the new race of angry young anthologisers was churning out paperback collections of bogus radicalese entitled *Whither Commitment?* and *Exercises In Existentialism* and *The Right to Know – Essays on the Obligations of*

Communicators in a Negative Environment. As for the more popular market, such classics as *A Knapsackery of Chuckles* or *A Wordsmith's Bouquet* had been thrown out in favour of *The Wit and Wisdom of MacDonald Hobley* and *Dora Gaitskell's Rugger Favourites.*

Ninety per cent of all anthological output was manufactured by the BBC, linked on the one hand to a vaguely similar broadcast, and on the other to a wide range of dangle-dollies and jocular tea-towels.

These were, in consequence, bleak years for me. My entire creative life to this point had been wasted, the art of anthology to which I had dedicated myself was no more. Not that I surrendered lightly: by day, I worked as stevedore, cocktail waiter, pump attendant, steeplejack, male model, by night I pursued my muse, working feverishly and without sleep to produce, in the space of five years, *The Connoisseur's Book of Business Poetry, The Big Book of Boer Operetta, A Nosegay of Actuarial Prose,* and, perhaps my own favourite, *We Called It Medicine: A Selection of Middlesex Hospital Correspondence Between the Wars.*

I was thrown out of every publishers in London. It was the same story everywhere, as the 1960s rolled inexorably on and television worked its equally inexorable way deeper and deeper into the culture — I was not a Face. For a new breed of anthologiser was abroad: the personality. Names like Michael Barrett, Jimmy Young, Robert and Sheridan Morley, David Frost, Antonia Fraser, Freddie Trueman, Des O'Connor, Henry Cooper and the rest, all represented the New School of English Anthology; they were household words who held the publishing world in enviable thrall.

It was upon this inescapable realisation that I finally threw in the creative sponge. I had reached that nadir which all anthologisers have at some time or another plumbed, when you feel you can never skim through a book again. Worse, my run of bearable jobs had come to an end with the installation of an automatic car-wash, and I had nowhere to turn but to a weekly humorous magazine, where I was employed to manufacture lengths of material which could be inserted in between pages of advertising in order to display them to advantage. It was, as can readily, I think, be imagined, lonely, grim and unrewarding work, relieved only by my access to a comprehensive library of published humour and the constant stream of new humorous books which paused briefly in the office of the Literary Editor before being wheeled around the corner to a Fleet Street bookseller prepared to exchange them for folding money.

I thus came to read every comic word that had ever been written. It has left me grey before my time, and I jump at the slightest sound, but it has produced one strange by-product, an effect unsettling yet at the same time curiously thrilling: when I had been convinced for the better part of two decades that every creative instinct within me had shrivelled and died back like a frostbitten rose, a glimmer of the immortal longings of my youth returned. On a chill November evening, as I huddled for warmth among the teetering piles of comedy, a tiny spark of – shall we call it – inspiration no bigger than a dog-end falling through the night flashed deep within my head and, a second later, hope blew upon it, and it glowed.

This book, then, is the result. Whether, given my time again, it would have been wiser to have spent the thirty years in humping barrels, I cannot say. I know only that it would have been a lot easier.

Southgate–San Francisco–
Fleet Street
1960–1969

MELVYN BRAGG

Introduction

When I first met Alan, he was heading for the library in the back quad at Wadham College. He was also headed, the word was, for a brilliant academic career. I still have no idea why he stopped to chat with a callow newcomer from the sticks, but I remember vividly the blast of bonhomie, the instant embrace into an unearned familiarity which turned to friendship, and the dazzle of his wit. This was Oxford on stilts.

I was quite alert to accents at the time, but Alan made it quite difficult. He had the breezy metropolitan machine gun manner, but it was already minced into a sort of Oxford ease. Not Upper but no longer WC or even LMC.

He had adopted the linguistic camouflage as immediately as he had put on the correct 1950s tweed jacket, and maybe even cavalry twills, and God help us perhaps a cravat.

Had he re-launched himself as gentleman Pip? Yes. But that was job done. Over the next decades of *Punch* lunches and the occasional posh dinners, he rested cheerfully in the berth he had made for himself so characteristically quickly, and the machine gun delivery never slowed down.

He carried his literary gifts into the columns and programmes which seduced him from scholarship, but scholarship blazes through his earliest pieces in the 1960s.

In 'Under the Influence of Literature', for instance, he

describes an awakening. One morning aged thirteen and three-quarters, he wrote to his mother: 'Please do not be alarmed but I have turned into a big black bug.' He had read Kafka, was 'in that miserable No-Man's-Land between Meccano and Sex', and was about to change heroes from Captain Marvel and Zonk to Raskolnikov and Werther.

In another early piece in the same period, in a single paragraph mocking the failure of the English to produce plausible Bohemians, he mentions more than twenty authors: 'Our seed beds have never teemed with Rimbauds and Kafkas and D'Annunzios . . . Our Bohemia is populated by civil servants, Chaucer and Spenser and Milton . . . by corpulent family men Thackeray and Dickens and Trollope . . .'

He then launches into the excesses which were to colour some of his best comic writing. 'Cowper mad among his rabbits, Swinburne, a tiny, fetishistic gnome as far from Leopold von Sacher-Masoch as water is from blood . . .'

Then he turns his guns on Wordsworth. I ducked.

It would have taken at least three years to write that up as a thesis, and another five to produce it as an academic masterwork, but an extraordinary speed of thought was Alan's great gift; the necessary tortoise pace of serious research would have driven him screaming mad. And he was blessed with what was almost a disease of humour. These two qualities gave him his take on the world.

Later, he begins to wean himself from the literary inheritance he conquered and subsumed so thoroughly. His 1970s pieces take off from a standing start, which can be seen in 'Let Us Now Phone Famous Men': Mao Tse-Tung, Kosygin, the Pope, full of Coren fantasy and phonetically convincing accents. Then there's a little masterpiece on alcohol and the artists which begins: '"Shrunk to half its proper size, leathery in consistency and greenish-blue in colour, with bean-sized nodules on its surface."Yes, readers, I am of course describing Ludwig van Beethoven's liver.'

As ever, he takes it for granted that his readers are as culturally clued up as he is, and the jokes work the better for that.

I think that what was tugging away at Alan in the 1960s was not so much academic regrets as fictional possibilities. He wanted to write novels. Perhaps he did, and didn't publish them. He was certainly sufficiently talented, inventive and energetic.

The only reason he didn't, that I can think of, is that he came to prefer the columns and the radio, which themselves became short fictions, unceasing figments of his imagination.

As a friend and someone to talk to (or more usually listen to), it never took him more than a few minutes to torpedo even the most serious conversation with wit meant to sink it.

He was one of the very few people who made me laugh out loud. He does still.

For which, old pal, much thanks.

2

No, But I Saw the Movie

Up until a very short time ago, no nation on earth enjoyed as splendid a popular Image in the United States as the English; the visiting Briton basked. And no one ever asked him actually to demonstrate those qualities on which his glory was based; he was simply required to Be. Whatever his personal appearance, whatever his character, or behaviour, or background, when he passed through a crowded room, hushes fell, beautiful women gnawed their lower lip, strong men dropped their eyes, and small boys lifted their shining faces, as to the sun. For all knew this man's inheritance. Not, necessarily, the facts of it; but this ignorance was unimportant to them. Across a thousand panoramic screens, they had seen his clouds of glory trailed, and now, encountering the Englishman in the flesh, they recognised the presence of something greater than they knew. And so they roared at jokes they did not understand, because the English Sense of Humour was a rare and precious thing, they nodded at his truisms, seeing immediately their hoary wisdom, they saw his inarticulacy as noble taciturnity amid the sounding brass; and husbands, noticing their wives' idolatrous looks, dashed in herds to their tailors to order suits made up from old army blankets, specifying the dashing trousers, flared at the knee, the cunningly asymmetrical jacket, the skilfully frayed shirtcuffs.

Americans, in that sweet not-so-long syne, knew where

respect was due. Millions of feet of celluloid had taught it them, and they had met nothing to say it was not so. They had seen the Englishmen in War, whistling dirty songs at the Japanese, escaping in guffawing droves from cretinous camp-commandants, knocking back bitter in the mess before going out with a boyish toss of the head to paste Jerry over Kent, while all the world wondered. Americans had gaped at the Miniver set, picking shrapnel out of their tea and fussing over the Young Conservatives' Picnic. In Peace, too, they had seen and doted; England was God's Little Acre, a thatch-dotted paradise of trafficless lanes where blithe spirits in veteran cars chugged from one hunt ball to another, swam in Piper-Heidsieck, watched the dawn come up over Pont Street, and spent their serious hours redecorating mews cottages. Just as Jack Hawkins had been everybody's CO, so now everybody's Daddy was Cecil Parker, and Basil Radford and Naunton Wayne were always running through the drawing-room on the way to Ascot. Between War and Peace, there were Times Of Stress, when the British, played by John Mills disguised as Richard Todd, or vice versa, tightened their belts, stiffened their lips, chased the natives out of the rubber, and went back to their airmail copies of the *Telegraph*. The Common Folk, of course, were a splendid bunch. In War, they died uncomplainingly like flies, sat in the ruins of their homes and told uproarious Cockney stories, and, adrift in a lifeboat with Noel Coward, were never at a loss for a spirited song. When Peace came, they all went back to being chauffeurs, bus-conductors, publicans, comic burglars, bank clerks, and Stanley Holloway. They were deliriously happy.

When I first came to America, this image still hadn't changed much. True, a backward glance from New York towards the horizon might have caught those little fistshaped clouds forming, but it was some time before the first cans of Truth were unloaded on the docks. At first, it was easy to argue my

way out of American suspicion. 'Look Back In Anger'? 'Room
At The Top'? Flashes in the pan, I said. I would laugh nervously.
Alarmist minorities, I said. But when the new wave of British
filmmaking broke across this continent and swamped Old
Albion in its scummy tide, I knew I was beaten. For, worst
of all, it hit at a time when some of the facts of English life
were finally filtering through to the average American; word
was out that the garlands were showing a tendency to wither
on the brow, and the films provided the clincher. America
knows. Over the last few months, San Francisco cinemas have
shown: 'Saturday Night And Sunday Morning', 'The
Entertainer', 'A Taste Of Honey', 'The Long And The Short
And The Tall', 'Sons And Lovers', 'The Loneliness Of The
Long Distance Runner', 'Term Of Trial' and 'A Kind Of
Loving'. In succession; to packed houses; and against the
background of *Time*'s articles on the decline of Britain, and
Mr. Acheson's penetrating twang.

Now, I'm not complaining. I'm delighted, Lord knows, that
English filmmen are at last making films. I can hold up my
head among the cognescenti. But not among the masses. And
this overnight switch of Image is hard to bear. Now these
Americans who once looked on me with awe, look with
derision, or pity, or revulsion. If they bother to look at all.
For they know the Truth. They know that I was born in a
narrow street, in a scrofulous terraced hovel, to a withered old
mother of twenty-four, her delivery screams drowned by the
roar of the machine-shop/pit disaster. As a child, I stumbled
wretchedly about in a pall of silicotic filth, unaware of the
sun, occasionally catching a dim glimpse of my father, an
emaciated creature in long underwear and a cloth cap, as he
was dragged home, stewed to the gills on dole-money, from
the local thieves' kitchen. I never had much of an education,
due to long absences from my hellish school after regular
beatings by me mum's fancy-man (tattersall waistcoat,

moustache, Vauxhall), and weekend jaunts to drizzleswept boarding-houses with the nubile milk-monitor in 5A. However, the educational problem was easily solved by sending me: (a) to Borstal, where I was thrashed by the staff, humiliated by Etonians, and ostracised by my fellows, or (b) to a bicycle factory where I got my kicks from dropping dead rats (with which England is bubonically overrun) into the packed lunches, or (c) – if I was a girl – down to the waterfront to watch the boats. A short time later, sex reared the ugliest head outside a Hammer Film; due to the constant presence of drunks in underwear mashing tea all over the hovel, I pursued love's young dream in bus-shelters, grimy cinemas, on canal-banks, behind bill-boards, and so on. My partners in the great awakening were diverse; every American schoolboy knows that I have: (a) Gone to bed with the foreman's wife and got her pregnant, (b) Gone to bed with the blonde from the typists' pool and got her pregnant, (c) Gone to bed with one of the sailors and got myself pregnant. This is the new Time Of Stress, and acting in the new True British Fashion, I faced the problem squarely by: (a) Nipping off to my auntie, the cheery abortionist, (b) Marrying the girl and promising her a life of loveless squalor, (c) Playing house with a young homosexual and waiting for the Day.

But suppose I managed to survive this *jeunesse dorée*; what then? Well, I might have gone into showbiz, and, living the glamorous life of a matinée idol in Bootle summer stock, entered my senior years without (from sheer luck) having got anyone pregnant, and with the comfy recognition that I was merely an alcoholic failure. Alternatively, had I gone into a respectable profession like teaching, I would have got all the plums the other fellows got (penury, frustration, domestic disaster, social rejection) simply by giving private lessons to a little girl to keep myself from the workhouse. Naturally, there was justice in all this – if I hadn't been a dirty pacifist, and had gone off to Burma to whistle with the rest of the lads, I could have landed a job in a public school. Mind you, I mightn't have got a look-in on the whistling routine; the Americans now know that I should have wound up in a grass hut with six typical British chaps, beating the living hell out of a senile Japanese until his mates turned up to square the odds and give us what we deserved.

Nevertheless, though I have been passing these last months with all the misery of an ad-man watching the Truth knock the stuffing out of a beloved Image, it wasn't until last night that I actually broke and ran. The cinema that had been responsible for most of the punishment suddenly interrupted its run of English films to show an American low-budget movie, called 'David And Lisa', and since this took as its subject two young inmates of a mental hospital, I went along with glee at the prospect of having the ball in my court for a rare hour or so. The manager smiled at me in the lobby.

'Hi there!' he said. 'Just in time for the short subject. You'll like it. It's an English documentary.'

'Splendid!' I said, with a touch of the old panache. After all, I was safe enough. It was probably a Pathé Pictorial, one of those delightfully exportable Technicolor furbelows full of Cotswold centenarians, and Chelsea Pensioners who've made the Brighton Pavilion out of matchsticks. I sat down. The lights dimmed. And onto the screen, in several shades of grey, came Waterloo Station, wrapped up by Edward Anstey and John Schlesinger in a package called 'Terminus'. Leaden-faced people milled about in the gritty air; a small boy sat on a battered trunk, and howled; queues of people moaned about trains that had left ages before, and failed to arrive. I pulled up my coatcollar. I heard the familiar dark laughter breaking out around me. And when a party of convicts appeared and shuffled into a carriage labelled: 'HOME OFFICE PARTY', I stood up slowly, mumbled; 'Excuse me' in a deep southern accent, and left. The manager was still in the lobby.

'Where're you going?' he said. 'You'll miss "Terminus".'

'You're wrong,' I said. 'I've been there before. It's where I get off.'

He looked at me. 'You British and your sense of humour,' he said, unsmiling. 'Personally, I never went for it. But, by God, I guess you need it, huh?'

'Yes,' I said. 'I guess we do.'

3

Through a Glass, Darkly

The man who owned the papershop came out onto the pavement and watched me copying down addresses from his board. He didn't say anything; he had been studying me from inside the shop for a long time; I'd seen his eyes in the slit between the halfdrawn blind and the Coca-Cola sign.

I took down half a dozen names and numbers and closed my notebook. He stepped forward.

'Excuse me,' he said, a little hesitantly. He was a short, tubby, midfortyish negro in a pinstripe blue suit, white shirt.

'Yes?' I said.

'Look buddy, maybe it ain't none of my business, but you sure – I mean, like absolutely *sure* – you wanna look up them addresses? What I mean is, you wanna *live* there?'

'That's right.'

'Y'ain't looking up for somebody else, maybe?'

'No. For me.'

He plucked a small cigar from his breast pocket, picked a hair off it carefully, struck a match on his window, and lit up, watching me through the smokeclouds.

'We – ell –' he said, soft southern, rolling the word, '– guess you know y'own mind. Good luck.'

'Thanks,' I said, and would have probed him, but he'd disappeared inside the shop again, and I was left on my blasted heath wondering whether, perhaps, he couldn't have fitted me out with a quiet little country thaneship somewhere.

Nowhere, actually, could be less like a blasted heath than Harlem; it is perhaps the most undeserted area in the world, if you know what I mean. Sixlane avenues are whittled down to alleyways by the permanent overflow from the pavements, solid, sluggish streams of people, whose reasons for being there at all seem incomprehensible – they walk too slowly to be actually *going* from A to B; they are too far from the shops and bars to have any possible interest in them; and they never appear to cross from one side of the street to the other; instead, they roll on, as if on some enormous conveyor-belt, with no apparent purpose, and no pause. Naturally, this sort of jay-walking would be treated in downtown New York as an offence located somewhere on the books between child-rape and dope-addiction; but here, a crack regiment would be needed to enforce the laws; it's left to the motorist to keep up a constant cacophonous alert to save himself from being devoured. It's an odd sensation to stand in the centre of one sidewalk looking across the slowly passing heads towards the other; the mass of humanity makes the traffic invisible, so that one seems to be cut off from the opposite bank by an open chasm filled with a perpetual honking moan, on either side of which the silent souls trudge on. Once, I thought I saw, across the gorge, Beatrice waiting in the crowd; but I must have been mistaken.

I find Harlem extremely disturbing, this sort of set-aside Negro metropolis, a sophisticated ghetto; although one rarely sees a white face, one constantly *thinks* one has, due to the fanatic attempts to approximate to the White Condition, through dress, and make-up, and hairstyling, and accent; the shops are stacked with advertised encouragement – with bleaching-creams and hairstraightening preparations and almost-white plaster models in tennis clothes. And the billboards flash products whose saleability depends upon the obvious air of success exuded by the figures depicted; and these are, without exception, the palest of negroes, often with blonde wavy hair, since these, in the hierarchy of shades which operates here, are the Top People. Constantly, the Madison Avenue stage-whisper is: This product will help you pass for White. Everything is angled towards the dispossession of the negro, towards making him a racial and cultural mongrel, towards offering him, in packet-form, an unrealizable dream. One knows that these techniques were developed to work within the tension of class-difference; but this is not the same thing at all.

I had decided to live in Harlem partly because of its proximity to Columbia University, partly to my eviction from my Greenwich Village broomcupboard, an eviction supposed to be temporary, but as the period stated was to allow the Exterminator to rid my room of cockroaches, I decided to forego the option. (I waited to see The Exterminator. I imagined a long cadaverous Kafka-esque terror with a stovepipe hat and a little black bag and an Instrument. He turned out to be two squat toughs from Brooklyn in green overalls, who were, without question, Steiger and Brando down on their luck.)

Anyway, I was tired of the Village; as in Hampstead, or Chelsea, rents rise relative to the immigration of wealthy non-artists hunting for charm, or social cachet, or whatever it is. But here there is no Belsize Park to retire to. I was getting pushed nearer and nearer the Bowery, and since I can do without this sort of pressure to follow my natural predisposition, I determined to get out for good. Harlem is cheap.

After I left the papershop, I tried five of the addresses. I was met with the same responses at each. Surprise (one woman laughed through the gap in the door, and vanished, and wouldn't come back; but I could hear her laughing in the hall); suspicion ('Look, fellah, thanks anyway, but we got so much goddam detergent in this house, we use it to stuff pillows!'); and finally, refusal. The room, sorry, was taken. Just this minute.

The sixth address was a tall brownstone, hung with black balcony-rails and fire-escapes, an external skeleton, like a scorpion's. The door was opened by a tall, slim, grey-haired, well-dressed negro. In his lapel was a N.A.A.C.P. button. He smiled, and it was the first straight smile I'd had all morning.

'I've come about the room,' I said.

'Oh!' He looked past my shoulder into the street. 'Afraid it's taken. Guy just left.'

'Are you sure?' He looked back at me. 'Yours is the sixth place I've tried, and they were all dated this morning, and they've all gone. Odd that, isn't it?'

'Kind of.' He shifted his weight, leaning on the door-jamb. 'Big demand for rooms, though.' He looked at me, hard. 'You English?'

'That's right.'

He pushed open the door with his shoulder, and stepped back into the dark hallway.

'Look, come in for a minute, anyhow. Maybe I can help you.'

I followed him into his living-room. On one wall, a huge photograph of Martin Luther King, and a daguerrotype of John Brown. On a side-table, the latest issues of *The Southern Patriot* and *Ebony*. I sat down, and at eye-level in the bookcase were volumes of Baldwin, and Ellison, and titles like 'The Negro Vanguard' and 'The Truth Shall Make Us Free'. The man sat down on the arm of the chair opposite.

'Look here,' he said. 'I lied. I got a room. It's still free. Only I'm not so sure I can let you have it.'

'How come?'

He picked up one of the magazines, and fiddled with its pages.

'Look, don't get me wrong – you're a foreigner, otherwise

I wouldn't have to explain. I don't want you to go thinking I'm – well, prejudiced, or anything like that.'

'You mean you don't take whites?'

'Don't say "you" like that.' He frowned, and put down the magazine. 'It's not just me. If I had my way, why, sure, I'd take you in. But I got other things to consider.'

'Such as?'

'Well, like I said, it's not me. It's the neighbours.' He looked at me, eyebrows raised in appeal. 'How're they going to feel about it? A man doesn't live alone, y'know. And this isn't just any old neighbourhood. No offence meant – but this is a pretty good-class street.'

'I know,' I said. 'That's why I like it.'

He shook his head.

'Man can't always have everything he likes. Take me – I get on fine with you people. I was in the war with white boys, fought right alongside 'em; you couldn't wish for better soldiers. I work with white people right now. They pull their weight same as the rest of us. I got white acquaintances – why, I count them among my closest friends. They come here all the time, we sit around, chew a lot of fat; you know the sort of thing.'

'Only you wouldn't have one living in your house?'

He sighed.

'I'm gonna level with you. Suppose you were to come and live here. You got white friends, right?'

I nodded.

'Okay. Pretty soon, they're gonna start visiting here regular. Maybe some of 'em'll get to like the area; why not? What then? Maybe they'll take it into their heads to move in. What the other people in the street gonna do? I'll tell you. They kinda respect me, know what I mean? I do a lot of work for them, address meetings, all that stuff. So they see I got a white boy living here. They'll reckon it's okay. So maybe they'll let your buddies move in. Pretty soon, we're gonna have us a – you'll excuse me – a white neighbourhood. I mean, let's face it, that's the way you folks are, am I right? Soon as a couple of you take hold, next thing you know there's a whole colony.'

'Well, would – I mean, is that so terrible, after all?'

He looked at me as if I were a child who'd misspelled 'cat'.

'Don't stop there, though, does it? I've lived in white areas, see? Like Greenwich Village. Now, I don't like those people who say that white men are all no-good drunks and loafers – but I've seen 'em on paynights down there, blind drunk, shouting and singing, running after women. I don't say there aren't good and bad, nor that coloured people don't behave that way sometimes. But there's no point, far as I can see, in having a lot of people like that coming in and raising hell.' He leaned forward. 'Lot of white men find coloured girls pretty attractive, huh?'

Caught either way. All right.

'Some. Like any other girls, I suppose.'

'That's just it! They're not. See what I mean? Pretty soon they're gonna start walking out together. Maybe even get married.'

'Well, even if things go that far, would that be so bad?'

He pursed his lips.

'Look, I'm liberal, like I say. I know all the reasons, too, and about love and all that, and skin not mattering, and the same blood, and so on. Except –' he shook his head, and gave a small laugh, '– it still kinda goes against the grain, thinking of a coloured girl going to bed with a white man. No offence?'

'No offence,' I said.

'If I had my way, I'd like to see everyone getting along together, next door to one another. But – I can see you're a man of the world, an intelligent human being – you don't expect me to be the first, do you? A man has to live.'

'I suppose you're right. I don't expect you to be the first.'

'Sure you don't.' He smiled comfortably now, relieved. 'It's been interesting talking to you.' He stood up, and we went into the dim hall. 'Good to see you understand. About the room and all. But I guess that's nothing new to you; a man who's been around must've run into this sort of thing from time to time?'

'Yes,' I said. 'It all sounds pretty familiar.'

We shook hands on the step, and he closed the front door. I walked down the stone stairway, and two little coloured boys chasing one another down the street sidestepped to dodge out of my way. I took the list of addresses out of my pocket, and screwed it up, and threw it in the gutter.

4

It Tolls for Thee

Manhattan's largest fallout shelter, the New York Telephone Company Building rising near the Hudson River, will have 21 storeys without a single window. The vertically striped fortress will house 3,000 workers, who will be capable of surviving a near-miss atomic attack for two weeks.

Life Magazine, November 9th, 1962

For the first few moments, I was convinced that some joker had directed me to the sanctum sanctorum of one of California's more esoteric sects. The doors sighed shut, sealing me into a huge pastel-coloured hall; on the facing wall was etched the outline of a bell, beneath which stood a long low table flanked by two gently revolving plastic bushes hung with pink, blue, olive and yellow telephones. A row of multi-coloured phones, doubtless freshly picked, garnished the table. Behind these sat a motionless young woman, smiling fixedly. In order to approach her, it was necessary to pass between two long rows of identical desks, on each side of which stood a telephone of a different colour, and a rack of pamphlets. No one sat at the desks, and, apart from myself and the votary at the far end of the hall, the place was empty. It is almost impossible to walk down a long aisle towards someone who has been trained to smile. I committed the miserable error of starting my own smile as I began to walk; consequently, by the time I reached the table, I had considerable difficulty in speaking through the grinning death-mask into which my face had been turned.

'Good morning,' I gritted. 'I should like to have a telephone installed in my apartment.'

'Yes, sir,' she murmured, softly. 'If you'll wait over there by the lavender instrument, I'll have someone help you with your problem.'

'I haven't got a problem,' I said. 'I want a phone. Can't I just leave my name and address with you?'

'I'm sorry, sir.' The same monotone coming through the glazed smile. 'Bell Telephone has found that the most efficient way of dealing with clients' problems is through the instrument.'

I sat at the desk, looking at the Instrument, wondering whether I ought to smile at it. I heard the girl murmuring on her own telephone. I casually opened one of the bright pamphlets in front of me, and found the familiar catechismal layout prescribed by PR departments of the great industrial organisms. I turned the pages with waiting-room languor, impervious by now to the frenetic hyperbole; after all, I had known before coming here that the net worth of Bell Telephone approximates to that of England, that it is wealthier than the five wealthiest states in the Union, that soon it will have a satellite all to itself, and so on. I was beyond surprise by Bell. And then, on the last page of the pamphlet, I came on this: 'At present there are more than 85 million phones in the U.S., and by 1975 there will be more than 160 million.' I went back and re-read it. And realised that the telephone was reproducing at approximately three times the rate of the population of China. This in itself, all other implications aside, had a staggering effect on me. Until then, I had, like almost everyone else, accepted as the two yardsticks by which all other quantities were to be measured, the distance to the Moon, and the population of China. (I have never needed any others, since, at fourteen, I spent two weeks in bed on glucose following a maths master's attempts to conceptualize infinity for me. We cornered it at one point, and had it belittled to the ignominy of one-over-nothing. I thought about this for a few moments; then I cracked.) Told that: 'The 1962 model was driven 250,000 miles on two quarts of oil and one tyre-change. This is the distance from here to the Moon', I am happy. Or that: 'In 1961, we manufactured one billion ballbearings, or enough to give every man, woman, and child in China two ballbearings each', I know where I stand. Or knew. Not any longer. Now that small fund of conversation-stopping statistics that I have hoarded for bad moments at parties will have to be completely revised in terms of telephones, lengths of cable, warehouse-loads of dials. I shall have to teach my sons that every fifth child born is destined to become a telephonist. Stuff like that.

The Instrument cut through this morbid reverie. A voice of metallic silk introduced itself, and elicited a file-full of irrelevant personal information before asking, finally:

'Now, sir, how large is the apartment?'

'Three rooms,' I said.

'So you should be able to get along with only one extension. Is that to be a wall-phone, or a Princess Bedside?'

'I want one instrument,' I said. 'With a long cord.'

A metal snigger.

'Oh, come, sir! Nobody has long cords any more. Our researchers found that so many accidents were caused by cords getting tangled up with children and pets and things of that nature.'

'I haven't got anything of that nature,' I said.

'Well, at least you'll need a Home Interphone. So that you can communicate with the party in the other rooms.'

'There aren't any parties. I live alone.'

'Don't you ever have guests?'

Of course, since she lived at the end of a lavender cable, the idea that people actually indulged in the gross obscenity of talking face to face could hardly be insisted upon by me.

'No,' I said meekly, 'No guests'.

A pause. I could see the inside of her brain visualising a banner headline: 'ONE-PHONE RECLUSE FOUND STRANGLED BY ANTIQUE CORD. BODY DISCOVERED AFTER THREE WEEKS BY JANITOR'. I wanted to meet her, I wanted her to see that I was healthy, that there was a spring in my step, that I smiled. But this was impossible.

'Oh, well,' said the voice. 'Of course, you can never tell when a party may drop by.' I wondered whether she was human enough to be trying to console me. The voice sighed, and went on: 'Well then, sir, perhaps we can decide on the colour of the Instrument'.

'Black.'

A tin gasp.

'Beige, green, grey, yellow, white, pink, blue, turquoise!' A pause. 'Nobody has black, sir. We couldn't guarantee a new Instrument in black. What is the colour-scheme of your room?'

In fact, it's pale-green. But I knew the consequences of my admitting this. So I joked. I thought.

'It's black,' I said. 'Black wallpaper, black ceiling, black fitted carpet. Black furniture.' I waited for her laugh.

'We-e-ell,' she said, 'Why not have a white Instrument to set it off?'

'All right,' I said running my tongue over my lips. 'All right, white.'

'Wish I could persuade you to have a coloured Instrument. Everyone else does, you know. They're so much more individual.'

'Yes. Well, that's all, I suppose?'

'But we haven't decided on the chime yet, have we?'

'The what?'

'The chime. You can have a conventional ring if you choose, but for the Discerning we are now able to offer a Gentle,

Cheerful Chime Adjustable To Suit Your Activities Or Your Mood.'

'But how do I know what mood I'll be in when it chimes?'

'But on some days, don't you just *long* for a Gentle Chime?'

I closed my eyes. For three weeks I have carried on a running fight with my landlord over my request to change my door-chime for a buzzer. And two weeks ago I bought, or, rather, was sold, a Discount House Bargain which keeps perfect time all day, and, having been set for nine a.m., awakes me up at 4.17 by chiming crazily and hurling scalding coffee over the walls and carpet.

'No, dear,' I said wearily, 'I'm something of a strident buzz man myself'.

'As you choose, sir.' I could hear her hesitate. I knew she was cracking. Finally she murmured: 'The Princess Bedside lights up at night.'

'Quite possibly,' I said, and replaced the receiver.

After I left the building, I stopped to buy the copy of *Life* from which I quoted at the beginning of this story. And suddenly I saw her, and her sad sorority, in their last hours, in their windowless concrete pillar above the rubble of New York. Three thousand telephonists, connected only by a web of lavender cable, frantically dialling and re-dialling, while the nightlights flash, and the bells chime gently, over a dead world.

5

. . . that Fell on the House that Jack Built

*The bombing of North Vietnam has had little or no effect
on the flow of men and materials from north to south.*
US Secretary of Defence McNamara

Five miles south of the DMZ, Major-General Sam
Kowalski, USAF, sopped up the last of his egg with the
last of his ham, sluiced it down with the last of his
coffee, and belched gently. It was good coffee. Not, he hastened
to remind himself (nostalgia being the better part of valour)
as good as the coffee in Topeka, Kansas, which was the best
coffee in the world. But good. He watched the morning sun
dissolve the white mists to the north, longingly: better flying
weather than this, you couldn't expect.

Except there was nothing to fly against.

It had been that way for a week now. Daily, Kowalski's
reconnaissance planes went out, daily they returned, with
nothing to report. The photographs showed hills and streams,
trees and cloud shadows on the grass. Nothing a man could
bomb. Not even a goat. A goat would have been *something*,
thought Kowalski; especially a moving goat. Now there was
a challenge! Out of the amethyst sky, Kowalski's spotless
Skyhawks would swoop, hedge-high over the dark grass, trim
as white playing-cards flicked across the green baize tables of
home, and BLAT! No more goat. One dead Cong goat.

Kowalski sighed, stood up, tugged his gleaming belt into
the soft movement of his breakfast, and notched it. At his right

hip hung a Smith & Wesson .45 Magnum, not Army Issue, but Kowalski's own side-arm. His mother's Christmas present. She had gone into Duckett's Hardware in Topeka and said did they have anything for her boy who was a Major-General in Vietnam, and the salesman had said nothing was too good for a guy like that and sold her the hand-gun for two hundred dollars. He threw in a hand-tooled cutaway holster, because that was the least he could do, he said; he would have been out there himself, he said, only he had this trick knee, had it since he was a kid, gave him hell.

On his left side, Kowalski wore a Bowie knife. It was the sort of thing the men appreciated, he knew. It gave him personality, it gave him colour, it placed him in a direct line of descent from Sam Houston and John Mosby and George Custer and Blackjack Pershing. He wanted the men to know that if the Cong ever attempted to overrun the airstrip, he, Kowalski, would be out on the perimeter, meeting them hand-to-hand. 'Remember the Alamo!' he would cry. 'Don't fire till you see the whites of their eyes!'

He walked out into the bright sun to where his Skyhawks were drawn up, combat-ready, gleaming-white. Bullpup AS missiles hung beneath their wings, slim, deadly, and Zuni launchers fat with 5-in. rockets, and AIM-9 Sidewinders, and plump napalm tanks like great grey footballs. Kowalski watched them through his smoked glasses, trembling with anticipation, feeling himself part of their functional mystery. Kowalski prayed for opportunity.

He was still there when the morning reconnaissance planes touched down.

'Nothing,' said the pilot in the de-briefing room.

'Nothing?'

'Looks like it, General.'

Kowalski flicked again through the blown-up photographs, still moist from the fixing-bath. He stopped suddenly, peered close, cursed the light.

'What's that?'

The pilot squinted.

'Some guy cutting wheat, I guess.'

Kowalski straightened up, triumphantly, looked at his assembled staff with bright eyes.

'Cong wheat!' he said. 'For Cong bread.'

A colonel shrugged.

'It's one peasant, General,' he said.

'Correction, Colonel! One Cong peasant.'

'North Vietnamese.'

'Cong, North Viet, what's the difference?' shouted Kowalski. 'He's cutting strategic wheat, right? To make strategic bread, right? To feed to Cong, so they got the strength to pull the triggers, right?'

Twenty minutes later, three Skyhawks roared off north. Sam Kowalski watched their black trails dissolve, willing them on, feeling in his muscles the faint recoil of cannon, seeing the shells stitch dark patterns in the earth.

Two planes came back.

'Who knows?' said the lead pilot. 'Small arms fire, maybe. I looked around, Harry wasn't there. Then I see this smoke, coming out of the trees. Maybe he just spun out. Who knows?'

Kowalski thought of the wreckage, the shattered wings, the dead engine, the wasted bomb-load. The Cong would take the tailplane and put it on a stick and take pictures of it.

'A million-dollar peasant,' he said savagely. 'Did we get him?'

'He wasn't there.'

Kowalski screwed the flight report into a ball.

'A trap,' he whispered. 'A goddam Cong trap!' He took out his gun and spun the chamber furiously while he thought. Also, he smiled, in a private, military way.

'Maybe the guy just went for lunch,' murmured the pilot. But Kowalski did not hear.

That afternoon, six aircraft took off on a seek-and-destroy mission to knock out the anti-aircraft sites Kowalski had pin-pointed for them. That done, a second strike was to go in and silence the peasant.

Three bombers returned. The Vietnamese, having found themselves suddenly in a strategic position, had called up a couple of heavy machine-guns to defend their village, both of which had survived the attack that had homed in on the largest building, the school.

'School, huh?' said Kowalski, with a certain amount of relief, due to his having originally attributed the smallness of the bodies in the photographs to some fault in his aerial cameras. He turned to his wireless operator. 'Send this: Major-General Kowalski to USAF HQ – In a pre-emptive strike against major supply dumps north of the DMZ, an A4F Skyhawk was downed by enemy fire. A retaliatory strike against anti-aircraft positions resulted in the loss of three further Hawks. However, a major VC training-camp was destroyed, with many – make that hundreds – dead. Ten thousand rounds of ordnance and one hundred tons of bombs were expended. Attacks continue. Message ends.'

The commander smiled triumphantly upon his staff.

'We got ourselves some war, gentlemen,' he said.

'For four Hawks,' said a captain laconically, 'they'll want results.'

'They'll get results. Tomorrow, we'll hit the missile sites.'

They looked at him.

'Missile sites?'

'If I know the Cong,' said Kowalski, 'and I know them, I can smell them, there'll be missile sites. They got the whole night to set 'em up.'

He was right. At dawn on the following day, twenty-four Skyhawks, heavy with HE and napalm, ran into a wave of North Vietnamese GAMs. Six were shot down, one crash-landed in the DMZ; two helicopters were lost trying to bring back the pilot, who died slowly, but was recommended for the Medal of Honour by Kowalski. It was good for morale.

'To the folks back home,' he told his men on the parade-ground the following morning, and his voice trembled through the loudspeakers, 'that medal isn't just Charlie Fitzgerald's medal. It belongs to every man out here fighting for liberty, justice, and the flag. To your mothers and dads, and sisters and brothers, every one of you is a hero.'

The airmen shuffled their feet, and blushed. Some of them were very young. Pride welled up in them, diluting fear. Reminded of what they were there for, they climbed back into their cockpits in good heart, knowing that death could have a purpose. Pride filled Kowalski, too, as he watched them go.

'This is a major offensive,' he told his 2IC. 'Vital to the war. Strategic. If we break here, we break everywhere. But,' he patted his holster, 'no-one's gonna break.'

That night, he went to bed happy. True, half his strike force had failed to return, but the day's sorties had racked up a tally of a thousand tons of bombs and rockets, which was a record for his sector of the front. Also, a large area of possibly strategic jungle had been defoliated, the district hospital had been razed, and innumerable chickens would not now find their way into the lunch-baskets of General Giap and his friends. Kowalski, wide-awake, was still calculating the size of reinforcements he would need to call up in order to maintain his escalation at the prescribed textbook level, when the first mortar shell hit the airstrip. Snatching his revolver and knife from beneath their respective pillows, Kowalski leapt out into the night.

It glowed bright as day. Burning fuel silhouetted planes for the few seconds necessary for their bomb-loads to explode, shells and flaming debris rained down, men in pyjamas ran about barefoot, shouting, firing at anything that moved.

Kowalski, trapped by the twin agony and joy of war, stood rooted to the spot, gun cocked, breathing in the heady fumes: it took two lieutenant-colonels and a cook to carry him away to a makeshift dug-out.

'I knew it!' cried the major-general. Beside him, a man fell dead, half his head shot away. 'I knew they'd have to come! They walked right into it.' His words were sucked away as an ammunition dump went up, tearing the night apart, but they came again '. . . what you call war, gentlemen! Tomorrow, we'll get three divisions in here, four, we'll get two hundred Hawks, we'll get ground-to-grounds, and whole batteries of Lazy Dogs, we'll get nuclear . . .'

A grenade blew out the side of the bunker, flinging what was left of his second-in-command against Kowalski. The man looked up at his commander, dying.

'I wonder,' he murmured, 'I wonder – whatever happened to that – to that peasant?'

'What peasant?' shrieked Kowalski. He looked round wildly. 'What's he talking about?'

But before anyone had the chance to answer, and despite Mrs Kowalski's expensive Christmas present, they were overrun.

6

Under the Influence of Literature

My mother was the first person to learn that I had begun to take literature seriously. The intimation came in the form of a note slid under my bedroom door on the morning of February 4 (I think), 1952. It said, quite simply:

> Dear Mother,
>   Please do not be alarmed, but I have turned into a big black bug. In spite of this I am still your son so do not treat me any different. It must have happened in the night. On no account throw any apples in case they stick in my back which could kill me.
>   Your son.

I hasten to add that this turned out to be a lousy diagnosis on my part. But the night before I had gone to bed hugging my giant panda and a collected Kafka found under a piano leg, and since, when I woke up, I was flat on my back, it seemed only reasonable to suppose that I'd metamorphosed along with Gregor Samsa, and was now a fully paid-up cockroach. The fit passed by lunchtime, but for years my father used the story to stagger people who asked him why he was so young and so grey.

Thing is, I was pushing fourteen at the time, and caught in that miserable No-Man's-Land between Meccano and Sex, wide open to suggestions that life was hell. My long trousers were a travesty of manhood, and shaving was a matter of tweezers and hope. Suddenly aware of how tall girls were, and of how poorly a box of dead butterflies and a luminous compass fit a man for a smooth initiation into the perfumed garden, I tried a desperate crash-programme of self-taught sophistication; I spent my evenings dancing alone in a darkened garage, drinking Sanatogen, smoking dog-ends, and quoting Oscar Wilde, but it never amounted to anything. Faced with the Real Thing at parties, I fell instant prey to a diabolical tic, stone feet, and a falsetto giggle, and generally ended up by locking myself in the lavatory until all the girls had gone home.

Worst of all, I had no literary mentors to guide my pubescent steps. For years I'd lived on the literary roughage of Talbot Baines Reed and Frank Richards, but the time had now come to give up identifying myself with cheery, acne-ridden schoolboys. Similarly, the dream heroes of comic-books had to be jettisoned; I could no longer afford to toy with the fantasy of becoming Zonk, Scourge of Attila, or Captain Marvel, or the Boy Who Saved The School From Martians – girls weren't likely to be too impressed with the way I planned to relieve Constantinople, it had become increasingly clear to me that shouting 'SHAZAM!' was a dead loss, since it never turned *me* into a muscle-bound saviour who could fly at the speed of light, and as for the other thing, my school seemed to pose no immediate threat to Mars, all things considered. I needed instead, for the first time, a reality to build a dream on.

But I wasn't yet ready for adult ego-ideals. Not that I didn't try to find them in stories of Bulldog Drummond and the Saint (Bond being, in 1952, I suppose, some teenage constable yet to find his niche), but experience had already taught me the pointlessness of aiming my aspirations at these suave targets. Odds seemed against my appearance at a school dance, framed in the doorway, my massive bulk poised to spring, my steely eyes flashing blue fire, and my fists bunched like knotted ropes. Taking a quick inventory, I could tell I was short-stocked on the gear that makes women swoon and strong men step aside. And, uttering a visceral sigh (the first, as things turned out, of many), I sent my vast escapist, hero-infested library for pulping, and took up Literature, not for idols, but for sublimation.

The initial shock to my system resulting from this new leaf is something from which I never fully recovered. Literature turned out to be filled, yea, even to teem, with embittered, maladjusted, disorientated, ill-starred, mis-understood malcontents, forsaken souls playing brinkmanship with life, emaciated men with long herringbone overcoats and great, staring tubercular eyes, whose only answer to the challenge of existence was a cracked grin and a terrible Russian shudder. I learned, much later, that there was more to Literature than this, but the fault of over-specialisation wasn't entirely mine; my English master, overwhelmed to find a thirteen-year-old boy whose vision extended beyond conkers and Knicker-bocker Glories, rallied to my cry for more stuff like Kafka, and led me into a world where bread fell always on the buttered side and death was the prize the good guys got. And, through all the borrowed paperbacks, one connecting thread ran – K, Raskolnikov, Mishkin, Faust, Werther, Ahab, Daedalus, Usher – these were all chaps like me; true, their acne was spiritual, their stammer rang with *weltschmerz*, but we were of one blood, they and I. How much closer was I, dancing sad, solitary steps in the Stygian garage, to the hunter of Moby Dick, than to Zonk, Scourge of Attila!

At first, I allowed the world which had driven me out of its charmed circles to see only the outward and visible signs of the subcutaneous rot. In the days following my acute disappointment at not being an insect, I wandered the neighbourhood dressed only in pyjamas, a shift made from brown paper, and an old overcoat of my father's, satisfactorily threadbare, and just far enough from the ground to reveal my bare shins and sockless climbing boots. By opening my eyes very wide, I managed to add a tasteful consumptiveness to my face, backed up by bouts of bravura coughing and spitting, and I achieved near-perfection with a mirthless chuckle all my own.

Suburban authority being what it is, I ran foul of the police within a couple of days, not, as I'd intended, for smoking reefers or burying axes in pensioners' heads to express the ultimate meaninglessness of anything but irrational action, but for being in need of care and protection. At least, this was how a Woolworth's assistant saw me. I had been shuffling up and down the aisles, coughing and grinning by turns, when a middle-aged woman took either pity or maliciousness on me, and tried to prise an address from the mirthlessly chuckling lips.

'What's your name?' she said.

'Call me Ishmael,' I replied, spitting fearlessly.

'Stop that at once, you horrid little specimen! Where do you live?'

'Live!' I cried. 'Ha!' I chuckled once or twice, rolled my eyes, hawked, spat, twitched, and went on: 'To live – what is that? What is Life? We all labour against our own cure, for death is the cure of all diseases . . .'

I took a well-rehearsed stance, poised to belt out an abridged version of *La Dame Aux Camélias*, when the lady was reinforced by a policeman, into whose ear she poured a resumé of the proceedings to date.

'Alone, and plainly loitering,' said the copper. He dropped a large authoritarian hand on my shoulder. I was profoundly moved. I had been given the masonic handshake of the damned. Already with thee, in the penal settlement, old K.

'I shall go quietly,' I said, wheezing softly. 'I know there is no charge against me, but that is no matter. I must stand trial, be condemned, be fed into the insatiable belly of the law. That is the way it has to be.'

I gave him my address, but instead of leading me to the mouldering cellars of the local nick, he took me straight home. My parents, who hadn't yet seen me in The Little Deathwisher Construction Kit, reeled and blenched for long enough to convince the constable that the fault was none of theirs. My father, who believed deeply in discipline through applied psychology, gave me a workmanlike hiding, confiscated the existential wardrobe, and sent me to my room. By drawing the curtains, lighting a candle, releasing my white mice from bondage, and scattering mothballs around to give the place the camphorated flavour of a consumptive's deathbed, I managed to turn it into an acceptable condemned cell. Every evening after school (a perfectly acceptable dual existence this; the Jekyll-and-Hyde situation of schoolboy by day, and visionary nihilist by night appealed enormously to my bitter desire to dupe society) I wrote an *angstvoll* diary on fragments of brown paper torn from my erstwhile undershirt, and tapped morse messages on the wall (e.g. 'God is dead', 'Hell is other people', and so on) not, as members of the Koestler fan-club will be quick to recognise, in order to communicate, but merely to express. I got profound satisfaction from the meaninglessness of the answers which came back from the other half of our semi, the loud thumps of enraged respectability, unable to comprehend or articulate.

However, the self-imposed life of a part-time recluse was

growing less and less satisfactory, since it wasn't taking me any nearer the existential nub which lay at the centre of my new idols. I was, worst of all, not experiencing any suffering, but merely the trappings. True, inability to cope with what the romantic novelists variously describe as stirring buds, tremulous awakenings, and so on, was what had initially nudged my new persona into life, but this paled beside the *weltschmerz* of the literary boys. Also, suburban London was not nineteenth century St. Petersburg or Prague, 1952 wasn't much of a year for revolution, whaling, or the collapse of civilisation, I was sick of faking TB and epilepsy, and emaciation seemed too high a price to pay for one's non-beliefs. Pain, to sum up, was in short supply.

It was *The Sorrows Of Young Werther* which pointed the way out of this slough of painlessness. Egged on by a near-delirious schoolmaster, I had had a shot at Goethe already, since a bit of *Sturm und Drang* sounded just what the doctor ordered, but I'd quickly rejected it. I wasn't able to manufacture the brand of jadedness which comes, apparently, after a lifetime's fruitless pursuit of knowledge, and the paraphernalia of pacts with the devil, *Walpurgisnachtsträume*, time-travel, and the rest, were not really in my line. While I sympathised deeply with Faust himself, it was quite obvious that we were different types of bloke altogether. But Werther, that *meisterwerk* of moonstruck self-pity – he was me all over.

The instant I put down the book, I recognised that what up until then had been a rather primitive adolescent lust for the nubile young bride next door had really been 22-carat sublime devotion all along. It was the quintessence of unrequitable love, liberally laced with unquenchable anguish. Sporting a spotted bow, shiny shoes and a natty line in sighs, I slipped easily into the modified personality, hanging about in the communal driveway for the chance to bite my lip as the unattainable polished the doorknocker or cleaned out the drains. I abbreviated the mirthless chuckle to a silent sob, cut out the spitting altogether, and filled the once-tubercular eyes with pitiable longing.

The girl, who must have been about twenty-five, responded perfectly. She called me her little man, underlining her blindness to my infatuation with exquisite poignancy, and let me wipe the bird-lime off her window-sills and fetch the coal. What had once been K's cell, Raskolnikov's hovel, the *Pequod's* poop-deck, now took on the appearance of a beachcomber's strongbox. My room was littered with weeds from her garden, a couple of slats from the fence I'd helped her mend, half-a-dozen old lipstick cases, a balding powder-puff, three laddered stockings (all taken, at night, from her dustbin), a matted clot of hair I'd found in her sink, an old shoe, a toothless comb, and a pair of lensless sunglasses that had once rested on the beloved ears. Daily, I grew more inextricably involved. I began to demand more than silent service and unexpressed adulation. I dreamed of discovering that she no longer loved her husband, that she had responded to my meticulous weeding and devoted washing-up to the point of being unable to live without me. I saw us locked in each other's arms in a compartment on the *Brighton Belle*, setting out on a New Life Together.

In April I discovered she was pregnant. For one wild moment I toyed with the idea of claiming the child as my own, thus forcing a rift between her and her husband. But the plan had obvious drawbacks. The only real course of action was undoubtedly Werther's. Naturally, I'd contemplated suicide before, but an alternative had always come up, and, anyway, this was the first time that I had something worth dying elaborately for. I wrote innumerable last notes, debated the advantages of an upstairs window over the Piccadilly Line, and even wrote to B.S.A. to ask whether it was possible to kill a human being with one of their airguns, and, if so, how.

In fact, if the cricket season hadn't started the same week, I might have done something foolish.

7

This Thing with the Lions

The result of a bed-ridden afternoon, in which a romp through Hemingway concluded with a coda of Elsa the Lioness and the belief that enough was as good as a feast, however moveable.

The windbrake crackled in a gust of hot breeze. She looked up but the leaves were still now. She could see the leaves through the open tentflap, and they were still. There was a lizard on the tentpole near the top. It was the colour of old sand, and it had one yellow eye that did not blink. She whistled at it, twice; but it did not move. A muscle twitched in its shoulder, but it did not move. It is one of the brave ones, she thought. It is one of the few brave ones left.

The boy padded in with the drinks. Not that she drank so much any more, because drink did not do the thing that it used to do. All the drink in the world will not do that thing now, she thought.

'There are vultures,' said the boy.

'Yes,' she said. She watched the soda bubbles rise in the long glass, and burst, impotently. 'They have made a kill.'

'Yes,' he said. He looked away. 'Missy not go no more kill?'

'No,' she said. 'Not any more.'

'It is good,' he said. He pulled a tick from his black neck and snapped it with his thumbnail, carefully. 'It is not for lady, the thing with the guns.'

'That's right,' she said. She took the tall glass, and the ice bumped against her lips, and she thought: they will be cold now, the lips. But she did not laugh. 'No,' she replied, 'it is not for lady.'

Now in her mind she saw the wet platform of the Estacion Norte, and the great black tank engines, and the shuffling lines of khaki puppets and the anaesthetized faces of men who have lain beside the dead, and have got up and walked away. She saw the bars of the Madrid-Floride, and the Metropole, and the others, which were all the same after a while; like the fresh-faced boys who would never quite be fresh anymore. It was a long war, but they had still gone to it, and they had come back, more or less. Mostly less. She remembered the purple Spanish nights when she sat up in the room smelling of ordinario and cartridge-belts, holding their hands and telling them it did not matter the way everyone said it mattered, and that this thing with the woman was not all it was cracked up to be, anyway.

She could hear the bearers singing now, and she wondered about the kill. I hope they got a water-buff, she thought. I hope they got a big black sweating buck, one of those that keep on coming, even with a couple of 220 solid-grain Springfields buried in their guts; one of those big, hard males with the great spread of horn. Those were the best ones, in the old days. George would not let her go for them any more. Not after the time she had gone into the bush after the bull that had tossed him. She had dropped it, finally, with one so clean you had to part the forelock to find the hole. When she got back, George had been lying in the sun for three hours.

'He was a tough one,' she said.

'I know', he said. 'I have lost a lot of blood.'

'Where did he get you?' she said.

He took his hands away.

'Oh.'

'That is the way it is, sometimes.' He laughed, briefly.

'Like Manolete,' she said.

'Yes.' He began to cry. 'Like Manolete.'

Things had been different between them after that, and he would not let her hunt the water-buffs any more. He did not like what it did to her, he said. So she sat around the camp, in the brass African heat, raising mongeese and crossbreeding scorpions. Sometimes she would stick pins in little clay models; but even that did not help.

She saw the first two boys come over the hill with the animal slung on poles between them. George walked alongside, carrying the big Remington by its strap. He waved at her, the way he always did, and she took another finger of scotch, and waved back. She got off the camp-bed and went towards them.

'It's a lioness,' she said, quietly. 'You son-of-a-bitch.'

'I didn't want to do it, but it happened that way. She came out of the bush, and no one had time to ask questions. She was a big one,' he said, 'and she was coming fast.'

She looked at the animal, with its guts torn open and its swollen teats hanging down, heavy with uselessness. She saw the belly full of old fertility, with the fat black flies buzzing around it.

'Cojones,' she said.

'I didn't want to do it,' said George again.

'I hate it when you kill females.' She looked at the bronze horizon. 'I hate it when you take it out on them.'

'Don't pity me,' he said, 'for Christ's sake.'

'She just calved. Is that why?'

'I didn't know she had cubs, I swear. When she came at us, I thought she was just one of the mean ones.'

'I hope it was a clean shot.'

He pumped a used shell out of the Remington.

'Some things you just don't lose.'

'You're so damned clever,' she said.

Two boys came up, grinning, with a basket between them.

'I brought you a present,' said George. He flipped open the lid. Inside there were three lion cubs; their eyes were still closed. There was something terrifying about their innocence.

'You and your goddamned metaphors,' she said.

He turned and walked into the tent. He pulled his bed a little further away from hers and sat down. He looked at the typewriter. Someday he would write about it, he thought. You can get rid of it when you write about it. He would write with symbols, so that when he was dead they would know he had been one of the big ones all the time. Turgenev was one of the big ones. And Flaubert. And Jack Dempsey. He was one of the big ones, too. And Ludwig von Beethoven. Turgenev and Flaubert and Dempsey and Beethoven and Peter Abelard and that old man in Key West who caught the biggest goddamned sailfish he'd ever seen in his life with a two-dollar rod. They were the great ones.

The next day he went up-country on a Government weevil survey. He did not get back for five months, and when he walked out of the bush, waving and calling the way he always did, it took six houseboys to get the lion off him.

'You didn't have to do that,' he said. He lay on his back in the tent, his one good eye bright among the bandages. 'You didn't have to alienate her.'

'I'm sorry,' she said. She smiled. She was looking better than she had for a long time. 'Elsa's funny with strangers. I had to send the other two away. I hope you don't mind?'

The eye glittered.

'As it turns out,' he said, 'you did the right thing.' He paused. 'How come you kept the third one?'

She did not answer. In the stillness, a baboon vomited. Elsa came in silently, lapped from a basin of pink gin, and padded out again.

'You got her pretty damned well trained.'

'We understand one another,' she said. 'That's all it takes. Understanding. And a little love.'

'That's fine,' he said. He tried to laugh, but the stitches dragged, and he fell back writhing. After a time, he said: 'You girls have to stick together. That's the way it is.'

'Yes,' she said, 'That's the way it is.'

That evening, they were closer than they had been since the time she worked the epidiascope at the Royal Geographic. They hand-wrestled, and laughed about the time he had smashed in the French ambassador's face with a bottle of Pernod on the train to Pamplona, and they went through the Book of Job together, looking for a title for that short story he planned to write some day; he felt good, with the old, half-familiar thing. At ten o'clock, he put his arm round her, and as he did, Elsa came in out of the dark and looked at him in a way that made him put his arm down again.

'What the hell,' he said. 'The stitches still hurt, anyway. I guess I'll just take a walk before we turn in.'

When he got back, the tent was dark. He sat down on his bed to take off his boots. There was a sudden roar of thunder in his ears, and a stench of stale caviare, and something heavy struck him in the back. He fell across his wife's bunk.

'What happened?' she said.

'There's something damned funny about my bed,' he said. '*Whose* bed?'

He paused. 'You're not serious?'

'I took your mattress out into the open,' she said. 'It's a fine night. There are shooting stars. You'll be happier there.'

At three a.m., the monsoon broke. It was a good monsoon, as monsoons go, but the thunder was loud, and nobody heard the shouting. The boys found George three days later, after the flood went down. He was stuck in a gau-gau tree eight miles away. After four months, the hospital in Dar-es-Salaam sent him home.

'How was it?' she said.

'Fine,' he said. 'They said plenty of people go around with one lung.'

'It's good for a man to know suffering,' she said. A locust flew past, and she drew the Luger he always kept under his bed for medicinal purposes, and hit it three times. 'Animals suffer,' she said. 'The strong survive. That is the law. That is the only law that counts.'

He looked at her.

'I did a lot of thinking while I was in there,' he said. 'It isn't good for Elsa to be brought up with human beings. She is a lioness. She is being deprived of her natural inheritance.'

'I thought of that,' she said.

They had raw okapi meat for lunch, but he let Elsa have his share, because she was a year old now, and had a way of crunching bones that put him off his food. After the meal, Elsa and his wife sat around roaring at one another.

'I wish you'd teach me that,' he said.

'It'd only make Elsa more jealous,' she said.

He did not see much of them after that. They went out hunting at dawn, and did not return until sunset. Once, he wanted to go with them, but they would not let him take his rifle or his trousers, so he stayed behind and thought about the good time before the war and the time Dominguin got both ears and a tail and the time before that when he was a zoology student in Camden Town and he knocked a policeman's helmet off in Regent's Park Road. That was one story he had saved to write. He looked across the dung-coloured scrub to the dead tree where the vultures waited, cleaning their beaks. Somewhere it had gone wrong, he thought. Something had come and it had waited a while, and then it had gone and it would not ever come back any more. And he was no nearer to knowing what it was than he had been on those pale mornings in Edgware in the days when his father had done that thing they did not talk about.

One evening, his wife came back alone. He saw her loping across the twilit scrub, growling. She stopped in front of him, and he saw the blood on her, and the bad marks, and the bald patch.

'It is over,' she said.

'Over?'

'She has found a mate.'

'That's how it is with kids,' he said. 'You bring them up, teach them everything you know, and they turn round and go off with the first creep who whistles at them.'

She laughed once, very high, and the vultures flew off in a rattle of black wings. She looked at him with eyes tinted yellow by the dying sun.

'Is that the way it is?' she said.

'Yes,' he said. 'That's the way it is.'

'I'm glad you told me,' she said.

8

Bohemia

E nglish Bohemianism is a curiously unluscious fruit. It does not belong in the great, mad, steamy glasshouse in which so much of the art of the rest of the world seems to have flourished – or, at least, so much of the pseudo-art. Inside this hothouse, huge lascivious orchids slide sensually up the sweating windows, passion-flowers cross-pollinate in wild heliotrope abandon, lotuses writhe with poppies in the rich warm beds, kumquats ripen, tremble, and plop fatly to the floor – and outside, in a neat, trimly-hoed kitchen garden, English Bohemians sit in cold orderly rows, like carrots.

In our Bohemia, there are no beautifully crazy one-eared artists, no *sans culottes*, no castrated epistolarians, no genuine revolutionaries, no hopheads, no lunatics, not even any alcoholics of note; our seed-beds have never teemed with Rimbauds and Gauguins and Kafkas and d'Annunzios and Dostoievskys; we don't even have a Mailer or a Ginsberg to call our own. Our Bohemia is populated by Civil Servants like Chaucer and Spenser and Milton; by tough-nut professional penmongers like Shakespeare and Dryden and Johnson, who worried as much about underwear and rent as about oxymorons; by corpulent suburban family men like Thackeray and Dickens and Trollope. And whenever an English oddball raises, tentatively, his head, he's a pitifully pale imitation of the real thing – Thom. Gray, sad, thin Cambridge queer, Cowper, mad among his rabbits, Swinburne, a tiny fetishistic gnome as far from Leopold von Sacher-Masoch as water is from blood. The private lives of our great powerhouses of passion, Pope and Swift, were dreary and colourless in the extreme, and Emily Brontë divided her time between *Wuthering Heights* and the Haworth laundry-list. And history, though it may offer our only revolutionary poet the passing tribute of a literary footnote, will probably think of William Morris mainly as the Father of Modern Wallpaper.

There was, however, one brief moment in this socially unostentatious culture of ours when we were touched, albeit gingerly, by the spirit of Bohemia. I am not (how could you *think* a thing like that?) referring, of course, to the Wildean shenannigans at the *fin* of the last *siècle*, which were the product not of an authentic Bohemianism but of the need to dig up a literature and a *modus vivendi* you could wear with spats and a green carnation: that Café Royal crowd was the first Switched-On, With-It Generation England ever had, and the whole megillah should be taken with a pinch of pastis. No, the gang I have in mind are the Lake Poets, who had, for once, all the genuine constituents of real adjustment problems, social malaise, illegitimate offspring, numerous tracts, a hang-out, a vast literature, and, most important of all, a date: 1798. And since at first sight, and for several thereafter, the Lake District, a sopping place of sedge and goat, seems as unlikely a Bohemian ambience as you could shake a quill at, much can be gained by examining the area itself; one can do no better than take the career of its most eminent son, a William Wordsworth, and relate it (as all the local tourist offices do) to every cranny, sheep and sod between Windermere and the Scottish border.

I realise, naturally, that the aforementioned bard left a

meticulous record of all that made him what he was, but since all writers are extraordinary liars, poseurs, distorters, and self-deceivers, I have chosen to ignore most of his farragos and interpretations; and for the background to this chapter, I am not indebted to *The Poetical Works Of William Wordsworth* (5 vols, Oxford 1940–49), *Wordsworth: A Re-interpretation* by F. W. Bateson (London 1954), *The Egotistical Sublime* by J. Jones (London 1954), or *Wordsworth and Coleridge* by H. G. Margoliouth (London 1953). In particular, I am not indebted to *Strange Seas of Thought: Studies in Wordsworth's Philosophy of Man and Nature* by N. P. Stallknecht (North Carolina 1945). However, I gather from friends in the trade that no work of serious scholarship is complete without a list of references and sources three times the size of the thing itself, so for devotees of this sort of *narrischkeit*, a fuller bibliography will be found sewn inside the lining of my old green hacking-jacket.

Cockermouth, Cumberland, was the spot where, on April 7, 1770, William Wordsworth first drew breath, and the location goes a long way towards explaining his characteristic lugubriousness. In the Old Hall, now derelict and seeping, Mary Queen of Scots was received after her defeat at Langside in 1568; her gloom was plumbless, and her host, Henry Fletcher, gave her thirteen ells of crimson velvet for a new dress. This could hardly have compensated for having her army trodden into the mud, but it ranks as one of history's nicer gestures to Mary. Nearby stands Harry Hotspur's house, contracts for which had just been exchanged when the new proprietor was butchered at Shrewsbury, in 1403, and within spitting distance can be found a few lumps of twelfth-century castle: this was captured in 1313 by Robert the Bruce, and spent the rest of the century under constant attack and bombardment by any Scots infantrymen who happened to be in the neighbourhood. During the Wars of the Roses, it was first Yorkist, then Lancastrian, and the catalogue of woe was finally brought to an end during the Civil War, when it was demolished by the Roundheads. A mile or so away, at Moorland Close, is the 1764 birthplace of Fletcher Christian, leader of the *Bounty* mutineers, and the 1766 birthplace of John Dalton, the physicist whose nefarious theories led ultimately to the destruction of Hiroshima.

Given this agglomerated misery, it isn't difficult to see how young Wordsworth could become aware, very early, of the general rottenness of intelligent bipeds, by comparison with whom the local trees, thorns, and general flora assume a commendable innocence. One imagines John Wordsworth taking his little offshoot on trots through the topography, pointing out the various scenes of butchery and nastiness, totting up the huge casualty list, and pondering aloud on the question of how long it would take that diabolical infant prodigy John Dalton to come up with a hydrogen bomb. It's little wonder that William decided early on who his friends were, and began associating with daffodils. Not that the idea of Nature possessing a mean streak escaped him, either; the news that Fletcher Christian got his come-uppance for interfering with the rights of breadfruit was undeniably traumatic for young Wm. – thereafter, as the *Prelude* indicates, he couldn't break a twig or step on a toadstool without feeling that the crime would be expunged in blood.

He went on to Hawkshead Grammar School, where little seems to have happened to him, except that he befriended a lad called John Tyson, who immediately died, aged twelve, to be later commemorated in 'There was a boy, / Ye knew him well, ye cliffs and islands of Winander . . .' This drove Wordsworth even further towards the mountains and shrubbery, who were obviously bound to enjoy a longer lifespan and weren't going to peg out just when William was getting to know them. This was now his period of greatest involvement with Nature, a time spent sculling about the lakes with which the area is infested and grubbing about in the undergrowth, one ear cocked for the song of earwig and slug, the other for That Still Sprit Shed From Evening Air. It rained most of the time. And, as the years rolled by and William grew to pubescence, talking the whiles to roots and knolls, he became more and more aware of humanity in general as a collection of blots and errors. One could rely on the crocus; every year it re-emerged from the turf, developed into its tiny, private perfection, and then quietly pegged out. And other mates of the poet, like Skiddaw and Scafell and Easedale Tarn, changed very little from year to year. But as the maturing bard pottered around Cumbria, he bumped inevitably into some of the area's human population, later immortalised and now available in paperback, who served only to convince him that after the fifth day, the Almighty's unerring talent for creating perfection deserted him: the life of Wordsworth the Teenager teemed with mad old women, decayed sailormen, idiot children, dispossessed cottars, impoverished leech-gatherers, bereaved lovers, unscrupulous potters, orphans, mutes, destitutes, and chronic bronchitics. Why the Lake District should have seethed with such sad misfits and sufferers to the point where Wordsworth never met anyone else is a question I gladly leave to medical historians or any similar forager with the necessary time on his hands. But I would just like to point out to all those scholars who have wondered why Wordsworth should have been a believer in metampsychosis (that dubiously scientific process whereby souls pass on from one corporeal form to another as the subsequent mortal coils get shuffled off) that he quite clearly needed the hope it offered: souls inhabiting the forms of Lake District inhabitants were so unfortunately lumbered, that only the belief in their ultimate trans- mogrification into a hollyhock or woodlouse sustained Wordsworth's faith in God's pervading goodness. There is, indeed, much evidence to show that the poet would have given his eye-teeth to have been a clump of heather.

In 1787, he went up to Cambridge. Everyone drank port and spoke Latin, and the nearest Cumberland beggar was three hundred miles to the NW. Wordsworth was desolate, left the university, utterly unnoticed, and took ship for the Continent. It was here that he burgeoned and ripened under the cucumber-glass of Italian culture and Gallic revolution, suddenly exposed to all that the Lake District was not: Bohemianism took root in the Cumbrian corpuscles, and in the general uproar following the coup of 1789, Wordsworth sang in the streets, went about with his shirt unbuttoned, and seduced the daughter of a French surgeon. Again, scholars have been baffled by the whole Annette Vallon business: why the mystery, the concealment of Wordsworth's bastard son, the failure to return with its father to England? What the scholars have in textual fidelity, they lack in imagination; even without dwelling on the unwholesome possibility that Wordsworth's boudoir techniques, picked up at secondhand from observations of Esthwaite sheep, must have left much to be desired, we can make a fair guess at Annette's response to the poet's suggestion that she accompany him back to the fells to meet Mad Margaret, Peter Bell, Old Matthew, and the rest of the gang. At all events, Wordsworth came home alone, and unable to face the quiet of the Lakes, took Dorothy down to Somerset, which by now had got a reputation for having Coleridge on the premises. The two met up. Coleridge had already collected a Lake Poet, Robert Southey, and together they had concocted a form of early communism which they called Pantisocracy, so that by the time Wordsworth fixed his wagon to their star, the nub of Bohemianism had been unmistakeably shaped: of these two ur-Marxists, Southey had already distinguished himself for his opposition to flogging, Coleridge was smoking pot and seeing visions, and the pair of them had been writing like things possessed. With Wordsworth in tow, the poetic output stepped up enormously, and in 1798, he and Coleridge hit the market with their *Lyrical Ballads*, and everyone took off for the Lake District. The years that followed were ambrosial for Wordsworth: at last he could stop mooning about and involving himself with the problems of the educationally sub-normal citizens of Westmorland and Cumberland, and throw himself into the serious business of Bohemianism. Night after night the fells echoed to revelry and pentameters as the wild poets of Cumbria entertained thinkers and versifiers from all over the civilised world. Scott came, and Lamb, and Hazlitt, and de Quincey, until the nights of riot and boozing and composition surpassed anything the literary world had seen since William Shagsper, Kit Marlowe, Francis Bacon, the Earl of Oxford and Robert Greene had all stabbed one another in the Mermaid Tavern, leaving the responsibility for Elizabethan drama entirely in the hands of a Mr. W. H. Grobeley, the inn's landlord, who subsequently wrote it to avoid suspicion falling on his hostelry. No visit to Dove Cottage, Grasmere, is complete without examining the outhouse where Hazlitt's father, a Unitarian minister of strong liberal views, attempted to put his hand up Dorothy Wordsworth's skirt, and at Greta Hall, Keswick, can be seen the faded, bloody marks following a fight over the rent-book by its two most illustrious tenants, Coleridge and Southey.

But ultimately, as it will, Bohemianism died. Coleridge left in 1809, went south, and died of opium poisoning. Southey became Poet Laureate in 1813, and took to wearing hats and drinking lukewarm herb tea. In the same year, Wordsworth became the Distributor of Stamps for the County of Westmorland at £400 per annum, and as befitted a civil servant, moved to Rydal Mount, turned his back on liberalism, and finally petered out in 1850, leaving his cottage to de Quincey, who hadn't touched a drop for the past thirty years.

Today, there are few reminders of those high and far-off times: the occasional grocer with the ineradicable Hazlitt family nose, or the Coleridge lip; fading graffiti on some derelict farmhouse wall, retailing bizarre local legends in the language and forms set down in the famous *Preface* of 1798; the empty gin-bottles that have bobbed on Ullswater and Bassenthwaite for the past century and a half; a crumbling gazebo on the outskirts of Keswick, built by Southey and from which he would pounce on passing milkmaids. Naturally, there are far more memorials to the more respectable aspects of the Bohemians' life and work, and during the summer, the roads of the two counties are filled with coachloads of people from Bromley and Philadelphia being driven to Gowbarrow Park to look at the descendants of the original daffodils.

The traditions, too, are dead. Not only is the local population conspicuously sane, sober, ungrieving, unstarving and totally unlike the *dramatis personae* of Wordsworth's records, the visitors are similarly unpoetic and unBohemian. They throng the Lake District between April and October in great tweed crowds; they wear sensible shoes, and corduroy knee-breeches, headscarves and duffle-coats, balaclavas and plastic macs; they carry stolid-looking walking-sticks, and rucksacks, and notebooks for pressing bog asphodel and saxifrage in, and Aer Lingus bags containing tomato sandwiches and flasks of Bovril; they have ròsy cheeks, and hearty, uncomplicated laughs, and sturdy calf-muscles; they eat ham teas, and hold sing-songs in Youth Hostels, and go to bed at nine o'clock to listen to the wind in the eaves. Or else they come in Ford Cortinas and Bedford Dormobiles, with primus stoves and Calor Gas and tents from Gamages, to take their children boating on Windermere. And every year, they pay homage at the verdant shrine of someone whom they vaguely remember as being a poet, or something, simply because the guide book has led them to his grave, and because all tombs demand equal reverence. So they stand, heads bowed briefly, in St. Oswald's churchyard, Grasmere.

Never for one moment realising that Wordsworth himself would have thrown up at the sight of them.

9

The Power and the Glory

Mr. Denis Healey, the Minister of Defence, promised today that Britain would not lose her world lead in the development of vertical take-off aircraft.

BBC News

The other morning, I was standing by the gas-stove, ears tensed for the first, fine, careless cackle of the percolator, and watching the new day creep feebly up the sky with that curious, droopy greyness that characterizes February in London. The days, at this bleak time, never quite make it, never quite manage to look like anything but a dispirited pause between one night and the next. Buses loomed out of the darkness, shouldering the veils of drizzle aside rather in the manner of Akim Tamiroff pushing his way through the hanging beads of some Casablancan clip-joint, and disappeared back into the snivelling gloom. Not, all things considered, a morning designed to render the waking heart delirious at the prospect of unknown delights to come. But one, nevertheless, sadly appropriate to the island over which it had chosen to break.

We live on the first floor, which puts us on an exact level with the upper decks of London buses. Since our flat fronts the road, this means that at any given breakfast brew-up, people pass slowly by, in groups of thirty, and watch me with emotionless eyes as I strive to keep the front of my pyjamas closed; while I, in turn, stare back at them with the cool superiority of a man who in happier days might have been out chopping his way through Sikhs and Boers with terse Victorian purpose. These moments are about the only chance I have to show that breeding still counts, now that the Empire turns out to be something on which the sun never rises.

As, on this particular morning, we stood there, all thirty-one of us, I noticed for the first time a strange, unsettling sadness in the sixty alien eyes. They seemed to be looking to me for hope, for some mute sign that life was more than a tale told by an idiot; but before I could come up with a glance of comfort, a smile of faith, the bus moved on, and, wobbling slightly, they vanished into the gloom. I was deeply moved. The look was a look I had seen before, over the past few months, on faces passing in the street, in eyes across a public bar, in the brave, unflinching gaze of friends and cops and grocers, it was a look which said, with all the terrible expressiveness of silence, 'What is to become of us?'

I turned again to the percolator, which by this time seemed to be sobbing in sympathy with the general mood, and as I did so I caught the wheeze of the bedroom radio plucking weakly at the ether; my wife was awake, and avid for news. In these post-lapsarian days since the Tories shuffled brokenly into the sunset, England has been gripped by a feverish need for information unmatched since VE-Day. Each dawn, red eyes pop open all over the queendom, tiny, terrified stars in the overwhelming greyness, and wait for the eight a.m. news. In the preliminary silence, one seems to hear the creak of the economy, and the occasional subterranean groan of the trade-gap widening, like some glacier running between Land's End and John O'Groats and threatening to swallow us all; then comes the Greenwich Time Signal, followed by a BBC voice intoning in old, noble accents the latest catalogue of horrors, the crash of stocks, the leaps of Bank Rate as it fights its way upstream, the rifts between and within political parties, the news that Britain has been bounced out of one more of the rooms in the fickle seraglio that is Europe today, stories of industrial dispute and international embarrassment, of crop failure and metal fatigue – the list seems endless. And, after it all, at ten minutes past eight, we drag ourselves pitifully from our beds with all-too-evident third rate power, and crawl away to work with the aforementioned look in our one hundred million eyes.

All right. I realise that many citizens of the United States, the Soviet Union, of France and Italy and Australia and Japan and all the rest of that gang of unprincipled upstarts currently touting their carpetbags around the market-places of the world and making the *Made in Britain* label an object of derision among men, I realise that these people, while sympathetic to our decline, tend to feel that we had a good run for everyone else's money, and that we're bitching unreasonably now that other flags want to get in on the act. Which is rather like tapping Billy Batson on the shoulder and saying 'Tough luck, Billy, but *Shazam* isn't the code word any more and we're not telling you what the new one is because we figure it's about time somebody else had a crack at the Captain Marvel title. Under the circumstances, our advice to you is to open a hardware store in Wichita Falls and leave Doctor Savannah to some of the younger fellahs.' Fair enough, unless you just happen to be Billy Batson, in which case you're stuck with a not inconsiderable problem of adjustment.

To return to specifics. I sloshed the coffee into a brace of Coronation Mugs, and, my upper lip a ridge of steel, padded into the bedroom to shore up my wife's wilting spirits with a few well-chosen words about the unconquerable will and study of revenge and similar snippets culled from our immortal heritage. She lay palely between the sheets, like one whose life has been frittered away on over-attention to camellias, listening to the newscaster reeling off reports of motions of censure on the Government, the wasting sickness of our gold reserves, the current protest march of aircraft workers, the latest lurch in the cost-of-living index, and other gobbets calculated to stick in the most optimistic craw. As the minutes flashed by, loaded to the gunwales with disaster, our commingled gloom deepened to a rich ebony, and I was on the point of hurling the radio through the window in the hope, perhaps, of felling a passing Volkswagen (a distinct statistical possibility), when the announcer paused suddenly, caught his breath, and said

'Mr. Denis Healey, the Minister of Defence, promised today that Britain would not lose her world lead in the development of vertical take-off aircraft.'

There might have been more news after that, but we didn't hear it. My wife sat bolt upright in bed, the colour hurtling through her cheeks, her eyes uncannily bright, and clutched at my arm with that reserve of energy normally associated with drowning men in the presence of a sudden boathook.

'Can it be true?' she whispered.

I bit my lip.

'It has to be true,' I said.

'A world lead? Of our very own?'

'And we have it already!'

'Pray God we can hold on to it!' she muttered. We looked at one another with new hope. Horizons began to open before us, albeit vertically.

'I think –' I said, very slowly, '– I think it's all going to be all right, after all. I think we're going to come through.'

We drank our coffee in one draught, flung the cups over our shoulders, and offered a brief prayer for those in peril on the drawing-board. We had seen, at last, the thin end of the wedge, and it was a good wedge. Without a weapon of one's own, you see, without an original working weapon, it's impossible to hope for greatness. All very well to moan about defence expenditure and the lack of funds for schools, hospitals, pensions, roads, universities and all the rest of that pointless paraphernalia. All very well to brag about your Shakespeares and your Dantes and your Racines and your Ella Wheeler Wilcoxes. But when the chips are down, the chap from Smith and Wesson is the one we turn to. Weapons are the only true curators of our culture, and what in recent months has sapped the vitality of the Island Race has been the increasing doubt as to whether our independent deterrent was worth the sack it came in. While other nations proliferated their Polarises, or lobbed their ICBM's willy-nilly between Novaya Zemlya and the Pole, we in Britain have gradually come to feel that the idea of having our own personal overkill was but an idle dream. We know that, called upon to swop punches with an Unnamed Foreign Power, we'd be hard put to to raise one megadeath among the lot of us. In all probability, the first day's hostilities would turn us into mere froth and flotsam; we should go down in history as no more than a patch of choppy water off the Irish coast. But not now. Now that we possessed a weapon in the development of which we led the world, to what glorious heights might we not rise?

'They ought to ring the churchbells,' said my wife, mopping her tears with a sheetcorner.

'By heavens!' I cried, smiting the mattress till the springs sang, 'The old lion lives to roar again! Let Russia tremble! Let China quail!'

My wife looked at the ceiling with passionate calm.

'And gentlemen in Osh Kosh, now a-bed
Shall think themselves accurs'd they were not here,
And hold their manhoods cheap . . .'

She lit a cigarette with a trembling flame. 'I say, my love, do you suppose it's too late to get the Empire back? Or, at least, some of the nicer bits?'

'Never!' I shouted. 'We are just entering the period familiarly known as the nick of time, and from here on in the going cannot be anything but good. Before the year is out, vertical take-off aircraft will be dropping like archangels all over the uncivilized world. Natives will run from the bush, crying 'What is that great shining bird that drops from the skies like Ukkra, God of Sleet?' and we shall answer 'It is a British vertical take-off aircraft, you heathen bastards, sent from the Great White Queen across the oceans, and you have ten seconds flat in which to start the grovelling routine.'

She clasped her hands ecstatically.

'Oh, think of it! There is trouble in the Straits . . . the natives are running riot through the rubber . . . mud has been thrown at the Flag . . .'

'. . . ten thousand miles away, a tall figure in mutton-chop whiskers hails a cab in Downing Street and clops rapidly . . .'

'Clops?'

'All right, roars. Roars rapidly through the night to Buckingham Palace . . . the Imperial Presence . . . the curt nods . . . the rasp of pen on parchment . . .'

'We have decided to send a vertical take-off aircraft!'

'Ah!'

'Ah!'

I strode to the window, hands clasped behind me, and looked into the coruscating future.

'What about this? De Gaulle criticises the movements of British hussars in the Sudan . . . our Ambassador hurries to Colombey-les-deux-Églises . . . the slap of glove on cheek . . . next morning, when the population of Marseilles awakes, there, bobbing on the tide, is a fleet of British vertical take-off aircraft . . .'

'Bobbing on the what?'

'I don't know why you have to quibble. Bobbing in the air, then. Shooting vertically up to five hundred feet, and shooting vertically down again, like great silver yo-yos, like . . . what's the matter?'

My wife was looking at me with every sign of fear.

'These vertical thingummies,' she said, quietly. 'What do they do except . . . except bob up and down?'

'What do you mean?'

'I mean, do they carry Ultimate Deterrents and stuff like that?'

'I suppose so.'

'But we haven't got any. Not anything Ultimate of our own.'

I said nothing. Something prickled against my tonsils.

'There isn't much percentage in just bobbing up and down, is there?' she said. 'Not unless you're in a position to improve on it. I mean, you're going to look pretty bloody ridiculous if in the middle of the yo-yo bit an Intercontinental What-not comes along horizontally and bowls you over like a row of skittles, aren't you?'

'They do fly on the level too, you know,' I said, with a scorn I was rapidly ceasing to feel.

'How fast?' she pressed.

'I don't know,' I said weakly. 'Quite fast, I suppose.'

'Fast *enough*?'

I looked down at the citizens romping about in the street below. There was a new bounce to their step, a new light in the communal eye. Here and there, a Union Jack fluttered. I turned away, pity and panic wrestling in my breast, to see her knuckles whitening on the edge of the blanket.

'It's all — it's all just another noble gesture, isn't it?' she whispered.

Slowly, I nodded. But the light, though waning fast, had not altogether passed from my eyes.

'All is not utterly lost, my love,' I said. 'One truth remains. When comes to noble gestures, Britain still . . .'

'Leads the world?' she murmured.

'That's right,' I said.

10

Mao, He's Making Eyes At Me!

*Love is a 'middle-class prejudice', a 'capitalist weakness',
and a time-wasting 'psychopathic occupation', according to
the latest Chinese Press pronouncements. In the Maoist
view, married life is an opportunity for studying the works
of Mao Tse-tung and maintaining a 'permanent atmosphere
of ideological struggle and criticism in the home'. Attempts
to reconcile family quarrels are considered unMarxist.*

Daily Telegraph

Lao Piu-Fong was singing as he walked up the grimy staircase of his concrete apartment block. He was singing a song about the need to produce more 3.2 millimetre rivets, thereby prolonging the life of Chairman Mao by at least another two thousand years. He was singing despite the fact that a bus had just run over his foot and a rat had eaten his ersatz prawn during the five minute Thought Break at the factory and his best friend had been decapitated by the authorities for losing his spanner down a drain. He was singing, above all, because it was seven p.m. in Peking and five million people coming home from work were singing, and it was a thing it was wise to do if you had any plans about waking up the next morning.

He reached the scrofulous hell of the upper landing, where he paused to thank a kindly Red Guard for spitting in his eye and bayonetting his hat, and passed on into his tiny, dark flat.

Lao Piu-Fong had been uneasy all day. That morning, on leaving for work, he had failed to remember not to kiss his wife goodbye, which was something which always upset her. What made it worse was the knowledge that he would be unable to apologise to her, since reconciliation was also unMarxist. The only course open to him was to hit her.

She picked herself up off the floor gratefully, took his threadbare hat and coat, and threw them on the fire. Lao Piu-Fong bowed, and began singing a song about the shortage of glue in Maintenance Area Fourteen, and how it was directly attributable to the presence of Chiang Kai-Shek on Formosa. Then his children came in and swore at him until it was time for bed; the main target of their abuse was the fact that in order for him to have become their father at all, he had found it necessary to indulge in a spot of capitalist messing about with their mother, whom they similarly reviled for allowing him to pull his right-wing deviationist tricks in the first place. With happy cries of 'Psychopath!' and 'Warmongering Revanchist Tart!' they ran off to bed, leaving the Piu-Fongs despising one another in front of the fire.

'Excuse, most horrible fragment of dung,' said Mrs. Piu-Fong, 'but what is this I am hearing from many comrades concerning your filthy neo-Wall Street practices behind factory canteen with Worker-Waitress Eighteen?'

'Is vile slander put about by agents provocateurs for purpose of sabotaging output,' said Lao miserably. He sighed. He found himself unable to put his heart into vituperation this evening; much as he recognised his marital responsibility in reducing his wife to the level of a treacherous maniac, his mind kept wandering to subversive memories of lip and thigh. Tiny beads of sweat squeezed out of his forehead, slid down his nose, and splashed onto the thumb-stained copy of Mao's Thoughts open on his lap. It was not easy being a perfect husband. But he tried.

'Sickening poisonous capitalist toad,' he said, 'I am also hearing of your politically destructive laissez-faire policy with the riceman. What have you to say, dissolute cow?'

Mrs. Piu-Fong flushed angrily.

'Is loathsome lie!' she cried. 'Riceman T'song and I are merely discussing Chapter XVIII, paragraph IX—'

'SO!' shrieked Lao. 'While back is turned, you are considering question of leek-rotation with Riceman T'song! While honourable first-class riveter husband is slaving over lathe all day, worm-eaten petty bourgeoise wife is sharing same sentence as pigfaced ricemonger!'

Mrs. Piu-Fong looked up at him, and sneered triumphantly.

'Now,' she smirked, 'we discuss cheap lousy middle-class jealousy of failed husband unworthy to sit in same room as genuine sepia-toned portrait of Chairman Mao, immortal father of his people. Please to begin, small thin dolt!'

Lao ripped his shirt, and began to keen.

'I have been jealous,' he moaned, rocking on his heels. 'True.'

'I have been possessive.'

'And worse!'

'Worse?'

'You have been guilty, unworthy morsel, of interfering in discussion of matchless gem-like Thoughts of Chairman Mao, and of attempting to subvert spiritual development of me and Riceman T'song.'

'Ah, so. I have been guilty of interfering in discussion of matchless gem-like Thoughts of Chairman Mao, and of attempting to subvert spiritual development of wife and Riceman T'song.'

'And?'

'And I have been having middle-class thoughts about female bus-travellers. And capitalist ideas about Postwoman Cho.'

'You are a psychopath.'

'I am a psychopath.' Lao Piu-Fong stared at the flickering grate. 'Mind you,' he murmured, 'I have not indulged in any perverted deviationist private enterprise for eight months. Is this not worthy?'

Mrs. Piu-Fong spat.

'You are complacent,' she snarled.

'I am complacent.'

'Also you have been guilty of not repairing leaking tap in kitchen, contrary to Chapter MCDXVI, sub-section IV, lines II–V: *Urban progress possible only if each individual citizen-soldier recognises responsibility to maintaining roof placed over head through foresight and generosity of Chairman Mao.* Similarly, you have neglected your duties with regard to faulty ball-cock, hole in bedroom window, and short leg on dining-room table.'

'All this I have not done,' groaned Lao Piu-Fong. 'Indeed, I am guilty of betraying great principles formulated on Long March.' His stomach rumbled. 'When are we eating?'

'First we sing magnificent chart-topper describing the joys of building new wing on public library,' said his wife. 'For has not peerless Chairman Mao written: *Hunger of soul cannot be satisfied with noodles?*'

'Probably,' muttered Lao, *sotto voce.*

After the song had died away at last, he looked down at his small wooden bowl.

'Excuse, please, obscene disaster in human form,' he said to his wife, 'but what is this esteemed muck I am supposed to eat?'

'It is from special Madame Mao recipe,' said his wife. 'With purpose of building healthy citizen-soldiers and at the same time destroying ugly capitalist greed-orientated appetite. Is sawdust foo yong full of nourishing synthetic protein, guaranteed free from artificial colouring.'

Lao forked a moist blob of the khaki paste into his mouth,

blenched, and pushed the bowl away. His wife, poised for ideological advantage, raised an eyebrow.

'Well?' she said dangerously.

'Oh,' cried Piu-Fong, 'how all-seeing and talented is the great mother of our people!'

She narrowed her eyes.

'What are you trying to pull, revisionist fink?' she grated.

'Nothing. But see how my former fascist greed and unMarxist appetite have disappeared through the wisdom of Mother Mao! Not one more mouthful need I eat, so successful has her policy proved.'

Mrs. Piu-Fong threw down her chopstick.

'Do you refuse, therefore, to give me the opportunity of self-criticism? Am I not to be allowed to repent for my deviation from the recipe as laid down by Madame Mao?'

'No,' said Lao. A tiny gloat ran across his lips. But it was short-lived.

'So!' cried his wife. 'Can it be, subversive louse, that you failed to notice the forbidden bean-curd, introduced by me for the sole purpose of testing your awareness of Madame Mao's edicts?'

A sob shook the mean little room. Broken, Lao Piu-Fong pushed back his stool and stood up raggedly, and bowed a small, pitiful bow.

'Am going to bed,' he said hoarsely. 'Am going to bed for purpose of self-castigation. Am indeed an unworthy husband and dialectician. So sorry.'

And, leaving her smiling terribly at the portrait on the wall, he trudged into the neighbour room and threw himself upon the unyielding palliasse.

But self-criticism would not come, no matter how hard he tried. Each time he began to enumerate his deviations, slim bodies danced out of his memory and writhed before him, a thousand faces rose up from his imagination to smile and kiss, a thousand slim, seductive hands reached for his unworthy flesh. Until, at last, the incorrigible capitalist spirit of Citizen-Soldier Lao Piu-Fong fell into restless slumber, to dream its dreams of counter-revolution.

11

Death Duties

Up until now, it may not have been generally known that I live in a flat whose previous tenant shuffled off this mortal coil owing Selfridge's 12/6. But eighteen months is long enough to live with the increasing burden that this debt has come to represent; and since, on the question of responsibility, I am less of an island than most men you run across, I feel the need to spread the weight a little.

I know almost nothing about my predecessor, except that she departed this life peacefully at a commendably advanced age; I learned only a little more from the sad trickle of uninformed post that kept turning up after I moved in – she did the pools, she voted, she read *The Reader's Digest*, and she once spent a holiday in Torquay at a hotel that persists in inviting her to Gala Gourmet Weekends which, from the manager's imploring circular, obviously won't be the same without her. At some time in her life, she purchased enough roofing-felt from a firm in Acton to warrant an annual calendar's gratitude, and, long before that, she had been a pupil at a girls' school in Roehampton which has now fallen on evil times and needs £5,000 to drive the woodworm from its ancient bones.

I dutifully sent these voices from the past back to the land of the living, marked 'Address Unknown', together with a brace of Christmas cards wishing her peace, a sentiment I feel bound to endorse. The only things I held on to (all right, this is probably a heinous crime under some sub-section or other, but, believe me, I have paid in full for it) were a series of polite notes from Selfridge's, requesting the coughing-up of 12/6.

I had my own nefarious reasons for this peccadillo. Back in the early days, it came to me (not unlike a shaft of pure white light) that here I was with an invaluable index of consumer-tolerance, i.e., How far was Selfridge's prepared to go before they cried havoc and let loose the dogs of war? Were I ever to consider running up a fat bill with them, this information would stand me in the best of steads, since, the longer one can delay the payment of bills the better, inflation being what it is. (I have never been too certain what it is, actually, but as a kid I used to buy 1930 billion-mark German stamps at threepence a hundred, and a thing like that sticks in your memory.) Whatever Mrs. X bought for 12/6 in 1962 doubtless goes out at around fifteen bob these days, and if she's reading this now under some Elysial hair-dryer, bless her, I hope she takes comfort from the thought that she got out while the going was good.

So, just to test the plan, I hung on, opening the three-monthly reminders, waiting for the sort of filthy innuendo *I* usually get in these circumstances about what a pity it is that I mislaid their bill and if I don't fork out in seven days, my humble and obedient servants will be round with the boys and have the telly back and no mistake. But nothing like that ever came. A year passed with the characteristic rapidity of its kind, leaves fell off the rubber-plant, the odd crow's foot stamped itself around my limpid eyes, and still Selfridge's continued to beg the pardon of the dead, and nothing more. I began to lay complex plans for capitalising on this inside knowledge. I walked the store, floor by floor, choosing one of them, two of those, fifty square yards of that, and so on, in order that when I came to make my move, I could draw up in an articulated truck by the goods entrance and be away from the place with a complete home in about ten minutes flat, with every chance of hanging on to luxury for a year or so. It was on one such drooling foray that my best-laid schemes ganged agley and withered on my brow in one fell metaphor; turning a sharp right at a bolt of Gustav Doré chintz, I came upon a scene that made the death of Little Nell look like a Groucho Marx routine; a tiny, lacey, delicate old lady, a butterfly emeritus exuding spiritual lavender, was pressing a small package on a salesman. She was going away, I heard her whisper, and she wanted to give him something to remember her by; he was, she said softly, not a salesman, but her dear, dear friend. I staggered out into, I believe, Gloucester Place, choking with Truth. She was, of course, *my* little old lady, or as near as made no odds; I'd become so enmeshed in the web of greedy intrigue currently on the loom that I had forgotten that there was more to my plan than just Selfridge's and I, two hard-boiled toughs who might one day face one another down at High Noon in Carey Street. Never for one moment had I paused to consider the old lady who had gone to join her ancestors with 12/6 worth of Selfridge's money. The one obvious reason why the store hadn't sent its bruisers round to collect the debt had up until then escaped me – that Mrs. X had no doubt been a customer in those far-off Edwardian days when Harry Gordon Selfridge was still worrying about his mortgage repayments. Quite probably, she had been all set to go through the store for the last time, distributing cuff links and panatellas when the call for the long trip took her unawares, and it is more than clear to me that no one had informed Selfridge's of her passing. Suddenly, I saw her, a sweet soul, full of the simple goodness which is honed to a fine smooth finish on the *Reader's Digest* lathes; in my mind she sat filling in her Littlewood's coupons and praying for a first dividend to save the school from termites and provide everyone in Selfridge's with enough roofing-felt to last a lifetime. They must have missed her at the store, the living image of Whistler's mum, first up the escalator at the Sales ('Put them ornamented bathmats aside for Mrs. X, Esmond, she's one of our reg'lars'), smiling at Uncle Holly year in, year out, remembering every liftboy at Christmas ('It's little Horace, isn't it? My, we've grown, haven't we?'), a favourite with all the waitresses in the cafeteria, a paragon of virtue to the Accounts Dept.

I turned into Baker Street, the iron in my soul, another Raskolnikov with guilt for an old lady red on his hands. No doubt she had been missed at the store for eighteen months; rumours would be seething in the staff canteen, and, finally, half-apologetically, looking down into his tea-cup, someone would bring up the issue of her outstanding debt. At first, it would be excused, laughed off; but before long fifty years of graciousness would be swept away, and she would be written off as just another lousy customer, at one with the welshers and the shoplifters and the people who knocked things off shelves in the china department.

It was when I decided to make amends that the real horror of the things struck, in true Dostoievskian fashion; actions are irreversible, sin cannot be structurally altered. There was no way in which I could straighten the mess out; if I wrote to the store, explaining that their debtor was in no shape to square the account, they would wonder why I had taken nearly two years to contact them. It was even on the cards that I'd find myself opening the door to a couple of characters in fawn raincoats demanding to know what I'd done with the body. Similarly, were I able to trace her descendants, what could I say? ('Look, I hate to stir old memories, but your dear mother/aunt/sister owes Selfridge's 12/6'). How would they react to the stain imprinted by me on their loved one's reputation? I was the one who'd made her, post-mortally, a rotten financial risk, and dragged the good name of X through the mire. For all I knew, they might take it out on me by having me sent down for tampering with the mails, or something, and I understand they're handing out thirty years for that these days.

Last week, another demand-note turned up. The tone had shifted slightly to one of gentlemanly bewilderment; I knew the omens of old. I had to forestall the ultimatum; like Macbeth, I was in blood stepp'd in so far, that, should I wade no more, returning were as tedious as go o'er. Only one course of action lay open; I put a ten-bob note and a half-crown in an envelope, together with a note explaining that I had been laid up for two years with a wasting disease and only now was I beginning to pull through, and I hoped they would understand, theirs, with every apology, Mrs. X.

That ought to hold them for a bit. But you can never be sure about these things, and if they decide to have a whip round in the Soft Furnishings and send me a Get Well card and a jar of crystallised ginger, I may yet have to go on the run.

'The Funniest Writer In Britain Today'

1970–1979

VICTORIA WOOD

Introduction

I was thirteen. I couldn't manage my breasts. I couldn't manage my eating. I never did my homework. I lived in a misbuttoned guilt-ridden fog most of the time. I had two consolations. One was food – which can, as we know, prove a false friend, but at thirteen one doesn't realise the many tedious years that lie ahead, as one tries to unpick the knotted relationship between comfort, joy and American hard gums.

My other consolation – and this remains a true pal – was comedy. Not television comedy, which for the most part in the mid 1960s was twee, leaden and over-reliant on canned laughter, but written comedy.

My house, which was an ex-anti-aircraft base on a windswept hill in Lancashire, had been made into an approximation of a family home by my mother, who had put up plywood partitions, not exactly at random but not in any way William Morris might have salivated over either. Having by this method formed about twenty rooms, she then proceeded to fill them all with books. Second-hand books. Sometimes she would chuck in the odd rogue item, like the costumes from a production of *The Quaker Girl*, or a sack of shoe lasts, but mainly it was books.

And because there was eff-all going on in my home, and because I was a compulsive person, and I didn't have enough money to eat all day long, and the telly didn't come on till four, I read. In the bath, while playing the piano, while watching *Magpie* and *The Man from UNCLE* – I read. And though I would read anything rather than nothing, what I really wanted to read was comedy.

I had a tattered paperback, I should think from the 1930s, called *Modern Masters of Wit and Humour* and this was my introduction to the comic essay, the funny piece. It didn't matter to me that these particular pieces were all by men, that there didn't seem to be any modern mistresses of wit and humour – I just loved the detail, the angle, the taking of some prosaic domestic situation and skewing it through a prism, so that something that presumably in life had been irritating or boring became something quite life-enhancing in print.

I went to the library every day after school – I had to wait an hour for my father to pick me up from the bottom of our lane. I wasn't supposed to walk home in case I got molested, though I think even a sexual nutcase might have thought twice about approaching my solid trudging figure with its flapping satchel of homework arrears and its trail of wine gums. Oh, get to the point, Wood. Yes: the library. Bury Library. Like a big old municipal crack house just sitting there full of my drug of choice. And what they had in the Reference section was *Punch*. Not the old bound volumes with their unhilarious yokels, cooks and curates, but the current magazine. *Modern Masters of Wit and Humour* thirty years on.

And that was where I first read Alan Coren. You might not think a thirteen-year-old girl with collapsing socks and a pocket full of chocolate with a street value of ninepence would have been his ideal reader. But I was. He made me laugh. It wasn't my world, but it was no less funny for that. For those two pages, I lived in his universe. I wasn't in Bury with a dull evening ahead of me – luncheon meat, beetroot and *The Forsyte Saga* – I was in Cricklewood wondering what was up with the central heating, or trying to get my raincoat back from the dry cleaner's.

Let's jump forward nearly forty years. Leapfrogging Dana, loonpants, perestroika, 'The Birdie Song' and red pesto. My homework's still not done, but my behaviour around Creme Eggs is slightly more under control, and there I was in my kitchen in London with the radio on and I was listening to one of those mad programmes you could only get on the wireless – it was Alan Coren and a friend going round London on buses, just maundering on about things and getting on and off when they felt like it, and just acting like boys, really – oldish boys. And I heard a bus number I recognised: it was the bus that goes up Our Hill and stops outside Our House. And I can't really explain what a thrill it was to hear that master of wit and humour, Mr Alan Coren – to hear him get off the bus at the top of Our Hill and actually hear the crunch of his humorous feet on Our Gravel. And if it had been live, and if I had been gawping out of my bedroom window, I would have been able to see him. And I meant, were I ever to meet him, to say: 'Hello, Alan, we've never been introduced, but you got off the bus onto my gravel, and you've made me laugh from when I was thirteen. Thank you.' But I didn't get that opportunity, so writing this is the next best thing.

12

Boom, What Makes My House Go Boom?

*One of the effects of the house-price spiral and the rush
to buy has been that estate agents no longer find it necessary
to disguise the truth about their properties.*

The Observer

I met him at the gate, as arranged. We looked up at the
house together. He glanced at his watch, not unobviously.

'It's rather nice,' I said. 'I've always wanted to live in St.
Johns Wood.'

'No point going in, then,' said the agent, taking a cigarette
from his packet and deftly avoiding my reaching hand. 'This
is Kilburn.'

'Oh, surely not! I understood that this area was traditionally
described as, well, as St. Johns Wood borders?'

He sucked his teeth. He shook his head.

'Not even Swiss Cottage,' he said. 'Not even *West* Swiss
Cottage.'

'Swiss Cottage borders?' I begged.

'Kilburn.' He put the watch to his ear. 'If that.'

'Oh.'

'What do you expect,' he muttered, 'for twenty-three-nine-
fifty?'

'Twenty-two-five,' I corrected. I showed him the specification
sheet.

He tapped it with a finger.

'Got yesterday's date on,' he said.

'I received it this morning,' I said, 'and surely—'

'Lucky we sent it express,' he said. 'Might be out of your range tomorrow.'

'Could we go in?' I enquired. 'It's rather chilly here.'

'What do you think it is inside?' he said. 'Bermuda?'

'The central heating must make a—'

'*Part* central heating,' he said. 'Plus small boiler, totally inadequate to the job. Especially bearing in mind the lack of double-glazing. The only way to tell if the radiators are on is to put your cheek up against them and wait for a minute or two. Still, at twenty-four-two-fifty, you can't really complain, can you?'

'I suppose not,' I said, 'these town houses are at a premium these days.'

'*Terraced* houses.'

'I always thought—'

'Call a spade a spade, that's our motto. When you've got a long line of nondescript jerry-built bogus-regency items leaning on one another to keep from falling down, they're known as terraced houses. Or, in some cases, back-to-backs. If the gardens are as tiny as this one is.' He opened the front door. 'Don't rush in,' he said, 'or you'll miss it, ha-ha-ha!'

'Ha-ha-ha!'

'See that crack in the hall ceiling? You'd think they'd take a bit more care with a twenty-six-grand property, wouldn't you?'

'It doesn't look too bad,' I said, 'probably just a fault in the plastering. A good workman could fill that in in two shakes of—'

'That's what the previous owner thought,' said the agent, stubbing his cigarette out on the wallpaper. 'His dog fell through it and broke its neck. Treacherous, these stone floors.'

'But sound,' I said. 'No chance of warp, dry rot, that sort of—'

'You wait till your plumbing packs up,' he said. 'Main

conduit's under there: one day your bath's cold, the next you've got six blokes and a pneumatic drill poking about in your foundations. Want to see the kitchenette?'

'Thank you.'

''Course,' he said over his shoulder as he forced the door, 'when I say foundations, that's only my little joke. Three inches of builders' rubbish and a couple of two-by-fours, and that's it. I wouldn't like to be here when the motorway goes through – one articulated truck, and you're liable to find yourself with half the roof in the downstairs lav.'

'Oh, I didn't realise there was a downstairs lavatory,' I said. 'That's rather encourag—'

'I wouldn't show it to you,' he said, 'I wouldn't even talk about it. Not so soon after breakfast. This is the kitchenette.'

'Kitchen*ette*?' I said. 'Mind you, I suppose it is a bit on the small side, but—'

'*Small?* It's lucky there's no mice here, otherwise you'd have to take turns going to the larder.'

'Well, you wouldn't expect mice in a modern house, would you?'

'Right. Rats yes, mice no.'

'Oh. Well, we've got a cat, so—'

'That's one bedroom out for a start, then,' he said. 'Big cat, is it?'

'Neutered tom,' I said.

The agent pursed his lips.

'Probably have to give him the master suite, in that case,' he said. 'At least he can shove open the bathroom door and stick his tail in if he starts feeling claustrophobic. Lucky it's on the first floor, really.'

'I'm sorry?'

'If the cat's on the first floor, you and the family can sleep above it. On the second. You don't want a bloody great moggy stamping around overhead all night, do you? Let alone watching you and the missus through the gaps in the floorboards. Lying on your back listening to the tubes rumbling underneath, with a bloody great green eye staring down at you.'

We left the kitchen, and came back into the hall. He opened another door.

'I imagine that's the dining-room?' I said.

'That's what you want to do, squire,' he said. 'Imagine. Mind you, it'd do for buffet suppers, provided the four of you all had small plates. The other door leads to the integral garage, by the way, if you were wondering what the smell of petrol was. You've got a car, I take it?'

'Yes.'

'Don't forget to leave it outside, then. Bloke two doors down made the mistake of changing his Fiat 500 in for a Mini. Brought it home from the showroom, drove straight in, had to spend the night there. Wife fed him through the quarter-light. I suppose you could always have a sunshine-roof fitted, though.'

'We'll leave ours out,' I said. 'It's more convenient, what with taking the kids to school every morn—'

'Oh, you won't need the motor for that, squire! School's only a stone's throw away.'

'Really? Well, that's a load off—'

'Very good glazier up the road, though. Mind you, you have to take the day off to let him in. He won't come out at night.'

'That's surprising.'

'In this neighbourhood? After dark even the police cars cruise in pairs.'

'Do you think we might go upstairs?'

'And that's only if there's a full moon.'

'Four bedrooms, I think you said?'

'Well, three really. The third one's been split into two with a party wall, but you could easily convert it back. Just slam the front door, and bob's your uncle.'

I started up the staircase, and it wasn't until I'd reached the first landing that I realised I was alone. The agent called up.

'You all right?'

'Yes,' I shouted.

He joined me.

'Hope you don't mind,' he said. 'Never tell with these stairs. I reckoned you were about my weight.' He patted the banister lovingly. 'See that workmanship? They don't make 'em like that any more!'

'It's certainly an attrac—'

'Not after *Rex* v. *Newsomes Natty Fittings Ltd.*, they don't. Christ!' he exclaimed, looking at his watch again. 'It's never twelve o'clock already!'

'Two minutes past, actually.'

'That's another half-hour off the lease, then.' He turned, and started down the stairs again, gingerly. 'I trust you have the requisite used notes in the motor, squire?'

I followed him down.

'I'd like a little time to think about it,' I said, 'and then, of course, my solicitor will have to make the necessary searches and—'

He laid a kindly claw on my arm.

'Do yourself a favour, son,' he said gently. 'Forget about searches. Tatty old drum like this, you can never tell what they might find. Now, look, am I going to be able to unload this or not?'

'Well, I'm not entirely certain, but—'

The agent wrenched open the front door. A queue stretched down the path, and into the street. Mute supplication blinked in their watery eyes.

'Says he's not certain!' cried the agent.

Instantly, the queue dismembered itself into a shrieking mob.

'One at a time!' yelled the agent, tearing a brassette carriage-lamp from the wall and beating a clearing among the grabbing throng. 'Let's do this proper! Now, I am not asking twenty-nine-five for this mouldering pile! I am not asking thirty-two-and-a-half, all I'm asking is—'

I edged through the pitiful clamour, and out into the road, and bent my steps towards the YMCA. It's warm there, and there's a nice peg for your anorak and a shelf for your clock, and it'll be weeks before the developers start bidding for the site.

With luck.

13

Suffer Little Children

According to a new publishing company, Enfance Publishing, 'every leading author has at least one children's book in him.' Every leading author?

From THE GOLLIES KARAMAZOV
by Fyodor Dostoyevsky

On a bitterly cold morning towards the end of November, 18—a pale young man left his little room at the top of a toadstool in one of the meaner tree-roots of the province of Toyland, and began to descend the dark and freezing stairs.

He was praying that he would not meet his landlady. Her burrow gave directly onto the corridor, and he had to pass it every time he went in or out. The door was usually open, and he would have to run past to avoid seeing Mrs. Rabbitoyeva, and when he did so he would experience a sensation of terror which left him shaking and sick to his stomach. Sometimes he would be physically sick. Other times, he would become possessed of a hacking and terrible cough, and his thin little body would grow luminous with sweat.

It was not merely that he was behind with his rent, living as he did in wretched poverty: it was simply that he had of late a horrible fear of meeting anybody, of engaging them in the lightest of conversations, of remarking upon the weather. This fear had itself become a sickness. Mrs. Rabbitoyeva, if she saw him, would wipe her paws on her apron (an action which itself brought an uncontrollable trembling to the young man's emaciated limbs, and set the pattern on his threadbare herringbone overcoat twitching like a nest of spiders), and smile, and nod, and say:

'Good morning, Noddy Noddeyovich! I have a nice worm ragout cooking on the stove for your lunch.'

Or:

'You should have a young lady, Noddy Noddeyovich! It is not right for a fine young man to spend so much time in the company of gnomes.'

At this, the young man would fall to the ground and kiss the hem of her garment.

But on this occasion, Mrs. Rabbitoyeva called Noddy Noddeyovich into her kitchen, and, despite the fearful trembling of his limbs which set the bell upon his cap tinkling like some derisory omen of imminent doom, he followed her. He counted his steps, as he always did – eleven, twelve, thirteen, to the table, fourteen, fifteen, to the workbench, where the knives were, and the big meat chopper. The kitchen smelt of boiled sedge, and old ferret offal, and the grey, fatty soup that Mrs. Rabbitoyeva always kept simmering for the pitiful little civil servants who inhabited her dark, cold building.

'Noddy Noddeyovich,' said Mrs. Rabbitoyeva, 'I wish to talk with you about the Gollies Karamazov.'

His trembling worsened. The Gollies Karamazov had recently moved in to the room next to Noddy Noddeyovich, and they came from the Big Wood, and their faces were black as round holes in the white winter ice. Whenever Noddy Noddeyovich saw them, he began to shake all over, and often he was sick down the stairwell, and sometimes he fainted altogether. He did not want to talk about the Gollies Karamazov. He listened for a while to the sound of Mrs. Rabbitoyeva, and it was of no sense, a heavy buzz, like the flies upon the far steppes when spring wakes the eggs.

And then he picked up the big meat chopper, and he brought it down on Mrs. Rabbitoyeva's old head, and she looked very surprised, and when the blood was all over his hands, their trembling stopped.

'I should not be here,' said Noddy Noddeyovich, possibly aloud. 'Soon Plod Plodnikov of the State Police will be here for his morning glass of tea, and he may engage me in some philosophical discussion about guilt, with reference to the words of Morotny, and it would be better if I were to get in my little car and go Beep! Beep! and seek the advice of Bigears Bigearsnitkin . . .'

From FIVE GO OFF TO ELSINORE
by William Shakespeare

ACT ONE, Scene 1
Cheam, a desert country near the sea. Before the gates of The Laburnums. Alarums off. Sennets. Keatons. Enter Julian.

Julian: Hung be the heavens with black, yield day to night!
              The hols are but a short week old, and now
              There comes such news as Hecate herself
              Would quake to hear of! Five years of study
                gone
              And now I learn that all I have to show
              Is two O-levels: one Eng. Lit., one Maths!
              Five subjects failed, and I one subject felled
              By failure to as fell a fall as folly
              Feels!

Enter Timmy, a dog.
                    Ah, Timmy! Had I but the joy
              Of e'en thy meanest flea, I were in luck!
Timmy: Arf! Arf!

Julian: Unmetric!

Timmy: Arf! Arf! Arf! Arf! Arf!

Julian (*weeps*): The very dogs do bend them to my pleas,
Though men do reck me not! But yet I'm
wrecked!

Enter Georgina.

Georgina: How now, sweet coz! I am this sec arrived
From Cheltenham Ladies' College for the vac!
And we shall do such things, we Famous Five—
Find maps, thwart thieves, have midnight feasts
In ruined castles, smugglers' coves, and more
Deserted cottages than you've had hot—

Julian: Eff off, Georgina! All has come to nought!
A sound career with ICI is lost!
And I must hie me with my measly two
And seek emolument as Clerk (Grade IV).
No longer mine, the tree-house and the barge,
The secret passage and − but ho! What comes?

Enter Dick and Anne.

Dick: Look, dearest Anne! We Five are now conjoined
As one, like some great Lyons Sponge Cake late
Divided, and now once more new enseamed!

Julian (*aside*): It is my younger brother. Dare I ask
How he has fared in this last GCE?
Holloa, sweet Dick! How goes the world withal?

Dick: Withal, indeed! With all six subjects passed,
Geog., Maths, Eng. Lit., French, History, and
Stinks!

Anne: Oh, rippin', Dick! Top-hole, spot on, good show!

Julian (*aside*): This little twit shall yet undo me quite!
          Replace me in our father's rheumy sight,
          And get a Morris Minor for his pains,
          The dirty swot! I say, chaps, what about
          A game of harry cricket?

All: YES!

Timmy: Arf! Arf!

Enter cricket bag. Stumps are set up. Julian bowls the first ball to Dick, who smites it mightily.

Anne: See Timmy run! Run, Timmy, run! Oh, look!
          He's caught the ball between his teeth. Good dog!

Timmy: Arf! Arf! (*Dies*)

Dick: That ball! 'Tis poisoned! It was meant for me!
          But what about this bat?

Julian: 'Tis poisoned, too!

Dick: Then have at thee, foul villain! Take thou that!

Julian: A poisoned off-drive! I am slain, alas! (*Dies*)

Dick: And so am I! Oh what a measly show! (*Dies*)

Flourish. Enter bearers. They bear the bodies and exeunt.

Georgina (*weeps*): Oh, world! The curse of thy eleven-plus!
          Two brothers minus! Shall it aye be thus?

From THE POOH ALSO RISES
by *Ernest Hemingway*

It snowed hard that winter. It was the winter they all went up to the Front. You could get up early in the morning, if you were not wounded and forced to lie in your bed and look at the ceiling and wonder about the thing with the women, and you could see them going up to the Front, in the snow. When they walked in the snow, they left tracks, and after they had gone the snow would come down again and pretty soon the tracks would not be there any more. That is the way it is with snow.

Pooh did not go up to the Front that winter. Nor did he lie in bed and look at the ceiling, although last winter he had lain in bed and looked up at the ceiling, because that was the winter he had gone up to the Front and got his wound. It had snowed that winter, too.

This winter he could walk around. It was one of those wounds that left you able to walk around. It was one of those wounds that did not leave you much more.

Pooh got up and he went out into the snow and he went to see Piglet. Piglet had been one of the great ones, once. Piglet had been one of the *poujadas*, one of the *endarillos*, one of the *noogales*. He had been one of the greatest *nogales* there had ever been, but he was not one of the greatest *nogales* any more. He did not go up to the Front, either.

Piglet was sitting at his usual table, looking at an empty glass of *enjarda*.

'I thought you were out,' said Pooh.

'No,' said Piglet. 'I was not out.'

'You were thinking about the wound?' said Pooh.

'No,' said Piglet. 'I was not thinking about the wound. I do not think about the wound very much, any more.'

They watched them going up to the Front, in the snow.

'We could go and see Eeyore,' said Pooh.

'Yes,' said Piglet. 'We could go and see Eeyore.'

They went out into the snow.

'Do you hear the guns?' said Pooh.

'Yes,' said Piglet. 'I hear the guns.'

When they got to Eeyore's house, he was looking at an empty glass of *ortega*. They used to make *ortega* by taking the new *orreros* out of the ground very early in the morning, before the dew had dried, and crushing them between the *mantemagni*, but they did not make it that way any more. Not since the fighting up at the Front.

'Do you hear the guns?' said Eeyore.

'Yes,' said Pooh. 'I hear the guns.'

'It is still snowing,' said Piglet.

'Yes,' said Eeyore. 'That is the way it is.'

'That is the way it is,' said Pooh.

14

Ear, Believed Genuine Van Gogh,
Hardly Used, What Offers?

*Next Tuesday, Sotheby's are to auction a lock of Lord
Byron's hair.*

The Times

I have a friend in Wells, Somerset, who has a hat belonging
to Isambard Kingdom Brunel. Not, of course, as a result
of a drunken post-prandial cock-up in some Victorian
bistro in which Marx went off with Thackeray's raincoat and
Dickens hobbled away in Emily Bronte's gumboots, but because
of some astute, or some would say idiot, bidding at an Oxford
sale some ten years ago.

The hat stands today on a small davenport in a house
belonging to the Abbey National Building Society, whose
financial acumen may be said to outstrip that of my friend.
However, the hat is more of a talking-point than the house,
I'll give him that. It is, indeed, the only object of interest in
the place. The first time I saw this moulting felt cylinder,
the soft Somerset sunshine highlighting the moth-grubs
feasting round its myriad holes, I said, quick as a flash, 'What's
that?'

Normally, it is only in the cheaper women's magazines that
a glint may be said to come into a man's eye. He may also
have drawn in his breath with a faint hiss.

'That's Isambard Kingdom Brunel's hat,' he said. 'He may
well have been wearing it when the *Great Eastern* sank.'

We looked at it together, as if it bore some tangible sign of engineering history.

'He may,' said its new owner, 'have taken it off to scratch his head while wondering—'

'—if it was possible to throw an iron bridge across the River Dart?'

'Exactly! Isn't it marvellous?'

In a curious way, I suppose it was. It was concrete evidence that history was more than fiction – few people, I'm sure, *really* believe that men fought one another at Flodden with long sharp swords, without benefit of television, antibiotics, or man-made fibres. One requires three-dimensional reassurance of events that took place before one's grandfather was born; that's what's good about Hampton Court Palace and Shakespeare folios. Here we were, in 1965, looking at Isambard Kingdom Brunel's hat; no surer proof of his existence could have been offered. In its very ordinariness lay its honesty. That is probably why my friend, who has no interest in shipping, ironfounding, or, indeed, I.K. Brunel, bought it.

Of course, there are innumerable reasons why people turn over large wads of negotiable lettuce every day in return for some tatty fragment of arcane reliquiae. This is not to mention museums, whose spies forage the sale-rooms like agents of Dr. Frankenstein, looking for likely bits to enhance their Samuel Johnson house, or Great Plague Of London room, making a jigsaw of time for the benefit of parties of yawning schoolchildren who file past these precious morsels snatched back from mortality and inscribe 'Norman Binns Form 3a 1970' on the escritoire at which Castlereagh blew most of his brains out. But museums apart, the list of reasons for which citizens rip out cheques in return for items of no intrinsic value must be endless, from the interior-decorating philistine – 'You know what the corner needs to pick up the Regency motif, Mrs. Greebs-Wibley? It needs the Duke of Wellington's bidet, that's what it needs, with a rubber-plant in it, and possibly a nice skull, *comme mémoire du Diable'* – to the intoxicated near-necrophiliac, who sits all day in Che Guevara's socks, weeping for gone glory and decomposing heroes. It may be that the lock of Byron's hair, unsold at the time of going to press, will be knocked down to one such fan, if the University of Texas doesn't get there first, because the God of Romanticism left countless worshippers to pass the bitter-sweet message on to succeeding generations: the old ladies rocking themselves back and forth on chintz upholstery, murmuring cantos of *Don Juan* and imagining themselves taken, firmly but tenderly, on the incense-smelling carpet of Lord B's Venetian bed-sitter, may look more respectable than the teeny-boppers who stuff each new Buddy Holly posthumous LP beneath their pillows, but they're no less potty. If the lock of hair has gone to one of them, it can count itself lucky: it's all velvet cushions and fond kisses from now on. If it's been snapped up by a male fan, it's in for a rougher time, and may well end up sellotaped to his forehead, being regularly tugged for inspiration as he paces back and forth in his carefully ruined Hampstead attic trying to find a rhyme for 'mat'.

Mind you, it may well have been bought by the time you read this, and if you're still listening, by a spry merchant bank, or Save-And-Prosper Unit Trust, something like that, with an eye to the main chance and a shrewd investment. Who knows what it might fetch in fifty years' time, split up, say, into one-hair lots to avoid the penalty of capital gains? There's always the chance, of course, that Byron may fall from favour and interest, or that the entire opus will turn out to have been written by Isambard Kingdom Brunel and published under an assumed name to avoid accusations of frivolity being levelled at a man who was trying to drum up money for his Channel Tunnel project (which would bang up the value of his hat overnight), but that's the investment game for you. Personally,

I'd go a bundle on Byron hair, whatever the *Financial Times* thinks: look at the case of Mahomet – his most Holy Relic is a mere two inches of one beard-hair, over which wars have been fought on a number of occasions. If you'd been wise enough to have bought that during the slack period, in around AD 600 and before he'd made a name for himself, you'd have more than money today. You'd have eight hundred million Muslims ready to follow you anywhere.

And that, friends, is the nub and crux. It's the case of Poseidon shares all over again – the world must be full of citizens kicking themselves for not having snapped up relics when the price was rock-bottom, only to see them soaring through the charts and turning canny paupers to lonely millionaires at the touch of a gavel. Sadly, as with so much else about history's heroes, it's the spotting of potential fame that's the difficulty, whether it's publishing their poems, or hanging their paintings, or buying their old underwear. Think of the great men whose lives passed in penury and hacking coughs due to public unawareness that their littlest possession would one day end up in Sotheby's or the basement of Fort Knox. Imagine poor I.K. Brunel, at the depth of his fortunes after the *Great Eastern* had gone down like a tin brick, rushing into a Burlington Arcade antiquerie with a brown-paper parcel and muttering 'Do you a very nice hat, brother, fraught with history, monogrammed inside, worn throughout the period I was inventing the watertight bulkhead?' What sort of response do you suppose that would have evoked, if not an assistant manager's boot up the backside of a pair of breeches which, had the fool realised it, would today be worth twice as much as the hat? And what of Byron, stuck in the middle of *Childe Harold* and the bailiffs about to carry off his quill? How would he have fared, had he attempted to put his sideburns on the market? Given his reputation at the time, terror of catching something off the precious locks would have had the floorwalkers shrieking for the Bow Street

Runners in nought seconds flat, who'd have chucked the shorn bard into a small dark room and thrown the key into the Thames.

Those of you who know me will by now, I think, have cottoned on to this matchless drift. Mine is no mere idle reflection on fame, or hair. Things have been a shade dodgy lately, what with the second instalment of Schedule D for the tax year 72–73 already overdue, and the Inland Revenue poised at the drop of a summons to distrain upon my chattels, so I'd like to let you in on the ground floor. Offer you an unprecedented chance to cash in on what, after the worms sit burping around my supine dust, will be a reputation fit to keep the encyclopaedia-writers in work for years and force the sale-rooms to take on whole armies of extra staff. Why wait for prices to boom beyond reach? Why fiddle around with building society deposits at five per cent after tax, when you could own a Coren shirt today, actually worn while this article (or, as it will later be known, British Museum MS 68854/ac) was being written, or a *matched pair* of Coren boots, as originally issued to Genuine Naval Officers, but now weighing down the feet of one of the greatest reputations which will ever be made?

The author will be signing vests at Austin Reed, Regent Street, between 10 and 5.30, weekdays only. Don't be late: the first edition is limited to 500 only.

15

Father's Lib

The City University of New York has offered its male staff paternity leave on the same terms as female staff get maternity leave. It is believed to be the first time such a provision has been offered in an American labour contract.

The Times

There are a number of things that are going to be wrong with this piece.

Some of them will be noticeable – a certain sogginess here and there; a tendency, uncharacteristic in the author, to use one word where two would normally do; arguments, if you can call them that, which start, falter, then peter emptily out; odd bits of disconnected filler, such as laundry lists, a reader's letter or two, notes from the inside cover of my driving licence, a transcript of my tailor's label; that sort of thing.

There will be phrases like 'that sort of thing'.

Some of the things that are going to be wrong will not be noticeable – the fact that the writer has a tendency to fall off his chair between paragraphs; to knock his coffee into his desk drawer; to rip the trapped ribbon from his typewriter and tear it to shreds, moaning and oathing; to wake up with a start to find the impression 1QA"ZWS/XED @ CRF£V on his forehead where it has fallen into the keys; to light a cigarette while one is still ticking over in the ashtray; to stop dead, wondering where his next syllable is coming from.

Nor will you notice, since the typographer, sturdy lad, will be backing up the young author like a seasoned RSM shoring a pubescent subaltern before Mons, that a good half of the words are misspelled, if there are two 's's' in 'misspelled', that is; and if it shouldn't be 'mis(s)pelt', anyway.

I'm glad that sentence is over; if it was a sentence. Was there a verb there?

But, for once, ineptitude will be its own defence; inadequacy its own argument. The very fact that readers this week are about to receive (have, indeed, already in part received) a substandard article with the tacks showing and the sawdust trickling out the back only proves the writer's thesis: which is that the concept of paternity leave has been a long time a-coming. That it has come to the United States, pioneer of the ring-pull can, automatic transmission, monosodium glutamate, the Sidewinder missile, and sundry other humanitarian breakthroughs should be no surprise to anyone; what is grievous is that there is little sign that the blessed concession is to be adopted on this side of the Atlantic.

Not in time for me, anyhow. And – hang on, that little light on the bottle-warmer that goes out when the teated goody reaches the required temperature has just done so. All I have to do now is unscrew the cap on the bottle, reverse the teat, replace the cap, shake the air out, nip upstairs, prise apart the kipping gums before she's had a chance to wake up and scream the plaster off the wall, whang in the teat, sit back, and,

Dropped it on the bloody floor.

That's what I like about the three a.m. feed – that deftness in the fingers that only comes after two hours' deep untroubled sleep, the clarity of the eyes rasping around behind the resinous lash-crust, the milk underfoot due to inability to find slipper and fear of turning on light in bedroom to search for same in case wife wakes up, thereby destroying entire point of self groping around in first place.

I'll come back to the argument in a minute. Now have to boil teat, mix new feed, screw, light goes on, light goes off, unscrew, reteat, rescrew, shake, nip upstairs, prise apart kipping gums, correction, prise apart screaming gums, that's my daughter, five weeks old and more accurate than a Rolex Oyster, it must be 3.01, must get feed done by 3.05, it takes exactly four minutes from first scream for three-year-old son to wake up, where's my panda, where's my fire-engine, I'm thirsty, I'm going to be sick, news that he's going to be sick delivered on high C, thereby waking up wife at 3.09 exactly, wife shouts What's going on? whereupon son shouts Mummy, father shouts Shut up, lights start going on in neighbouring houses . . .

3.04 and fifty seconds, breath coming short and croaky from stairs, got feed mixed, teat boiled, all screwed down, whip out miniature daughter with .001 to spare, pop in teat, falls on it like Peter Cushing on an unguarded throat. I lean back in nursery chair, feet tacky from old milk, left fag burning beside typewriter on kitchen table, know fag will burn down on ashtray rim, like Chinese torture in *Boy's Own Paper* – 'When frame leaches thong, Blitish dog, thong tighten on tligger, burret brow blains out, heh, heh, heh!' – fag will fall off ashtray, burn hole in table, possibly burn down house, Family Flee In Nightclothes.

I am actually writing this an hour later, madness recollected in tranquillity, if you can call tranquillity thing involving cat which has woken up in filthy mood to find milk on floor, therefore licking up milk off floor, therefore in middle of floor when I come back to kitchen, therefore trodden on.

Anyhow, back to an hour ago, still feeding daughter, she beginning to drop off halfway through feed, terrible sign meaning can't go on with feed since daughter asleep, can't not go on, because if she goes down half-full, she'll be up again at 4.38, screaming, son up at 4.42, where's my panda, where's my fire-engine, wife up at 4.46, saying If you're incapable of doing a simple thing like a feed etcetera to sleeping form, thereby transforming it into waking form, fall out of bed in netherworld confusion, thinking fag burning house down, look around for something to Flee In, since don't wear Nightclothes, subeditors all change headlines for 5 a.m. edition, Nude Phantom Terrorises Hampstead Third Night Running.

Wake daughter up, she cries, must be colic, hoist on shoulder, legs all colicky-kicking (I'd like to see James Joyce change a nappy), pat on back, crying goes up umpteen decibels, bring down again, mad gums grab teat, bottle empties like a Behan pint, relief.

Change daughter, all dry, smooth, cooing, give final burp with little rub, daughter hiccups, sick drenches dressing-gown sleeve, daughter's nightdress, change daughter again, can't find new nightdress, walk around numb and sicky, daughter shrieking now, since, having displaced part of feed, requires topping up, else valves will grind or crankshaft seize up, or something, back downstairs with daughter on shoulder wailing, feel like mad bagpiper, mix new feed one-handed, screw, light goes on, light goes off, unscrew, reteat, rescrew, shake, carry out with daughter, slam kitchen door with foot. Wake up cat.

Get upstairs, son wandering about on landing with dismembered bunny, I want a pee, can't explain holding daughter and feeding same is priority, since Spock says AVOID SUCH CLASHES THIS WAY TO JEALOUSY ETCETERA, lead son to lavatory with spare hand, holding bottle against daughter, daughter can now see bottle like vulture over Gobi, windows rattle with renewed shrieking, leave son peeing in sleepy inaccuracy on seat, back to nursery, finish feeding daughter, son roars I CAN'T GET MY PYJAMA TROUSERS UP, try to rise with daughter, bottle falls, teat gets hairy, hammers start in skull, but thanks, dear God, daughter now full, asleep, plonk in crib, turn out light, hurtle sonwards, son not there.

Son in bedroom, shaking wife, I CAN'T GET MY PYJAMA TROUSERS UP.

I creep, broken, downstairs. You know about treading on the cat. I look at the garbling in the typewriter. It stops at 'hang on, that little light on the bottle-warmer that goes out.' Sit down, smelling of regurgitation and panic, stare at keyboard, listen to dawn chorus going mad, man next door coughing his lung into the receptacle provided, far loos flushing, new day creaking in on its benders.

What I was going to write about before I was so rudely interrupted was, I see from the first tatty gropings, an article about how enlightened America was to introduce paternity leave for new fathers so that they wouldn't have to work for the first few weeks and could help cope with the latest novelty item, instead of going off to the office, the shop, the surgery, the factory.

Or the typewriter.

I had all these great arguments in favour of introducing the system over here, I had all the points worked out, it was all so lucid, so right, so uncounterable: I should bring about an instant revolution.

What arguments they were!

And if I only had the strength left to get them down on paper.

16

Let Us Now Phone Famous Men

A child's game, at root, like all good things. After all, could anything match that first fine discovery of the telephone and all it stood for? That first realisation that, contained within ten simple digits, lay the infinitely possible? Out there – the information seeped into the infant brain in all its diabolical clarity – lay six billion ears, all the people in the world, available for contact and mystery and insult, unable to resist the beckoning of one small and villainous forefinger. We used, my tiny evil friends and I, to congregate at the nearest parentless house, and dial into the void, and innocent mouths would answer, and gullible ears would wait. Ah, to be only eight and wield such limitless power over adults! To fell a vicar with a practised oath, to turn bass breathing on a solitary spinster, to order fourteen tons of coal from Rickett Cockerell and have it delivered to the schoolmaster of one's choice – what could match this for delirious joy? Only the pièce de résistance of scouring the phone-book for a citizen called Dumm or Barmie and phoning him to enquire if he was. What nights we spent in illicit spinnings of the dial, tottering helplessly about our living-rooms, gasping at our own wit and ingenuity and smashing our milk-teeth on the fender in the thrashing throes brought on by such hilarity!

I wonder, sometimes, if the men who were boys when I was a boy still do it. It's not a question you can ask of bald, august solicitors, of doctors nursing kids and mortgages, of paunched executives: but do they, a quarter of a century on, creep down, perhaps, at 4 a.m. and ring their enemies to offer six free foxtrot lessons, or scream indecencies at subscribers doomed to names like Bott and Hoare?

I thought of them last week, those tiny swine who helped misspend my youth. Because it suddenly occurred to me to crank the whole game up to a more sophisticated notch: perhaps it was the opening of direct dialling to New York, perhaps it was the acreage of puerile posters by which the Post Office whips us on to take advantage of their miracle offers, but, whatever the spur, I decided to spend the day trying to telephone the leaders of the world. Why not? After all, they had ears like anyone else, they had desks with phones on, they were put in power, more or less, by insignificant souls like me: surely they could set aside a few seconds for a chat, an exchange of gossip, an acknowledgement that the silent majority had a right, occasionally, to speak?

So I phoned Mao Tse-Tung.

'Who?' said the girl on 108 (International Directory Enquiries).

'He's the Chairman of the Chinese People's Republic,' I said. 'It's probably a Peking number.'

There was a long silence. I could see her there, repolishing an immaculate nail, shoving a wayward curl back beneath her head-set, sucking a Polo, wondering whether she should go on the pill.

'I'll get the Supervisor,' she said, finally.

'Nobody ever phones China,' said the Supervisor.

'Why not?'

'I don't know,' she said. Her voice was diamantine. 'I only know why people phone places, I don't know why they don't, do I?'

Ruined by syntax, I pled help.

'You could phone the Chinese Chargé d'Affaires in London,' she said. 'The number is 580 7509.'

580 7509 yielded a high-pitched moan. My Chinese may be less than flawless, but even I could tell that no human larynx was involved.

I phoned the Operator.

Who phoned the Engineer.

Whose Supervisor phoned me.

'It's NU,' he said. For a moment, I felt excitingly privy to some piece of inside dope about Post Office/Chinese Legation affairs: clearly, from the man's weary voice, it was old Enn-Yu up to his tricks again, Enn-Yu the phone-bugger (I don't mean that the way it looks), the tamperer, the Red Guard saboteur; Enn-Yu, the man who had plagued the GPO for years with his intercepted calls and weird Oriental devices fitted out in the Legation basement.

'Who's Enn-Yu?' I said.

'Not In Use,' he said, and a small world crashed. 'They're always switching their lines down there. Every six weeks, they want a new phone number. Hang on,' he said, and voices muttered in the background, and far bells rang. He came back. 'It's 636 9756 this week,' he said.

'Harro!' shouted a voice at 636 9756.

'Hallo,' I said. 'I want to know how I can telephone China.'

'Why?'

'I want to speak to Chairman Mao.'

'Why?'

'I have a personal message to deliver.'

Breathing. Whispering. A new, more senior voice.

'Not possible terrephone China!' it shrieked. 'Not possible terrephone Chairman! What you want?'

I explained again. It turned out that there were no lines between England and China. Nobody ever telephoned China. Nobody *would* ever telephone China.

'How do *you* speak to China?' I asked.

A third voice came on.

'GET OFF RINE!' it screamed. 'GET OFF RINE QUICK NOW!'

And rang off. The whole thing had taken forty-seven minutes. More than enough time for thermonuclear gee-gaws to have wiped both Asia and Europe off the map. I knew the PM didn't have a hot line to Mao, and it bothered me.

I dialled again.

'Yes?' said 108.

'I'd like,' I said, 'to speak to Mr. Kosygin.'

She muffled the phone inadequately.

'I think it's him again,' I heard, distant and woolly. There was giggling. I waited. The Supervisor came on.

'Are you,' she said, and the syllables fell like needles, 'the gentleman who just wanted to speak to Mao Tse-Tung?'

'Yes,' I said.

I sympathised. She had, I knew, a vision of this solitary loonie who had let himself loose on the telephonic world, prior, no doubt, to rape or suicide. I wondered if they were playing for time with their long, reflective pauses, trying to trace the call, trying to dispatch a van-load of GPO male nurses to my gate. But all she said was:

'Russian Inquiries are on 104.'

'Have you got his address and phone number?' said 104.

'No,' I said, 'I thought you'd have it.'

'They never send us directories,' she said. 'It's only them and the Rumanians that don't. Everyone else sends us their directories.'

'Then how do you phone Russians?'

'You have to have their number. We keep,' she grew confidential, 'a list of hotels and factories, a few things like that. We're not supposed to, but we do. I've got the Kremlin number. Do you think that would do?'

'Yes, that sounds very good.'

'There's an hour's delay to Moscow. I'll get them to ring you back, and he might come to the phone. That'd be nice, wouldn't it?'

'That would be very nice,' I said. 'In the meantime, as you're European Directory, could you get the Pope for me?'

'Oooh, you are *awful*!' she shrieked. Her voice faded, and I could just catch it explaining the situation to the other girls. Time passed. She came back.

'You're not going to say nothing dirty to them, are you?' she said. 'Excuse me for asking, but we have to.'

I reassured her.

'I'll have to keep your number by me,' she said, 'in case there's complaints, you know, afterwards, like. No offence meant, but you'd be surprised how many people ring up foreigners and swear at them.'

I agreed, wondering who. Insights were bursting in on every hand. It clearly wasn't all beer and skittles, being a world leader, trying to keep up the balance of payments and build new schools and hold back the opposition, with Englishmen phoning you up all hours of the day and night, shouting 'Eff off!'

She gave me the Pope's residential number. I dialled direct, 01039 6 6982. It was engaged. Odd. Was he, perhaps, on The Other Line? Or just on the balcony, waving? I tried again, trembling slightly at his proximity – five hundred million subjects under his thumb, and that thumb about to curl over the receiver in response to a far, agnostic call.

'Allo.'

'Your Holiness?'

Pause.

'Wod?'

'Am I speaking to the Pope? *Il Papa?*'

Scuffling.

'Allo, allo. Can I 'elp you?'

'May I speak to the Pope?'

A long, soft sigh, one of those very Italian sighs that express so much, that say *Ah, signor, if only this world were an ideal world, what would I not give to be able to do as you ask, we should sit together in the Tuscan sunshine, you and I, just two men together, and we should drink a bottle of the good red wine, and we should sing, ah, how we should sing, but God in His infinite wisdom has, alas, not seen fit to . . .*

'Can the Pope,' I said, determined, 'come to the phone?'

'The Bobe never gum to the delephone, signor. Nod for you, nod for me, nod for Italians, nod for nobody. Is nod bozzible, many regrets, 'Is 'Oliness never spig on delephone. You give me your name, I give mezzage to 'Is 'Oliness, 'e give you blezzing, okay?'

'Okay,' I said. A blessing, albeit proxied, was something.

'Don menshnit,' he said, kindly, and clicked off.

By great good fortune (or even the grace of God: who knows how quickly a Pope's blessing might work?), there was a different operator on 108 when I tried to reach Richard Nixon. He put me on to 107, who got me the White House in three minutes flat, which gave tricky Dicky a thick edge over Mao, Kosygin and Il Papa when it came to accessibility. I thought you'd like to know that, Dick, since I didn't get the chance to tell you myself. Accessibility, as Harry Truman might have said, stops here. Or almost here. The lady secretary at the White House was extremely kind, incredibly helpful and understanding; doubtless because, given America's readiness to empty magazines at those in power, you can't be too careful with nuts who phone up to speak to the President. Fob them off with a 'Get lost!' one minute, and the next they're crouched on a nearby roof and pumping away with a mail-order Winchester. The President, she said, was down in Florida, at Key Biscayne, where his number was 305 358 2380; someone there would speak to me. They did, and they were just as syrupy and sympathetic, and who knows but that I mightn't have got into the Great Ear if I hadn't played one card utterly wrong? What happened was, the call from the Kremlin, booked, you'll remember, an hour before, suddenly came through on my other phone, and I was mug enough, drunk with bogus eminence, to say to the American voice:

'Sorry, can you hold on a sec, I've got Kosygin on the other line?'

It was a nice moment, of course, but that's as long as it lasted. America hung up. Tread carefully when you step among the great, friends, their corns are sensitive.

I rather liked the Kremlin.

'Is that Mister Coren?' they said.

It's no small thrill to think one's name has echoed down the corridors of Soviet power, from room to room, while nervous men, fearful of the punishment that follows bureaucratic cock-ups, have tried to find out who one is, and what one wants with the Prime Minister. After all, so much is secret, so much unknown. I might have been anybody, even the sort of Anybody whose whisper in a top ear could send whole switchboardsful of comrades to the stake. Who was this Coren, this cool, curt international voice who seemed to be on such good terms with Alexi N. Kosygin that he thought nothing of phoning him person-to-person? For men who remembered Lavrenti Beria, no kindness to strangers was too much. Which is no doubt why I actually got to Kosygin's private secretary, who was himself extremely civil.

'I merely want to present the Prime Minister with my good wishes,' I told him.

He was heartbroken that the Prime Minister was inextricably involved at present, but swore to me that my message would be passed on immediately. And I have not the slightest doubt that it was. It's a long way to Siberia, after all, and the cattle-trains leave every hour, on the hour.

131

Which left me with just two numbers in my little black book: Havana 305 031 and Cairo 768944. It took me a day to get through to one, and three days to reach the other (all calls to Egypt are subject to censorship), and when I finally did make contact, Fidel and Anwar were, needless to say, busy elsewhere. Both, however, promised faithfully to ring me back, which is why I leave them till last. Courtesy I like. Not, though, that they actually *have* rung back, but who knows? Even now, the dark, dependable forefingers may be poised over their respective dials, groping along the cables for a chance to chew the fat and swop a joke or two. If not, and if they read this first, don't worry about it, lads. It's nothing urgent.

I just wanted to say hello.

17

The Rime of the Ancient Film-maker

There has been much speculation as to why, when Ken Russell's first film on the Lake Poets was so uncharacteristically restrained, his second was so characteristically extravagant.

Part I

An ancient director meeteth three viewers about to watch *Match of the Day*, and detaineth one.

It is an ancient Film-maker,
And he stoppeth one of three.
'By thy long grey script and glittering
                                              lens,
Now wherefore stopp'st thou me?

The telly's doors are open'd wide,
We've got the Guinness in;
There's cheese'n'bacon Krunchimunch,
And peanuts by the tin!'

He holds him with his podgy hand,
'There was a film,' quoth he.
'Eff off! It's Stoke v. QPR!'
Retort the Viewers three.

The viewer is spellbound by the old man's Arriflex. There may be money in it.

He holds one with his glittering lens –
The Viewer stood stock still:
'Is this for *Candid Camera?*'
The film-man hath his will.

133

The Viewer sat down on the step:
This could be fame at last!
And thus spake on that ancient man,
The mad-eyed cinéaste.

Mr Melvyn Bragg is
hired, and works for an
entire morning. The
book is finished.

'The script was cheer'd, the treatment
                                        clear'd.
Granada coughed up loot!
I grabbed my crew and off we blew,
Bound for the first day's shoot.

The Sun came up upon the left,
Into the lens shone he!
A blood-red smear, a crimson tear,
Was all the lens could see!

The film-maker gets
to the heart of
Wordsworth.

'Cut! Print!' I cried; for in that shot
Was all I asked, and more:
A sense of doom, in that one zoom;
All Nature steep'd in gore!

'Lake poetry is pain and lust
And death!' the old man roared.
'And—' here the Viewer turned his
                                        head,
For QPR had scored.

Warming to his theme,
he hires six helicopters
and abattoir.

'And then—' the Viewer's head jerked
                                        back
'—we cut across to France.
In every scene, the guillotine:
Well, why pass up the chance?

A sonnet is carefully interpreted.

The fat heads roll'd, and, green with
                                        mould,
The rotting torsos lay;
While, nude, the Eskdale Shepherd
                                        gasped
And rutted in the hay!'

The viewer is amaz'd by the sheer vision of the ancient director.

'Stone me! Is all *that* poetry?'
The Viewer cried. 'By heck!
I only know The Boy Stood On
The, wossname, Burning Deck!'

'You have to read *between* the lines!
Between the *words*, forsooth!
For what *I* read is what *I* know:
There is no other Truth!

Granada, hearing rumours, despatch a studio spy.

But fools' – and here his face grew
                                        black –
'Will ne'er let genius be:
A man was sent from Manchester;
His brief: to check on *me*!

Each day, he scribbl'd telegrams
Back to Granada's boss;
Each day, his calculator clicked.
His name was Albert Ross.

The spy, in a vision, foresees ratings.

And when he saw what we had shot,
His flannel chops turn'd white!
'You call *this* family viewing, son?
You call *this* Sunday night?'

135

Thereafter, sat he with our crew;
Thereafter, every day,
They fawned to do his every whim,
For they had heard him say,

The spy takes control of
the project.

That if the film did not pass *him*,
If there was one more shot
He could not show his grandmother,
Then he would scrap the lot!

The ancient director is
sold for a mess of
pottage, plus overtime.

And they were men with mortgages,
And they were men with wives:
There was no room for genius
Within their little lives!

I stood apart, as in a dream,
And let them shoot at will;
They filmed each lousy skylark, shot
Each stinking daffodil!

Yet, while I stood, my brain did not:
It, fertile, laid a plan;
A perfect crime, to wait the time
The film was in the can!

The ancient director
draws his own
conclusions!

And, as it left for Manchester,
I left to cut my loss;
And, with a Props Department bow,
I shot that Albert Ross!

Part II

A free man, the ancient
film-maker launches into
*The Rime of the Ancient
Mariner.*

'The Sun now rose upon the right:
We went to film Part Two.
But when they scann'd the scene I'd
                    plann'd,
Rank terror gripp'd the crew!

They look'd behind, to ease their
                    mind,
But no fat fink did follow!
Nor any day, with bonus pay,
Came to the film crew's Hollo!

Sheer brilliance
overwhelms doubt yet
again.

They did not guess; nor did they press
For further explanation:
Since genius brooks no challenge, and
Technicians know their station.

But Friday came; it brought no cash.
Their nagging made me cross.
And like a fool, I blew my cool:
Confess'd I'd murder'd Ross!

The film crew are
deeply stricken by news
of the poor wretch's
death.

They shriek'd! They swore! They tore
                    their hair!
They fell down in their woe!
For all averr'd I'd kill'd the bird
That made the cash to flow!

And when, next morn, I found my
                    teeth,
Arose, and quit my bed;
There came no sound from all around:
The camera crew had fled!

And yet, and yet: my actors stood,
Waiting in serried ranks;
Thank God, I thought, that actors are
As thick as two short planks!

They stared at me, made-up and dress'd,
With simple, empty eyes.
And what I saw when I stared back
Were blessings in disguise!

The ancient film-maker
recognises his own
supreme qualities.

Who needs a camera crew? I cried;
Who needs their bleating moan?
I took the kit, and shoulder'd it,
And went to film alone!

And oh, the reds! And oh, the greens!
And oh, the clever angles!
And, bless my wig, is that a twig,
Or something Coleridge dangles?

The ancient film-maker
pre-empts critical
acclaim, wisely.

Was ever documentary made
So bravely to defy sense?
Is, surely, this not what is meant
By sheer poetic license?

For am I not a poet, too,
Indeed, not far less boring
Than all those Lakeland buggers—' he
Broke off. The man was snoring.

He jabbed his ribs; the Viewer woke.
'Who won?' he cried, 'Did Rangers?
I know Stoke's bleeding midfield play,
It's full of hidden dangers.'

The ancient film-maker still struggles to communicate, with no more than usual success.

The ancient film–man grasped his
                                    throat!
'I talk of Art!' he cried;
'Of Culture for the masses!' 'Stoke's
A bloody tricky side,'

The Viewer said. 'they're all up front,
I've mentioned it before.'
A sadder (but no wiser) man,
He went to find the score.

18

Good God, That's Never The Time, Is It?

The weather would pick tonight to break. Just when I thought the whole dread moment might pass un- noticed, one day sliding into another without even a perceptible click. And now the sky is full of thunder, lightning, raindrops the size of golfballs, and hot golfballs, at that, dogs are going mad in the explosions, the cat's under the stairs, nightbirds are shrieking themselves hoarse at the thought of all those worms belting up through the topspit to greet the end of the drought . . . the entire galaxy is rotten with augury. If this were Fiji instead of Hampstead, you wouldn't be able to see for flying beads, there'd be blokes jumping up and down on hot coals, and senior civil servants tuning in to their local volcanoes to see what had set the gods off this time, and remittance men from the Home Counties sweating the stitches out of their seersucker suits and praying that the demented house-boy's kris might find an alternative place in which to sink itself.

It can't all be because I shall be thirty-five at midnight. I don't know Anyone with that kind of pull.

I had intended the whole thing, as I say, to pass unnoticed. Thought I'd go to bed at around eleven, aged thirty-four, and wake up in the morning with it all over. Like having your appendix out. Never expected to sit through midnight, June 26, watching everything turn into mice and pumpkins. And here I am, an hour off the end of Act One, and can't sleep for the thunder rattling the rooftiles, threatening the gutters.

I'll be fifty-eight when the mortgage is paid off. Pass like a flash, those twenty-four, all right, twenty-three years, if I'm any judge. Last twenty-three went by like *that*.

Sorry for the paragraph break. I snapped my fingers at *that*, and pain shot all the way up to the elbow; no doubt, arthritis sets in at thirty-five. A few years ago, I could snap my fingers, oh, a dozen times on the trot. Where was I (senility setting in, too, half a million brain cells been conking out annually since twenty-one, that's seven million brain cells, wonder how many I started with, maybe the entire skull is empty, like those joke ashtrays where you put the fags in the eye-sockets, just a couple of doz assorted brain cells left, huddling together like stranded amoeba, watching one another die)? Oh, yes, about the shooting-by of twenty-three years – I was twelve. I can still feel being twelve. Looking forward to the Festival of Britain. I went down to watch the Skylon going up, in short trousers. Me, that is; the Skylon went around in a sort of tin slip. I can exactly recall the feeling of chapped legs, wind coming over Waterloo Bridge. I went up the Shot Tower and spat off it. Tonight, I feel as if the spit hasn't hit the ground yet – *twenty-three years?*

Of course, thirty-five may not be significant at all. I might go on to ninety-six, in which case I ought to be writing this article at forty-eight, i.e. in about ten minutes' time. The thing is, one thinks in terms of three score years and ten. It's about all I have left of formal religious belief. That and a lingering guilt about non-payment of fares. One of the few things I don't have instant recall over: what it was like to believe in God. Stopped believing circa 1953, don't know why.

Other things I find it impossible to remember, (1) Virginity (2) What it was like not smoking (3) Being unable to drive (4) Not shaving.

The point is, am I about to become half-dead, or should I consider myself as being half-alive? I am extremely aware of deterioration tonight; I can see it spilling over the belt, feel it when I run my fingers through my hair. It's a short run, these days, barely get off the blocks and you're through the tape. Also, I appear to have more moles on my forearms than heretofore. I may be growing gnarled: finger-joints seem to be taking on angles, quite arbitrarily, which probably explains why my typing has been falling off. It's as accurate as ever, but the fingertips whang down on the neighbouring keys as often as not. Line up on a "g" and an "f" appears on the paper.

Eleven-thirty.

Deterioration is the last thing I worry about, normally. What I feel most is psychic age. It manifests itself most clearly in the sudden awareness that one is actually part of history, and therefore disappearing fast. I look at old newsreels, Stalin and Roosevelt and Churchill chuckling away at Yalta, it could be an eon ago, it might as well be the Treaty of Utrecht they're wrapping up, they could be ceding Mercia to Wessex, it's all dead time; but I was *alive when they did it*, six, going on seven, fully formed, you can see it in the school photographs, same head. I'd already seen Hatfield House, had teeth filled, eaten Radio Malt, fallen in love, caught fish. At bloody Yalta!

We all got a plate from George VI and a framed message congratulating us on our war effort. George the Sixth – it looks like William Rufus, when you write it down. Twenty years since the Coronation, we bought our first telly for it, 12″ Murphy with doors, somewhat larger than a wardrobe, used to stand oakenly in the corner like a coffin at an Irish wake, blowing valves faster than you could say Joan Gilbert; twenty years, and I can recall the exact clatter of Muffin's hooves on the piano-lid as if it was . . . in twenty years' time, I'll be fifty-five, Without A Pension I Really Do Not Know What I Shall Do.

It isn't that thirty-five is old in itself; merely that it is, as it were, the hinge, Halfway House, with Death sitting in the snug, biding his time over a brown ale, under the clock. An index of what's left, how long it will take, life's little Rorschach, you just fold it across the middle, and each mirrored blot is thirty-five years long. Or short. I got here so quickly; I was at Oxford yesterday, took O-levels Monday morning, learned to ride a two-wheeler over the weekend, and was it Friday I was dry all night, for the first time? I can't be sure, but I remember my father was in uniform; an old man, nearly thirty.

I wish more had changed, it would endow my degeneration with more significance; jet travel, sliced bread, colour TV, automatic transmission, professional tennis, and golf on the Moon – it isn't much, really. I would like, I don't know, England's coastline to have altered beyond all recognition, dolphins to have taken over the world, something of that order. I'd like to have had an Ice Age or two, been through the Jurassic Period, watched man climb down from the tree, grow less prognathous, discover the wheel – '*Hey, Al, you'll never believe this, ha-ha-ha, I just made something that rolls downhill!*' I don't seem to have been here very long, that's all, and shan't be for much longer.

It could be my fault, of course; maybe I ought to have done more. Not that I haven't done a considerable amount, I've eaten almost everything there is to be eaten, play most card games passing well, visited all forty-nine of the continental United States, written four million words, many of them different. But nothing solid. Mozart, Keats, Jesus Christ, Bix Beiderbecke, they were all dead by this point. 'And now, ladies and gentlemen, here to introduce his new opera, *The Eve Of St. Agnes*, is Alan Coren, son of God and first cornet.'

Can't be sure it'd be any better, of course. Achievement need not be a hedge against decay. Look at Ozymandias; or, to be more precise, his feet. I grow melancholic (it is five to

143

midnight) at a thought no more complex than that I like it here; it's a good dance, a good movie, a good match, and I glance at my watch and discover that it's half-way gone already: life's little irony number eight, there's no pleasure, however intense, that cannot be flawed by a brief reflection upon its inevitable transience.

Midnight. There we are, then. I'll be all right in a minute. Feel better already, as a matter of fact. Well, it's easier downhill, if nothing else.

19

Going Cheep

This week, I need hardly say, nine birds have been added to the schedule drawn up under the Protection of Birds Act 1954, that list of feathered items which persons of curious taste may not legally kill, steal, or, for all I know, train to whistle the *Toccata and Fugue in D Minor*.

These birds, as I know you have read, are the short-toed tree-creeper, the little gull, the Mediterranean gull, the gyr falcon, the purple heron, the scarlet rosefinch, the shore-lark, the green sandpiper and Cetti's warbler, and millions of you have written to me in considerable excitement, asking for enough information about them to be able to drop their names with confidence at this weekend's cocktail parties and dole queues.

I have, in consequence and knowing where my professional duties lie, made some investigations, not to say speculations, and am now well able to give you a few salient facts with which to start your conversation off and, I trust, stimulate further ornithological enquiry. To take them in order, then:

SHORT-TOED TREE-CREEPER
This is a small shifty bird, mottled brown in colour, that hangs around tree roots and sneers at anything that passes. It does not work at all, believing song to be a mug's game, and makes a point of getting up for the dawn chorus only to lean against

its roots, examine it claws with studied nonchalance, and occasionally spit out of the corner of its beak. It does not, of course, tear about building its own nests, but squats in those of other birds foolhardy enough to have migrated south without putting their premises in the hands of a reputable agent. It does not go out of its way, in spring, to preen, woo, or otherwise seek a perfect partner, but instead attempts to mate, for form's sake only and out of an instinct it personally finds an irritating drag, with anything it happens to bump into while creeping about. Many have been killed, as a result, by affronted mice, large bees, and the occasional sprightly toad. It is interesting mainly for its supporting role in interminable shaggy-dog stories about Long-Toed Tree-Creepers.

LITTLE GULL
The little gull is to be found mainly in supermarkets, where it is a sucker for special offers on unlabelled tinned goods. Unlike the Big Gull, which will believe anything it hears about Concorde, North Sea oil, reflation, détente, and so forth, the little gull is conned only by small operations: it will, for example, listen to encyclopaedia salesmen for hours, and often comes home with little things it has picked out of open suitcases in Oxford Street. It is despised by other birds, who are always off-loading unwanted junk on it and, in spiteful mood, telling it tall stories. The little gull, in consequence, believes that the world is flat, and lays its eggs under gooseberry bushes.

MEDITERRANEAN GULL
The Mediterranean gull is bigger than the little gull (*q.v.*) but no brighter. As its name suggests, it flies to the Mediterranean for the winter, but frequently fails to arrive, since it asks directions from any bird it passes. Mediterranean gulls can, as a result, be found anywhere, at any time of the year; in 1974,

three hundred of them spent Christmas in Preston, and a permanent colony now inhabits Tierra del Fuego in the belief that it is Majorca.

Occasionally, however, they do arrive in the Mediterranean, only to discover that they have once more been fooled and that their winter colony is only half-built, miles from the sea, and that they have to sleep twelve to a nest. When they examine the small print in their insurance, they invariably find that they are indemnified only against cycling accidents.

GYR FALCON
According to p. 788 of the *Shorter Oxford Dictionary* (which I borrowed from a little gull who owned forty-seven copies), the gyr falcon, or gerfalcon, is a native of Iceland, and the *gyr* describes (from the Latin *gyrus*) its habit of flying in circles. From this solid information, we can only induce that it has come here to negotiate, although watch your newspapers for reports that its negotiating circles have widened to two hundred miles in diameter and that it has taken to ramming any English birds found within that limit.

PURPLE HERON
The purple heron is the latest miracle offering from Heron Birds Ltd. Feathered in tasty purple skivertex, with an elegant machine-tooled simulated goldette spine, it spends its life flying into people's homes on ten days' approval, telling them about the sexual passages in Tolstoy. If attacked, its method of defence is to fall apart. Attractive on its own, the purple heron in fact looks best when standing on a shelf with ten others like it.

SCARLET ROSEFINCH
The most intriguing features of this bird are that it is neither scarlet nor a rosefinch. It is more like a large green starling than anything, but not much. Its nomenclature, however, is

quite without precedent, and won't happen again, either, if I'm any judge of these matters. Its name was given to it by an ornithologist in debt to a tailor called Sam Rosefinch to the tune of £86. Sam Rosefinch's wife, on the other hand, had always been driven by dreams of show business, and in 1940, following the overwhelming success of *Gone With The Wind*, cut her hair like Vivien Leigh's, changed her name from Lily to Scarlet, and took up drawl lessons. Since there were now three million women in a similar position, Scarlet Rosefinch's career came to nothing, and she went back, in deep depression, to cutting out waistcoat linings. Hearing of this, and instantly seeing it as a way out of his financial difficulties, the ornithologist called on Sam Rosefinch and offered to name his latest discovery after Sam's wife, in return for the £86, plus a spare pair of trousers for his blue worsted. Everyone ended up happy, except for the thing like a green starling, which spends its life answering embarrassing questions from other rosefinches.

SHORE-LARK

During the week, the shore-lark works in the City and flies home every night to its mate in Wimbledon, where it is a model husband and father. At weekends, however, it migrates briefly to Brighton, on any one of a hundred pretexts, where it meets female shore-larks under the pier and seeks to recapture its lost youth.

GREEN SANDPIPER

The green sandpiper differs from other sandpipers in that it never learns from its experiences. Many are so green, in fact, that they do not even *have* experiences. In consequence, the male green sandpiper frequently fails to consummate its spring-time relationships, while the female green sandpiper is just as frequently taken down to Brighton by shore-larks. This means that while both the green sandpiper and the shore-lark are understandably rare, and protected, the Greenish Shorepiper is just about the most common bird there is, and shot at all the time.

CETTI'S WARBLER

Often vulgarly known as the dead warbler, from its habit of sleeping twenty-four hours a day, this bird's correct name was coined in 46 AD, when the Cetti, of Eastern Marathon, were besieged by the Zuccini under their leader Caius Gnocchi the Indecisive. The Cetti, unable to maintain the round-the-clock vigilance necessary to prevent the breaching of their walls, decided to use geese, as was then the custom, for watchdogs. This decision having been taken, the Cetti leaders were then horrified to discover that their geese had been eaten by the starving townspeople the day before. The only birds left in the city were the warblers, who were too small and fiddly to eat. These were gathered up, and stationed at strategic positions on the ramparts, after which the soldiers retired to their desperately-needed rest. That night, the Zuccini mounted their attack, entered the city, and slew the Cetti to a man. The warblers slept through it all.

20

Go Easy, Mr Beethoven, That Was Your Fifth!

'Shrunk to half its proper size, leathery in consistency and greenish-blue in colour, with bean-sized nodules on its surface.' Yes, readers, I am of course describing Ludwig van Beethoven's liver, and I do apologise for going over such familiar ground, but I wanted to put the less musical members of my flock in the picture right from the start. I think they also ought to know that his spleen was more than double its proper size: far too many *soi-disant* music-lovers these days, when they drop the pick-up on *Egmont* or the *Eroica* and retire to their chaise longue for a quick listen, think to themselves *Poor old sod, he was deaf as a brick*, and leave it at that, entirely neglecting the fact that beneath the deaf-aid on his waistcoat Herr van Beethoven sported as misshapen a collection of offal as you could shake a stick at, including a pancreas the size of a pickled walnut and a length of intestine that could have been mistaken for pipe-lagging by all but the most astute German plumber.

I am reminded of all this internal strife by today's *Guardian*, which, in its copy-hungry turn, quotes from the current issue of the *Journal of Alcoholism*, a periodical of which I had not previously heard. Which is odd, since if I'm not on their mailing list, who is? At all events, this bizarre broadsheet has clearly decided that it is not going to be outdone in Ludwig's bicentenary year by all the other mags, and has hopped aboard the wagon, if they'll pardon the expression, with a succinct length of verbiage by one Doctor Madden, consultant psychiatrist at a Chester hospital addiction unit. He it is whom I quote at the beginning of this *feuilleton*, and if I may say so, Doctor, as one stylist to another, I have rarely encountered so well-turned a memorial to a great man. Why that sentence was not chiselled on Ludwig van Beethoven's gravestone, I shall never know. I gather you've translated it from the report of his autopsy, and it may be that it reads even better in German, but I doubt it: poetry is what 'bean-sized nodule' is, and don't let anyone tell you otherwise. Indeed, you may well have altered the listening habits of an entire generation: how shall any of us be able to tune in to *Fidelio* again, without the tears springing to our eyes at the memory of the greenish-blue liver behind it? Will our rapture at the *Emperor* not be intensified beyond measure by the thought of that gigantic spleen, throbbing away like a ship's boiler under the composer's vest?

One flaw, however, mars the sunny scholarship of your piece: not content to commemorate the bicentenary merely by your thrilling evocation of distorted bowel and giblet and leaving it at that, you insist, I'm afraid, on going on to moralise. And it's none of your business, Doc. Having broken the unethical news that Ludwig's organs got this way through a daily consumption of booze that could have floated a Steinway down Kaiserstrasse, you then wind up the scoop with the homiletic clincher: 'Beethoven had a brain and mind capable of many years of musical productivity, had his life not been shortened by alcohol.' Now, I realise that this oleaginous aside may have been the result of editorial pressure, and that if you hadn't put it in all your readers might have rushed out immediately and begun hitting the sauce in the hope of coming up with a quartet or two, but couldn't you have turned the sentiment a little less harshly? And aren't you being just a teeny bit demanding? Aren't nine symphonies, thirty-two piano sonatas, seven concertos, two masses, sixteen string quartets, and two suit-casefuls of quintets enough for you and the rest of mankind?

And don't you perhaps feel that, after that lot, posterity owes Ludwig a little snort or two?

I suppose not. All human life is divided between those who order by the crate and those who believe that sherry trifle leads to the everlasting bonfire, and never the twain shall meet except on the sodden salient of the *Journal of Alcoholism* for such brief and bitter skirmishes as the one filleted above. You're on one side, Doc, and Ludwig and I are on the other. My own conclusion would be diametrically different from yours, viz, that if Beethoven had *not* been a regular supplier of empties to the trade, he wouldn't have written anything at all, and how does that grab you, abstemious musicologists? If the great man had been confined to Lucozade on the advice of Chester's addiction unit, my bet is that he'd have thrown in the towel at *Chopsticks* and gone down in history as a mediocre hosier.

Because it is no accident that all men of creative genius have toiled in the shadow of the corkscrew – how else is a giant to survive among pygmies, make the mundane tolerable, fence himself off from the encroachments of numbing normalcy? How but through regular intakes of fermented anaesthetic are we – there, I've said it – artists to stave off the canvas jacket and the screaming abdab? How must Beethoven have felt of a morning, his head full of whirling crotchets and jangling semi-breves, to have his housekeeper running off at the gob about the price of vermicelli, or shrieking through his blessed deafness in an attempt to bring home to him the immutable truth that if you send six pillow-cases to the laundry, you only ever get five back? Is it any wonder that he followed up his Special K with a few quick chasers of schnapps? Do you for one moment imagine that the Piano Concerto No. 4 in G Major was written by a teetotaller, given the fact that the decorators were in the haus at the time, Beethoven's shoes hadn't come back from the cobblers, he was four months overdue on his Schedule D payment, his mistress had run off with a door-to-door wurst salesman, and the dog had just trodden on his glasses?

And, worst of all, people like you, Doctor Madden, were constantly nagging him to get on with the bloody music, what about a couple of quick symphonies to follow up the 9th, shouldn't take you more than an hour or so to rattle 'em off, mate, and how would you like to address the Rotarians next Wednesday night, dress formal, and isn't it time you did a personal tour of Silesia, and by the way it's the Prime Minister's birthday coming up, so could you see your way clear to knocking out a little celebratory sextet, no fee naturally, oh yes, I nearly forgot, my wife's brother plays the triangle, not professional of course, but we all think he's rather good, so I've arranged a little dinner-party next Friday to give you the chance of hearing him . . .

I'm amazed his nodules didn't get any bigger than beans, all things considered.

It's a dodgy tightrope along which we creators wobble, Doc: enough booze to close the world off and keep us inventing, but not so much that we allow the golden haze to settle on us permanently, while the piano-strings slacken, and the typewriter rusts, and the brushes dry out and go stiff, and the public yawns and goes off in search of fresh fodder, muttering about what an inconsiderate bleeder that Shakespeare was, snuffing it in his fifties and leaving us with little more than *Lear, Hamlet, Macbeth, Othello, Anthony and Cleopatra*, well I'm not surprised, you know what they say, he couldn't leave the stuff alone, liver like a dried pea, well that's the trouble with artists, isn't it, hoity-toity, too good for the rest of us, they've got to be different, haven't they, bloody bohemians the lot of them, load of boozers, junkies, fairies, layabouts, I mean to say, *only nine symphonies, only thirty plays, only ten novels, only ONE Sistine Chapel* (they say he was so pissed he couldn't get up the ladder), I mean, what do you expect?

Et in El Vino ego, Doc. In a small way, of course. What might *I* not have done, be doing, were it not for the lure of the barmaid's pinny and the brass-handled pump? Ah, the first chapters I have! What prolegomena! What flyleaf notes! A thousand words of the best, then it's off to the local for a self-congratulatory belt, and when I roll home, in a day or two, all is ashes, forgotten, dead. How was it going to go on, this trilogy, before those bottles intervened? Who was this character, and this, and who cares, now? Ah, those publishers' lunches, yes, I'll do a novel, yes, I have this wonderful idea, he meets her, see, and they go off to Ensenada, and her husband, broken by drugs and a lifetime of inferior diplomacy, kills his mistress, let's have another bottle of this excellent Mouton Cadet, but their son returns from the Congo where his mercenary activities have involved him with none other than, my goodness this *is* an amicable cognac, oh yes, you should certainly have the first draft by February, as you say, it's a natural, film rights alone should bring us in . . .

And I wake up in a Turkish bath, some time later, and can only remember that I had my umbrella when I left the house, but was it in the cab, or was it in the restaurant, or am I thinking of my raincoat?

Well, that's it, Doc, another thousand words, another bottle. And that's all you'll get from me today. All I ask is that when my liver and I kick off, and the *Journal of Alcoholism* rings up for a few succinct remarks on posterity's loss, you'll recall all this, and understand a little.

It may surprise you, but I'd hate to be remembered as just another greenish-blue liver, shrunk to half its proper size.

21

Take the Wallpaper in the Left Hand and the Hammer in the Right . . .

You live with a woman for ten years, not an intimacy remains unshared, and where are you?

It was Christmas morning, possibly with a capital M, so auspicious was the time, and the house re-echoed to the Yuley joy of children breaking their new toys over one another. Since dawn, the air had been filled with flying cogs, the walls of the upstairs hall shone with new day-glo graffiti, and on the stairs the pitiful shards of model soldier lay thick as on the field of Omdurman, their little swords and broken rifles still game for a last kamikaze jab at the bare parental sole as it lurched, hung-over, through the inimical pile towards the reviving caffeine.

I hobbled eventually to a breakfast table that would have left Oliver Wendell Holmes himself speechless. A doll's eye glared up from the porridge, rubber insects were all over the toast, and beside the coffee-pot stood the remains of an electric dog. Cobbled together in far Nippon by deft saffron digits, the animal had been a masterpiece of delicate invention a half-hour earlier, when my small daughter first flung herself at its wrappings. In theory, when you pulled its leash, two batteries in its cunningly hollowed bowels sprang into energy, and its little tail wagged while its little legs waddled it forward and its little head nodded as its little mouth yapped.

In practice, however, you pull its leash, and a little tin flange clicks up and down obscenely in its hindquarters, the tail having fallen off, and its little legs waddle it forward at a slow limp; but its little head does not nod, because its little head is now on the other side of the table. The decapitated torso, in fact, is crawling towards its severed skull, and, illogically, barking at it. As the high point of a Hammer film, the thing now has few equals, but as a cuddly toy it has all the winsome appeal of a clockwork boil.

I was still staring at the furry wreckage and musing on the whims of economic history whereby Japan's fiduciary sun was allowed to rise on such insubstantial collateral as this, when I heard my wife say: 'Never mind, you'll be able to mend all their toys now.'

How shall I describe the nudgy emphasis of that *NOW*? She is a subtle girl, and when she slips into italics, every hackle I have tells me there are difficult times ahead.

'I'm sorry?' I riposted wittily.

'You haven't opened your present,' she said.

'Oh!' I cried, having practised; and having painstakingly ignored the large parcel beside my chair which contained a half doz shirts, at the very least, possibly a brace of sweaters, and who knew how many ties, cravats, matching foulards? What the sequitur might be bridging them to the dismembered doggie, I could not begin to guess; but it had been a pretty heavy night, and I might well have lost a syllogistic rivet or two along the way.

I threw my remains upon the parcel and, having broken a forenail on the knot and gashed a thumb on the paper (co-ordination is one of my shorter suits: I am one of the few men I know to bang his head on seven-foot lintels), I came to a book. A book with a lock and a handle on it, yet.

'Hurrah,' I murmured. I brightened. Shirts it wasn't, but a *fake* book it might well be, a piece of snappy packaging for the literary cigar-smoker, say, under which head I fall.

'It's like a little suitcase,' I said.

'Isn't it, though?' she replied. 'What an eye for detail you have, and all self-taught.'

Detecting a coppery tang of disappointment here, and instantly tracing its source, I cranked up my enthusiasm a couple of notches.

'Wow!' I cried, hefting the bogus vol, 'How exciting to have a package *within* a package! Ha-ha-ha, it's passing itself off as – let me see – *The Reader's Digest Complete Do-It-Yourself Manual*!'

'Is it?' she said.

'Isn't it?' I replied.

I snapped back the catch, and opened it, and it contained a million or two loose-leaf pages, cleverly ring-bound for maximum inaccessibility. They fell open at a page of circular saws.

'Oh, look,' I said, 'circular saws.'

'There you are,' she cried happily, 'and you've always maintained you weren't technical.'

'I can, however, recognise any tool you care to name,' I replied. 'I have learned to, just as mice come to learn about mousetraps. It is almost an instinct with me, now.'

'It will be a whole new skill,' she countered. 'With this book, anyone can learn how to build anything. Look,' she continued, turning a leaf with enviable dexterity, 'a sideboard! All you do is saw wood up and fit it together.'

'Well, well! And think of all the fuss they made of Sheraton!' Many things were seething in my head at this moment, the least of them being my utter ineptitude when faced with anything constructional. The only thing I ever succeeded in making in school woodwork, and that after a year of rib-tickling failed attempts, was a toast-rack, and even then you had to put a rubber band around the toast to keep the whole thing from falling apart. I transferred to metalwork after that, where they would give me steel plates which I turned into shrapnel. But this drear practical record, as I say, was nothing to the deeper significances with which the gift was fraught.

'Darling,' I said, 'I had always believed that you thought of me as a sophisticated homme du monde, dashing scourge of croupiers and sommeliers alike, a two-fisted wit over whom lissom dollies sighed and suffered, a young god who could hold his liquor and his own with Freddie Ayer! Look here, upon this picture, and on this – and how many joiners do you know who could hit you with an apt Shakespearian reference at this early hour? – and tell me what you see.'

She looked at the proffered page. A man in a leather apron was demonstrating the correct method of squinting at a rebating plane. He had several ball-points in an upper pocket, no doubt of different hues, and a short-back-and-sides he had clearly manufactured himself, possibly with adze and chisel.

'Is that,' I cried, 'how you see me? A shaper of matchless dovetails, an adroit recycler of cotton-reels, a host to keep his guests enthralled, as they sip their Emva Cream, with tales of tile and bookcase? You know me,' I hurtled on, 'the only craft I have is gluing, and that imperfect. We have shared a life for ten years, you have watched me glue shelves to walls, and seen them fall, you have lain awake and listened while glued slates detached themselves from the roof, you have reeled back as wardrobe doors came unstuck from their hinges – and at the end of it all, *this*?'

'It's just a question of the proper tools,' she said, 'saws and chisels and – things.'

'Wounds is the word you were looking for,' I said, 'that is what goes with saws and chisels, a floorful of thumbs, the squirt of arteries, overworked surgeons converting my body into a Fair Isle masterpiece!'

Whereupon, wordless, she shoved back her chair, and left.

I sat for a while, staring at the table (how did they fit the legs in, how did they get the top on, to what arcane glue secrets were cabinetmakers privy?) and the ruined toys, and I thought: would it not, in truth, be cool to wave mystic implements over these remains, bring old British skills to bear upon Jap tattiness, return the toys, new-perfect, to the kids and accept their squeals of joy and love? Or knock up – I flipped the book – a cocktail cabinet or two, some bunk beds, even a summer house? Put in (page 41) a swimming-pool, relay the parquet floors, convert the loft?

Would this infringe upon the image of Renaissance Man? On the contrary, it would enhance it, endow new facets, why, I could paint the Mona Lisa with my left hand while my right was inventing the helicopter! I would buy gorblimey trousers, a crusty briar, learn how to hold nails in my mouth and tell the consistency of cement by the smell alone, and gawping neighbours would come to point out the matchless gabling, the new storey, the fresh bow windows—

I rushed out, borne on the boiling enthusiasm, into the garage which was to be my workshop, carrying the manual by its handle (perhaps, now, I should always carry it with me, and when crowds formed around some fallen masonry or shattered window or the torn woodwork of a bomb-blasted pub, I would elbow them aside, holding it aloft and crying 'Let me through, I'm a handyman!'), and, as luck would have it, there in an old tobacco tin on the window ledge I found a threaded hook, just the thing to hang the book on for easy reference, so I screwed it into the plaster, and I found a piece of string, and I looped it through the handle, and I hung the book up on the wall, *and it did not fall off!*

Until I slammed the garage door, that is.

I looked through the window, and there seemed to be a lot of plaster on the floor. But it did not faze me. A little thing like fallen plaster doesn't bother me any more.

Why, I'll have it glued back up any day now.

22

Owing to Circumstances Beyond our Control 1984 has been Unavoidably Detained . . .

in which I set out to prove that totalitarianism in Britain could never work. How could it, when nothing else does?

Winston Smith lay on his mean little bed in his mean little room and stared at his mean little telescreen. The screen stared back, blank. Smith eased himself from the side of his mean little blonde, walked across his dun and threadbare carpet, and kicked the silent cathode. A blip lurched unsteadily across it, and disappeared. Smith sighed, and picked up the telephone.

'Would you get me Rentabrother Telehire?' he said.

'They're in the book,' said the operator.

'I haven't got a book,' said Smith. 'They didn't deliver it.'

'It's no good blaming me,' said the operator. 'It's a different department.'

'I'm not blaming you,' said Smith. 'I just thought you might get me the number.'

'I was just going off,' said the operator, 'on account of the snow.'

'It's not snowing,' said Smith.

'Not *now*, it isn't,' said the operator. 'I never said it was snowing *now*.'

'Perhaps I might have a word with the Supervisor,' said Smith.

'She's not here,' said the operator. 'She gets her hair done Fridays.'

'I only need the Rentabrother number,' said Smith, 'perhaps you could find it for me. You must have a book.'

'I'd have to bend,' said the operator.

'I'd be awfully grateful,' said Smith.

'I've just done me nails.'

'Please,' said Smith.

There was a long pause, during which a woman came on and began ordering chops, and someone gave Smith a snatch of weather forecast for Heligoland. After that, there was a bit of recipe for sausage toad. Eventually, after two further disconnections, the operator came back.

'It's 706544,' she snapped.

Smith put the receiver down, and dialled 706544.

'809113,' shouted a voice, 'Eastasian Cats Home.'

He got a Samoan ironmonger after that, and then a French woman who broke down and screamed. At last 'Rentabrother Telehire,' said a man.

'Winston Smith here,' said Smith, '72a, Osbaldeston Road. I'm afraid my telescreen seems to be out of order.'

'What am I supposed to do?' said the man. 'We're up to our necks.'

'But I'm not being watched,' said Smith. 'Big Brother is supposed to be monitoring me at all times.'

'Ring Big Bleeding Brother, then,' said the man. 'Maybe he's not suffering from staff shortages, seasonal holidays, people off sick. Maybe he's not awaiting deliveries. Not to mention we had a gull get in the stockroom, there's stuff all over, all the labels come off, broken glass. People ringing up all hours of the day and night. You realise this is my tea-time?'

'I'm terribly sorry,' said Smith, 'It's just that . . .'

'Might be able to fit you in Thursday fortnight,' said the man. 'Can't promise nothing, though. Got a screwdriver, have you?'

'I'm not sure,' said Smith.

'Expect bleeding miracles, people,' said the man, and rang off.

Smith put the phone down, and was about to return to the bed when there was a heavy knocking on the door, and before he or the little blonde could move, it burst from its hinges and two enormous constables of the Thought Police hurtled into the room. They recovered, and looked around, and took out notebooks.

'Eric Jervis', cried the larger of the two, 'we have been monitoring your every action for the past six days, and we have reason to believe that the bicycle standing outside with the worn brake blocks is registered in your name. What have you to say?'

'I'm not Eric Jervis,' said Smith.

They stared at him.

'Here's a turn-up,' said the shorter officer.

'Ask him if he's got any means of identity,' murmured the larger.

'Have you any means of identity?' said the constable.

'I'm waiting for a new identity card,' said Smith. 'It's in the post.'

'I knew he'd say that,' said the larger officer.

'We're right in it now,' said his colleague. 'Think of the paperwork.'

They put their notebooks away.

'You wouldn't know where this Eric Jervis is, by any chance?' said the taller.

'I'm afraid not,' said Smith.

'Who's that on the bed, then?'

'It's certainly not Eric Jervis,' said Smith.

They all looked at the little blonde.

'He's got us there,' said the shorter constable.

'I've just had a thought,' said the taller, 'I don't think people are supposed to, er, do it, are they?'

'Do what?'

162

'You know, men,' the Thought Policeman looked at his boots, 'and women.'

'I don't see what that's got to do with worn brake blocks,' said his colleague.

They tipped their helmets.

'Mind how you go,' they said.

Smith let them out, and came back into the room.

'I'll just nip down the corner,' he said to the little blonde, 'and pick up an evening paper. Shan't be a tick.'

It was crowded on the street. It was actually the time of the two minutes' hate, but half the public telescreens were conked out, and anyway the population was largely drunk, or arguing with one another, or smacking kids round the head, or running to get a bet on, or dragging dogs from lamp-posts, or otherwise pre-occupied, so nobody paid much attention to the suspended telescreens, except for the youths throwing stones at them. Smith edged through, and bought a paper, and opened it.

'COME OFF IT BIG BROTHER!,' screamed the headline, above a story blaming the Government for rising food prices, the shortage of underwear, and the poor showing of the Oceanic football team. It wasn't, Smith knew, the story the Government hacks had given to the printers, but you could never get the printers to listen to anyone, and challenged, they always blamed the shortage of type, claiming that they could only put the words together from the letters available, and who cared, anyhow? The Government, with so much else on its plate, had given up bothering.

It was as Winston Smith turned to go back to his flat, that he felt a frantic plucking at his knee, and heard a soprano scream ring through the street. He looked down, and saw a tiny Youth Spy jumping up and down below him.

'Winston Smith does dirty things up in Fourteen B,' howled the child. 'Come and get him, he's got a nude lady up there.'

The youth spy might have elaborated on these themes, had

its mother not reached out and given it a round arm swipe that sent it flying into the gutter: but, even so, the damage had been done, and before Smith had time to protest, he found himself picked up bodily by a brace of uniformed men and slung into the back of a truck which, siren wailing, bore him rapidly through the evening streets towards the fearful pile of the Ministry of Love.

'Smith, W,' barked the uniformed man to whom Smith was manacled, at the desk clerk.

'What's he done?' said the clerk. 'I was just off home.'

'They caught him at a bit of how's-your-father,' said Smith's captor.

'It's Friday night,' said the desk clerk. 'I go to bingo Fridays.' He turned to Smith. 'Don't let it happen again, lad. You can go blind.'

'I've written him in me book,' said the guard. 'It's no good saying go home. I'd have to tear the page out.' He put his free hand on Smith's arm. 'Sorry about this, son. It'd be different if I had a rubber. We're awaiting deliveries.'

'You'd better take him up to Room 101, then,' said the clerk.

'NOT ROOM 101,' screamed Smith, 'NOT THE TORTURE CHAMBER, PLEASE, I NEVER DID ANYTHING, I HARDLY KNOW THE WOMAN, CAN'T ANYONE HELP ME, DON'T SEND ME UP . . .'

'Stop that,' said the clerk, sharply. 'You'll start the dog off.'

Smith was dragged, shrieking, to the lift.

'Ah, Smith, Winston,' cried the white-coated man at the door of Room 101. 'Won't you come in? Rats I believe, are what you, ha-ha-ha, fear most of all. Big brown rats. Big brown pink-eyed rats . . .'

'NO,' screamed Smith, 'NOT RATS, ANYTHING BUT RATS, NO, NO, NO.'

'. . . Rats with long slithery tails, Smith, fat, hungry rats, rats with sharp little . . .'

'Oh, do shut up, Esmond,' interrupted his assistant wearily. 'You know we haven't got any rats. We haven't seen a rat since last December's delivery.'

'No rats?' gasped Smith.

Esmond sighed, and shook his head. Then he suddenly brightened.

'We've got mice though,' he cried. 'Big fat, hungry, pink-eyed . . .'

'I don't mind mice,' said Smith.

They looked at him.

'You're not making our job any easier, you know,' muttered Esmond.

'Try him on toads,' said Esmond's assistant. 'Can't move in the stockroom for toads.'

'That's it!' exclaimed Esmond. 'Toads, Big, fat, slimy . . .'

'I quite like toads,' said Smith.

There was a long pause.

'Spiders?'

'Lovely little things,' said Smith. 'If it's any help, I can't stand moths.'

'Moths,' cried Esmond. 'Where do you think you are, bloody Harrod's? We can't get moths for love nor money.'

'Comes in here, big as you please, asking for moths,' said Esmond's assistant.

Smith thought for a while.

'I'm not all that keen on stoats,' he said at last.

'At last,' said Esmond. 'I thought we'd be here all night. Give him a stoat, Dennis.'

So they put Winston Smith in Room 101 with a stoat. It was an old stoat, and it just sat on the floor, wheezing, and as far as Smith was concerned, things could have been, all things considered, a lot worse.

23

Foreword to Golfing For Cats: *An Apology to the Bookseller*

One of the major headaches with which booksellers are invariably racked is the astonishing intractability of authors. The division between these twin curators of our literary heritage is over which of the two syllables of the word 'bookshop' is the more important. How rarely can an author be found who considers, before even setting pen to paper, the marketability of his product! How often has an author rung a bookshop to say: 'I'm thinking of doing a book, what's the best weight to go for?' or enquired as to the exact dimensions of the bookseller's most popular paper bag, so that something may be written to fit it?

Hopefully, *Golfing For Cats* will change all that. A new era of inter-literary co-operation, it is not too much to say, may well be dawning. For not only has this book been put together at the optimum size and weight, it also concerns the three most perennially popular subjects currently to be found on the bedside tables of the reading public, viz. golf, cats, and the Third Reich.

Unfortunately – but, then, one cannot have everything, all revolutions are by nature imperfect – it doesn't concern any of them very deeply. In fact, glancing through the material, I found nothing to do with golf, cats, or indeed the Third Reich. However, they are all there on the cover, which may well be enough: the majority of books sold are given as presents, and the givers, only too glad to have the rotten problem settled, rarely give more than a perfunctory glance at the dust-jacket. I cannot but believe that this book will find its way onto the bookshelves, not to say into the wastebins, of golfers, cat-lovers, and students of military history, in incalculable numbers. (These would be even larger had I managed to get 'Book of Records' somewhere in the title, but this proved to be impossible: *The Golfing Cat's Book of Records* runs cumbrously off the tongue. Similarly, I have been told that even more books about fishing have been sold than books about golf, but *Fishing For Cats*, conjuring up as it did the vision of someone leaning over a bridge with a mouse on the end of a string, stretched, I felt, ambiguity to an intolerable limit.)

Why, then, I hear you ask, should I apologise to the bookseller, having bent over so far backwards, not to mention sideways, to please him? Well, it is simply that some confusion may arise, this book having been ordered in the vast numbers necessary to satisfy the giant trifurcated public for it, when it comes to putting it on the shelves: should it go under GOLF, or under CATS, or under THE THIRD REICH; or, indeed, under none of these? (There is, I quietly submit, a good commercial case for putting it under BOOKS OF RECORDS, but I shall not push it.)

I leave, I'm afraid, the decision to the bookseller himself. If he chooses to opt for the safest course, and buy three times as many copies as he would otherwise have done, I should prefer, in the interests of modesty and good taste, that the suggestion did not come from me.

24

Baby Talk, Keep Talking Baby Talk

Harvard's Social Psychiatry Laboratory has been analysing the special language adults use when talking to children; and it doesn't like it. Children, it believes, should be spoken to as adults. And vice versa?

*T*he Savoy Grill. An elderly diner has pushed his plate to one side and is staring absently into the middle distance. To him, a waiter.

'You haven't eaten up your blanquette de veau, sir.'

'I don't want it.'

'Don't be a silly diner. It's delicious.'

'It isn't.'

'It is.'

'*Isn't!*'

'*Is!*'

'*ISN'T! ISN'T! ISN'T!*'

'I'm going to turn my back, sir, and I'm going to count up to ten, and when I turn round again I want to see all that nice blanquette de veau eaten up. ONE – TWO – THREE –'

'I'm going to be sick.'

'– FIVE – SIX –'

'I'm going to stick my fingers down my throat and I'm going to be sick on my new dinner jacket and I'm going to be sick on my new shoes and I'm going to be sick on my new mistress and I'm going to be sick on the tablecloth, and I *DON'T CARE!*'

'Look, sir, shall I tell you what we're going to do? You see that great big boiled potato? Well, that's Mount Everest. And the brussels sprouts are going to climb right up it.'

'Why?'

'Because they're mountaineers.'

'Why?'

'Because it's there.'

'Why?'

'Because it is, and because I say so. But when they get to the top, they're going to be eaten by a Yeti. And do you know who the Yeti is?'

'No.'

'You are, sir! You're a big brave Yeti, and you're going to eat all the mountaineers up!'

'I'm *not* a Yeti, I'm not, I'm *not*! I want some pudding.'

'Sorry, sir, no pudding until you've eaten your blanquette de veau all up.'

'I'll scream!'

'That's quite enough of that, sir. Do you want me to call the Head Waiter?'

'No.'

'You know what the Head Waiter does to naughty diners, don't you, sir?'

'Yes.'

'So you're going to eat up your nice blanquette de veau, aren't you?'

'Can I have some pudding afterwards?'

'If you're very, very good.'

'All right.'

The Manager's office, Barcloyd's Bank. A knock on the door.

'Yes? Ah — it's Hopcroft, isn't it?'

'Hoskins, sir.'

'Speak up, boy!'

'*Hoskins*, sir!'

'Have you got something in your mouth, Hoskins?'

'It's a – no, sir – I mean, yes sir, it's my pipe, sir.'

'And you think you can come in here smoking a pipe, do you, Hoskins? You think you can *afford* a pipe, do you?'

'Well, sir, I—'

'Don't lie to me, Hoskins, you snivelling little beast! And stop scratching yourself. What's that in your hand?'

'It's my m–monthly statement, sir.'

'Is it, Hoskins, is it indeed? And are you proud of your monthly statement, Hoskins?'

'No, sir.'

'No, sir. Well nor am I, sir. And I've asked you to come and see me, Hoskins, because I'm very disappointed in you. Very disappointed indeed!'

'I'm sorry, sir.'

'Stop whining, Hoskins! If there's one thing I can't stand, it's a customer who whines. I had great hopes for you, Hoskins: I pride myself on being able to pick a promising customer, a customer who'll go far, a customer who will be a credit to Barcloyd's. A credit, Hoskins. Do you even know what the word means?'

'Yes, sir.'

'I doubt that, Hoskins. I doubt that very much. You will please conjugate the verb *to be in credit*.'

'I am in credit, thou art in credit, he is in credit, we are in credit, you are in credit, they are in credit.'

'And *are* you in credit, Hoskins?'

'No, sir.'

'I despair, Hoskins, I truly despair. Look at the other customers, look at Sibley, and Greene, and Maltravers, look at Finnegan – credit accounts, deposit accounts, special accounts, joint accounts, all in credit, all improving every day, all rising to the top, all customers I can be proud of. And look at your younger brother, Hoskins Minor: he's just become Hoskins & Gribble Ltd. He'll go far.'

'Yes, sir.'

'Now, Hoskins, your teller informs me that you want to buy a bicycle. Is this true?'

'Well, sir, I thought—'

'I know what you thought, Hoskins, you thought you'd sneak off at every opportunity and go gallivanting about on your wretched machine instead of working. Well, Hoskins, I am not having it, do you hear? Now, unfortunately, our rules only permit me certain penalties, and since you are already paying eleven per cent on your wretched scroungings – God, if the Founder had lived to see a Barcloyd's chap beg! – there is only one other course open to me. You will stay behind after work, Hoskins, and you will do one hour's overtime per day. Is that clear?'

'Yes, sir.'

'And think yourself lucky you live in so-called enlightened times, Hoskins. In my day, you'd have been hauled up in front of the whole bank and made bankrupt! Now get out!'

'Yes, sir. Thank you, sir.'

A Surbiton bedroom. Afternoon. The blinds are drawn. The door bursts open.

'ALICE! You're playing with that awful milkman again! What did I tell you would happen if I ever caught you with him after last time?'

'You said you'd divorce me.'

'And did I say I would never ever play with you again?'

'Yes.'

'I only come up 'ere about the one doz large brown eggs as per note, I never—'

'You shut up! You just shut up! You're a nasty horrid person and we don't want you playing in our house! Alice is *my* friend!'

171

'I wasn't doing nothing, I was only talking, I didn't touch nothing, I never—'

'That's a double negative! You're a stupid uneducated little snot, and you live in a council estate, and you're not allowed to play with nice people! That was a double negative, Alice, did you hear it? That's what happens when you ask them in. You'll be picking up all sorts of things.'

'He's not common, Reginald, he's not, he's NOT!'

'He's still got his socks on, Alice. He's in bed with his socks on!'

'So what?'

'Har, har, har! Who's in bed with his socks on? Har, har, har! You wait till I tell your mother about this, Alice, you wait till I tell her about him with his socks on in bed!'

'*Your* mother used to wear a wig! Reginald's mummy used to wear a ginger wig, Dennis!'

'Wun't surprise me. Wun't surprise me at all. Wun't—'

'You just shut up! Your feet smell.'

'So do yours, with brass knobs on, and no returns.'

'*And* you haven't folded your trousers! He hasn't folded his trousers, Alice, he's just thrown them down all anyhow, he's just thrown them on the floor! You've just thrown them on the floor, you horrible little bogie!'

'Knickers!'

'Horse stuff in the road!'

'Wee-wee!'

'There we are, Alice, he's swearing, he's saying filthy things, what did I tell you? Why are you playing with him?'

'It's your fault, Reginald, you won't play with me anymore, you're always going out or too tired or something, and he's got all sorts of new games, it serves you right, so there!'

'But he's not even a member of our *gang*, he's never played Conservatives in his life, he's got hairs in his nose, and—'

'If you let me in your gang, you can 'ave a go on the float.'

'What? I mean, pardon?'

'You can drive it up Winchmore Crescent and back.'

'Oh.'

'You can blow the 'ooter and rattle the crates, and everything.'

'Can I wear your cap?'

'Yes.'

'And the satchel with the change in?'

'Yes.'

'Super!'

'Can Dennis come to play again, then, Reginald?'

'Well – only if he's very, very good.'

'He is.'

'All right, then.'

25

The Hell at Pooh Corner

From Christopher Robin Milne's recent autobiography, it turns out that life in the Milne household was very different from what millions of little readers have been led to believe. But if it was grim for him, what must it have been like for some of the others involved? I went down to Pooh Corner – it is now a tower block, above a discount warehouse – for this exclusive interview.

Winnie-the-Pooh is sixty now, but looks far older. His eyes dangle, and he suffers from terminal moth. He walks into things a lot. I asked him about that, as we sat in the pitiful dinginess which has surrounded him for almost half a century.

'Punchy,' said Winnie-the-Pooh, 'is what I am. I've been to some of the best people, Hamley's, Mothercare, they all say the same thing: there's nothing you can do about it, it's all that hammering you took in the old days.'

Bitterly, he flicked open a well-thumbed copy of *Winnie-the-Pooh*, and read the opening lines aloud:

'"Here is Edward Bear, coming downstairs now, bump, bump, bump, on the back of his head, behind Christopher Robin. It is, as far as he knows, the only way of coming downstairs."' He looked at me. 'The hell it was!' he muttered. 'You think I didn't want to walk down, like normal people? But what chance did I stand? Every morning, it was the same story, this brat comes in and grabs me and next thing I know

174

the old skull is bouncing on the lousy lino. Also,' he barked a short bitter laugh, 'that was the last time anyone called me Edward Bear. A distinguished name, Edward. A name with *class*. After the king, you know.'

I nodded. 'I know,' I said.

'But did it suit the Milnes?' Pooh hurled the book into the grate, savagely. 'Did it suit the itsy-bitsy, mumsy-wumsy, ooze-daddy's-ickle-boy-den Milnes? So I was Winnie-the-Pooh. You want to know what it was like when the Milnes hit the sack and I got chucked in the toy-cupboard for the night?'

'What?' I said.

'It was "Hello, sailor!" and "Give us a kiss, Winifred!" and "Watch out, Golly, I think he fancies you!", not to mention,' and here he clenched his sad, mangy little fists, 'the standard "Oy, anyone else notice there's a peculiar poo in here, ha, ha, ha!"'

'I sympathise,' I said, 'but surely there were compensations? Your other life, in the wood, the wonderful stories of . . .'

'Yeah,' said Pooh, heavily, 'the wood, the stories. The tales of Winnie-the-Schmuck, you mean? Which is your favourite? The one where I fall in the gorse bush? The one where I go up in the balloon and the kid shoots me down? Or maybe you prefer where I get stuck in the rabbit hole?'

'Well, I—'

'Hanging from a bloody balloon,' muttered Pooh, 'singing the kind of song you get put in the funny farm for! Remember?

> "How sweet to be a cloud,
> Floating in the blue!
> Every little cloud
> *Always* sings aloud."

That kind of junk,' said Pooh, 'may suit Rolf Harris. Not me.'

'Did you never sing it, then?' I enquired.

'Oh, I sang it,' said Pooh. 'I sang it all right. It was in the script. *Dumb bear comes on and sings*. It was in the big Milne scenario. But you know what *I* wanted to sing?'

'I have no idea,' I said.

His little asymmetrical eyes grew even glassier, with a sadness that made me look away.

'*Body and Soul*,' murmured Pooh, 'is what I wanted to sing. *Smoke Gets In Your Eyes*. Or play the trumpet, possibly. It was,' he sighed, '1926. Jazz, short skirts, nightingales singing in Berkeley Square, angels dancing at the Ritz, know what I mean? A world full of excitement, sex, fun, Frazer-Nash two-seaters and everyone going to Le Touquet! And where was I? Hanging around with Piglet and passing my wild evenings in the heady company of Eeyore! *The Great Gatsby* came out that year,' said Pooh, bitterly. 'The same year as *Winnie-the-Pooh*.'

'I begin to understand,' I said.

'Why couldn't he write that kind of thing about *me*?' cried the anguished Pooh. 'Why didn't I get the breaks? Why wasn't I a great tragic hero, gazing at the green light on the end of Daisy's dock? Why didn't Fitzgerald write *Gatsby Meets A Heffelump* and Milne *The Great Pooh*?'

'But surely it was fun, if nothing else?' I said. 'Wasn't the Milne household full of laughter and gaiety and—'

'A.A. Milne,' Pooh interrupted, 'was an Assistant Editor of *Punch*. He used to come home like Bela Lugosi. I tell you, if we wanted a laugh, we used to take a stroll round Hampstead cemetery.'

Desperately, for the heartbreak of seeing this tattered toy slumped among his emotional debris was becoming un-endurable, I sought an alternative tack.

'But think,' I said cheerily, 'of all the millions of children you have made happy!'

He was not to be shaken from his gloom.

'I'd rather,' he grunted, 'think of all the bears I've made miserable. After the Pooh books, the industry went mad. My people came off the assembly line like sausages. Millions of little bears marching towards the exact same fate as my own, into the hands of kids who'd digested the Milne rubbish, millions of nursery tea-parties where they were forced to sit around propped against a stuffed piglet in front of a little plastic plate and have some lousy infant smear their faces with jam. "O look, nurse, Pooh's ate up all his cake!" Have you any idea what it's like,' he said, 'having marmalade on your fur? It never,' and his voice dropped an octave, 'happened to Bulldog Drummond.'

'I'm sorry?'

Pooh reached for a grubby notebook, and flipped it open.

'"Suddenly the door burst from its hinges, and the doorway filled with a huge and terrible shape.

'"Get away from that girl, you filthy Hun swine!" it cried.

'"The black-hearted fiend who had been crouched over the lovely Phyllis turned and thrust a fist into his evil mouth.

'"Mein Gott!" he shrieked, "Es ist Edward Bear, MC, DSO!"

'"With one bound, our hero . . ."'

Pooh snapped the notebook shut.

'What's the use?' he said. '*I* wrote that, you know. After Milne packed it in, I said to myself, it's not too late, I know where the pencil-box is, I shall come back like Sherlock Holmes, a new image, a . . . I took it to every publisher in London. "Yes, very interesting," they said, "what about putting in a bit where he gets his paw stuck in a honey jar, how would it be if he went off with Roo and fell in a swamp, and while you're at it, could he sing a couple of songs about bath-night?"'

He fell silent. I cleared my throat a couple of times. Far off, a dog barked, a lift clanged. I stood up, at last, since there seemed nothing more to say.

'Is there anything you need?' I said, somewhat lamely.

'That's all right,' said Winnie-the-Pooh. 'I get by. No slice of the royalties, of course, oh dear me no, well, I'm only the bloody bear, aren't I? Tell you what, though, if you're going past an off-license, you might have them send up a bottle of gin.'

'I'd be delighted to,' I said.

He saw me to the door.

'Funny thing,' he said, 'I could never stand honey.'

26

And Though They Do Their Best To Bring Me Aggravation . . .

'Did you bring back something special from your holiday? Why not enter our Grand Souvenir Competition?'
Daily Telegraph

When Sir Henry Souvenir (1526–1587) at last returned to the court of Queen Elizabeth from his ten-year tour of the Orient, he little thought that their opening exchange would pass into history.

'What have you brought for me?' asked his queen.

'It's a box made from the liver of an elephant, your majesty,' replied Sir Henry, 'wrought in strange fashion by the natives and covered in sea-shells. You can keep fags in it.'

'Where did you get it?' she inquired.

'I can't remember,' he said.

And thus it was that the pattern of the next four hundred years was firmly laid. Ever since that fateful day in 1570, people have been coming back from distant parts carrying things to put cigarettes in, which they give to other people to remind them of places that neither of them can recall. The word "souvenir" has, of course, slightly extended itself in meaning until it now denotes almost anything either breakable or useless; but even today, ninety per cent of the items covered by the word are forgettable objects in which cigarettes can be left to go stale.

Some people don't actually give their souvenirs away,

preferring instead to build up a vast collection with which to decorate lofts; it is not immediately clear why they do this, but a strong ritualistic element is clearly involved, no doubt because the objects are themselves closely associated with the passing of time and take on a totemistic quality from this association. Souvenirs, for example, can never be thrown away, probably because to do so would be to wipe out the past of which they are the only extant record. They are, however, moved around the loft every five years or so, when their lids tend to fall off or, in the case of clocks, when their cuckoos fall out.

The cuckoo clock, in fact, may be said to be the quintessential souvenir, in that it exists purely to be bought, sold, wrapped, carried home, unwrapped, and put in lofts. It never hangs on walls. It is usually purchased in Switzerland, where it never hangs on walls either. How it became involved with Switzerland is a horological mystery of a high order, but experts have suggested that since Switzerland has nothing else to identify it (i.e., Eiffel Towers, Taj Mahals, castanets, lederhosen, chopsticks), and since both its national products, snow and chocolate, melt, the cuckoo clock was invented solely in order to give tourists something solid to remember it by. The undeniable success of the cuckoo clock has led the Swiss to branch out with typically cautious adventurousness: removing the tiny house from which the cuckoo emerges, they have enlarged it in recent years and inserted a music-box inside it, which, when you lift the lid, starts to play 'O Mine Papa' and breaks.

It's for keeping cigarettes in.

Mention of the Eiffel Tower and the Taj Mahal lead me naturally to point out an important secondary characteristic of the souvenir. It is invariably an imitation of something else. Even when it's original. Inventiveness of a remarkable kind often goes into this imitation, and accusations of vulgarity by citizens like Lord Snowdon (who has himself been called a vulgar imitation, though not by me) do not detract from the brilliance of the minds that, for example, saw in the Eiffel Tower not a thousand feet of iron, but six inches of salt-cellar with a nude in the base and a thermometer up one side. Not that our own English craftsmen have been left behind in the race for international kudos: a mere mile from where I am writing this, you can buy a midget guardsman with ten fags in his busby and a gas lighter on his rifle, or a pygmy beefeater out of whose cunningly constructed mouth twenty different scenes of London may be pulled, in full colour. All over Kansas, at this very moment, recent visitors to Britain will be trying to glue its head back on.

Souvenirs also have an invaluable role to play as conversation pieces, even though there will usually be more pieces than conversation. The talk is often quite fascinating, viz:

'Yes, we bought that in Brussels, ha-ha-ha, amusing isn't it? When you switch it on, it pees. Oh. Well, it did. Perhaps it needs a new batt— now look what you've done, it's come off in your hand. We'll never get the cigarettes out of it now.' Or;

'This nut-dish is constructed entirely out of a single piece of elkhorn, by the way, and the crackers are made from the ribs of an okapi. Yes. O–K–A–P–I. And now, if you care to pick up that pin-cushion in the shape of the Great Pyramid, you will find— oh, really? But it's only nine o'clock, and of course you haven't even seen our Nefertiti door-step yet, THAT CARPET YOU'RE RUNNING DOWN IS AN EXTREMELY FASCINATING EXAMPLE OF VERY EARLY SUDANESE . . .'

It's not always easy to choose souvenirs, of course, and many people swear by clothes. I myself have sworn by a suit I bought in Hong Kong some years ago, and hope one day to bring out the oaths in book form, as soon as permissiveness establishes itself a little more securely. As everyone knows, Hong Kong has some of the finest tailors in the world, but what they actually do there is open to question, since all the clothes are made by some of the worst. My own suit, hacked from a wonderfully dirt-absorbent length of, I think, Kleenex, is loosely piled on the floor of the loft, being unable to stay on its hanger. It was, of course, cheap – less than four times as much as a similar article picked up in Savile Row when, due to a light shower in Piccadilly, the Hong Kong item started gripping my flesh with all the enthusiasm of an under-nourished vampire – and this probably accounts for the way in which it was cut, since malformed Oriental dwarfs do not, I'm sure, carry much ready cash upon their persons. It's a wonderful conversation-piece, mind. People I'd known intimately for years suddenly began pointing out that they'd never realised I had one shoulder five inches lower than the other or that my inside leg measured fourteen inches. Osteopaths would approach me in the street and offer their services free in the interest of science.

Not that I'll be entering it in the *Telegraph* competition, though. The suit has competition enough at home, and my initial problem is selecting exactly which rare and precious item to blow the dust off in order to pick up the six quid with which the *Telegraph* hopes to console me for the misspent years of haggling in bazaars and dragging crates through airports and lashing out enough customs dues to turn the *real* Arc de Triomphe into a musical needlework cabinet and knock the bottom out of the French souvenir trade for ever. What shall I choose from the matchless hoard? The genuine Matabele shield, riddled with moth-holes? (No wonder Rhodesia is run by a white minority, if that's all there was between the natives and the Maxim gun.) The elephant's foot wastebasket, perhaps the most macabre thing ever to pass across a counter? (When we came home from India and unwrapped it, the toenails fell off.) The solid brass table-top we bought at the same Delhi

Alan Coren, war child

With his parents, Sam and Martha

In America, 1961

Literary editor of Punch, 1964

Proof-reading, 1970s

Two classic 1970s
book covers

'Had he re-launched himself
as a gentleman Pip?'

A Punch lunch.
Apparently they were great fun

The News Quiz team: with John Wells, Barry Took
and Richard Ingrams

Crossing Downing Street in lederhosen

The Prime Minister admires the canapés

Call My Bluff, with Bob Holness and Sandi Toksvig, 1990s

Mid-bluff, watched by Michael Gambon

The News Quiz in the 21st century: with Jeremy Hardy,
Francis Wheen, Linda Smith, Simon Hoggart
and Andy Hamilton

shop which peeled on the plane, and rusted in the cab back from Heathrow? The hand-sewn slippers from Alexandria which gave rise to a condition which has baffled chiropodists throughout the civilised world? My genuine Dutch meerschaum, that glows in the dark, blisters, and flakes off on to the authentic Bokhara rug which is supposed to have taken two generations of Uzbeks to weave and which it took the cat one evening to unravel?

On second thoughts, I don't think I'll bother. Let someone else take the *Telegraph*'s money with his walrus-tooth-letter-opener-barometer-and-shoehorn combined, I'm hanging on to my stock. Some day soon, the Martian package tourists are going to start arriving, and I'm going to be down there at the saucerport handing out my copper-plate business cards.

Give 'em a free glass of mint tea, and those people'll buy anything.

27

Life mit Vater

A man claiming to be one of Adolf Hitler's sons has turned up in France, intending to sell his memoirs. One of the other ones has not been slow to follow.

I was born on January 18, 1923, at 17, Bolitha Villas, SE26. It was an ordinary little Sydenham terraced house, flanked to the left by Dunlookin, and to the right by Fredberyl. Ours was called Arbeit Macht Frei.

It was distinguishable from the rest only by virtue of its paintwork. The front door was puce, the downstairs windows were yellow, and the upstairs were variously blue, green and beige. They were painted thus by my father, this being his trade; but he was constantly going abroad on business, leaving the job partially done, and finding upon his return that the paint in the open pots had gone hard.

He would then throw the pots at my mother and run up and down Bolitha Villas in his bare feet shrieking that the Jews had left the lids off. By evening, he had invariably calmed down, and would be found, weeping, in the shed, muttering that he had gone off beige, or blue, or eau-de-nil, or whatever it happened to be. Towards midnight, I would be awoken by the strains of Wagner, and would tiptoe to the window and stare out towards the shed, through the tiny window of which I would be able to see my father in a flaxen wig beating the cat with the flat of his wooden sword.

Years later, recalling such memories, I asked my mother

what had attracted her to him in the first place. She explained that she had met him at a dance in Leytonstone, where he was the only man in a helmet; halfway through the evening, he took the head of a conga line and marched it nine miles to Dagenham, in driving hail. She was, she said, carried away by his natural authority. He also had a lighter side, she maintained, and was well known, before his broody period set in, for his impressions of Charlie Chaplin.

None of this, of course, was known to me in my childhood, and my father remained, in consequence, something of a puzzle. I did not, for example, know why he slept on the roof in all weathers, and I was acutely embarrassed, being but four years old, when he took me to the Natural History Museum and insisted on goose-stepping to the bus-stop. He also, when we arrived, screamed at the dinosaur skeleton for some minutes on the grounds, as I recall, that it had given up without a struggle. He calmed down somewhat upon the arrival of three uniformed attendants, pausing only to inspect their buttons, feel their biceps, and pat them on the head affectionately, before taking me away to look at a stuffed gorilla beside which he delivered, to my total incomprehension, a long lecture about the decadence of jazz.

That Christmas, an aunt gave me a golliwog, which my father hanged. When I asked him why, he jumped out of the window.

In the spring of 1929, on my father's insistence, I joined the Cubs.

Although, initially, I was a figure of derision (I was the only one in a brown shirt; and also, try as I might, I could not fully disguise the fact that my cap had a spike on it), before long my little playmates were treating me with more and more respect. This was largely on account of my accoutrements; each time my daddy returned home from one of his foreign trips, he would bring me a new piece of equipment, until, by midsummer, I was turning up at meetings in riding-boots, Sam Browne belt and a gas-mask, carrying a Schmeisser machine-pistol. Where other boys wore cheap blunt penknives on their belts, I wore a grenade pouch; where they sported a woodcraft badge, I bore the Iron Cross.

Akela, our leader, was very decent about it: not only was she trained in the Montessori method, and thus responsive to self-expression irrespective of its prime motive, she also had steel spectacles gummed together at their broken bridge, thinning hair, a concave bust, and legs like Indian clubs. When my father, therefore, clasped her to him on collecting me one evening, kissed her on both sallow cheeks, and informed her that she would be the flower of the New Sydenham, a mottled glow suffused her entire visible surface.

Thereafter, I could do no wrong. When, the following week, I led my patrol away from its ostensible mission to pluck four-leaf clovers on Sydenham Hill and took them instead on a house-to-house search of Dulwich looking for Bolshevik printing presses, she awarded me the Blue Max with Oak Leaves and Crossed Swords, and allowed me to blow her whistle.

There is no guessing the heights to which I might have risen, had it not been for a characteristically over-enthusiastic blunder on my father's part. That autumn, our group went away to weekend camp. My parents took me down in our old Morris Ten, my mother driving and my father standing on the seat beside her with his head and shoulders poking up through the sunshine roof. Upon our arrival, my father dismounted and, catching sight of the tented camp, immediately began encircling it with a roll of barbed wire he always carried in the boot.

It was while he was attempting to construct a makeshift searchlight tower by lashing one of the Morris's headlamps to a telephone pole that an assistant to the Chief Scout ran up and insisted that he come down and explain his behaviour.

Daddy then threw himself to the ground and began biting the grass. Soon afterwards, we received a brief note informing us that Sydenham Cub Pack 1374 was being reconstituted under new leadership and that my membership of the group would not be looked upon with favour.

Of the subsequent career of Akela, I have little first-hand information: between her departure from SE26 in 1929 and her suicidal single-handed attack on General Vasilevsky's 4th Armoured Division outside Stalingrad, history has drawn a disappointing blank.

For two years thereafter, I saw little of my father. There had been some local unpleasantness on Guy Fawkes' Night 1929 when, by dint of a nocturnal raid on the files of Sydenham Public Library, he managed to steal enough tickets to allow him to take out its entire stock, which he then piled in our back yard and ignited, having first topped the heap with a stuffed effigy of Issy Bonn; and as the result of this he once more left the country.

Apart from one notorious flying visit to Bolitha Villas in the winter of 1930, when he showed up proudly on the arm of an aristocratic English girl — it ended in chaos when she laughed at our three china ducks and Daddy in consequence attempted to garotte Mummy with his armband — I did not see him again until late on Midsummer's Day, 1931.

It is an occasion which remains embossed upon my memory, despite the passage of almost fifty years.

I was coming home from school, and upon turning into Bolitha Villas from Pondicherry Crescent, I noticed a large crowd outside Fredberyl. Most of them were neighbours, but there were policemen in the crowd, too, and a fire-engine was drawn up at the kerb. Fredberyl being the house next to Arbeit

Macht Frei, I was therefore amazed, upon drawing nearer, to see my father at an upstairs window of it, shrieking and waving a makeshift flag.

'What's going on?' I enquired of an elderly police sergeant, whom I had met when my father, during one of his many bursts of wild enthusiasm, had written to Scotland Yard applying for a submarine licence.

'It's your old man,' he replied. 'He has annexed Fredberyl. As I understand it, he intends to knock down the dividing wall and use the combined premises for a spring offensive against Dunlookin.'

Being only eight, I could not of course grasp the full implications of the situation; I was, however, understandably concerned for the welfare of my father.

'Oh dear!' I cried. 'What will happen to my daddy? Will you have to go in there and drag him out and all that?'

The sergeant stared down at me in some irritation.

'*Me*?' he said. 'Intervene in a domestic wossname? You must be joking, son! I don't know what your old man's got against Fredberyl and Dunlookin, but one thing's for bleeding sure, I have not come all the way here from Tulse Hill to interfere in a quarrel in a faraway street between people of whom I know nothing.'

28

Dr No will See You Now

'CIA agents who lose the qualities that make good spies are retired at fifty under special pensions, according to testimony yesterday before a House Intelligence Sub-Committee. "A 70-year-old James Bond is kind of hard to imagine," said Republican Senator Sam Stratton.'

Herald Tribune

Bond tensed in the darkness, and reached for his teeth. There was something in the room.

You did not train for fifty-three years without developing that imponderable acuity that lay beyond mere observation. Indeed, you found that as the years went by, this sixth sense came, perforce, to replace the others: these days, he could hear dog-whistles, with or without his batteries in.

At least, he assumed they were dog-whistles. Nobody else seemed to hear them.

The teeth fell exactly to hand, there between the senna and the Algipan on his bedside table. He waited a calculated split-second for the cement to cleave snugly to his palate. It felt good. It should have: it was made for him by Chas. Fillibee of Albemarle Street, the world's premier fixative man. Senior British agents had been going to Fillibee since before the War; he knew their special requirements. When Witherspoon 004 had gone into the London Clinic to have his prostate done and the KGB had taken the opportunity to lob an Ostachnikov nuclear mortar into his grape-box, the only thing left intact between Baker Street Station and the Euston underpass had been Witherspoon's upper plate.

Very carefully, Bond slid his hand beneath his pillow and closed it around the ribbed butt of his Walther PPK 9mm Kurz with the custom-enlarged trigger guard by Rinz of Stuttgart which allowed the arthritic knuckle of Bond's forefinger to slide smoothly around the trigger. His other hand took the light switch.

In one smooth, practised move, Bond snapped on the light switch and simultaneously peered around the room.

There was a shadowy, half-familiar figure by the dressing table. Bond fired, twice, the fearful reports cracking back and forth between the walls, and the figure reeled.

'So much,' murmured Bond coolly, 'for Comrade Nevachevski!'

Miss Moneypenny sat up in bed, her grizzled bun unravelling, her elegant muffler in fetching disarray.

'You silly old sod,' she said.

Bond beamed, deafly.

'Yes, wasn't it?' he said. 'Inch or so wide, mind, should've been straight between the eyes, but, my God, he didn't even have time to draw!'

'YOU'VE SHOT YOUR WIG-STAND!' shouted Miss Moneypenny. She stuck an ephedrine inhaler in her left nostril, and sucked noisily.

Bond put on his bi-focals.

'Ah,' he said. He brightened. 'Still a bloody good shot, though, eh?'

'I should cocoa,' said Moneypenny. 'It ricocheted off the hot-water bottle. God alone knows what it's done to your rubber sheet.'

'Bloody hell,' said Bond.

He switched the light out again, and lay back. As always,

after untoward events, his wheeze was bad, crackling round the room like crumpling cellophane.

'Shall I rub you in?' murmured Moneypenny softly, from her distant cot.

'Don't start,' said Bond.

Moneypenny sighed. At sixty-eight, it seemed, her virginity was moving slowly but surely beyond threat.

Bond shuffled nonchalantly into M's office and tossed his hat in a neat arc towards the polished antler. The hat fell in the waste-bin. 007 stared at it for a time, and finally decided against picking it up. On the last occasion upon which he had attempted a major stoop, it had taken four osteopaths to unwind him.

'Good morning,' said M, 'if you're from Maintenance, I'd like you to know that the roller towel is getting harder and harder to tug. I don't know what they're doing with them these days. I think they put something in them at the factory. When I was a lad, you could pull them down between thumb and forefinger. Possibly the KGB has a hand in it. Also, I have great difficulty in pulling the soap off that magnetic thingy.'

'It's me, sir,' said Bond, '00—'

He frowned.

M stared at him glaucously from nonagenarian eyes.

Bond took off his James Lobb galosh, and removed a slip of paper.

'7,' he said. '007.'

M trembled suddenly. He tugged at a drawer, but it did not budge.

'I've got a gun in here somewhere,' he said. 'By God, you'll know it when I find it! You're not 007, you swine, I've known 007 fifty years, he's bright ginger!'

'I shot my wig,' said Bond, gloomily.

M relaxed.

'No good getting angry with a wig,' he said. 'It's only doing its job.'

'You sent for me,' said Bond.

'In the CIA,' murmured M, 'I'd have been retired forty years ago. I would have one of those thermal pools with a thing that makes waves in it. I would have my own genito-urinary man coming in on a weekly basis. A TV hanging from the ceiling, mink linings for the cold snap, a hollow cane with Remy Martin in it, a rare dog.'

'About this job,' said Bond.

M blew his nose, ineptly.

'Usual thing,' he said. 'MIRV-launching Russian satellite has been brought down by a defecting Albanian inter-galactic tail-gunner in the pay of the Irgun Zwei Leomi. As you would expect, it has fallen down inside Vesuvius: crack KGB, CIA, Mafia, Triad, and IRA teams are already racing to the spot. I promised the PM we'd send our best man.'

'Oh, good,' muttered Bond. 'You don't think Snuggley might fit the bill better?'

'003?' said M. 'His leg's gone in for its annual service. No, James, it's you – bags of parachuting, ski-ing, scuba-diving, unarmed combat, all that, right up your street.'

'Quite,' said Bond.

'Pop along and see Charlie in Special Equipment,' said M.

'This,' said Charlie, 'is probably the most advanced truss in the world.'

'It's snug,' said Bond. 'What are all these pockets for?'

'Spare surgical stockings,' said Charlie, ticking off his fingers, 'international pensions book, collapsible alloy crutches, Sanatogen capsules, arch supports, emergency pee bottle, mittens, underwater deaf-aid, thermal liberty bodice, and a handbell in case you fall over somewhere and can't get up.'

'Super,' said Bond.

'Also,' said Charlie, 'we've been over your Morris Traveller and, ha-ha, tarted it up a bit. Apart from the fact that you'll now be able to get it up to fifty-five—'

'Christ!'

'—there's an emergency inertia brake that brings it to a dead stop in the event of the driver having a heart attack, plus two big orange lights on stalks in both wings enabling you to drive it through narrow spaces, a foot-button that throws your window out instantly in the event of nausea, an inflatable anti-haemorrhoid ring set in the driver's seat that activates at the first scream, and a 3x magnifying windshield that enables you to read road signs without getting out of the car.'

'Fantastic,' muttered Bond.

'Good luck, 007,' said Charlie, 'and good hunting!'

He shook Bond's hand, but gently.

Bond nosed forward out of the roundabout, onto the Dover road.

People hooted.

The Traveller lurched forward, stalled, lurched on again. 007 ground into third gear. He glanced in his mirror, for the tenth time. Somebody was following him. They had been following him since Blackheath, almost two hours ago.

At the next traffic light, Bond got out, and walked back.

'I don't sell off the float, grandpa,' said the milkman.

'Why have you been following me?' said Bond levelly.

'I got no option, have I?' said the milkman. 'First off, we're the only two vehicles doing fifteen miles a wossname, second off, every time I bleeding pull out to overtake, you start wandering all over the road.'

'Evasive action,' snapped 007. 'Don't tell me you weren't trying to force me into the ditch. You're with SMERSH, right?'

The milkman took his cap off.

'It says Unigate on here,' he said.

'Ha!' cried Bond, and sprang into a Nakusai karate crouch, his left hand a club, his right fingers a dagger.

The milkman got out and helped him up.

'It's this knee I've got,' said Bond.

'Shouldn't be out, old geezer like you,' said the milkman. 'It's freezing.'

Bond laughed one of his short dry laughs. Once, men had gone white at the very sound.

'Be warm enough, soon, eh? I trust you're bound for Vesuvius?'

The milkman looked at him.

'I got Mafeking Crescent to do, and a bulk yoghurt up the telephone exchange,' he said, 'then I'm off home for *Pebble Mill.*'

'A likely story!' cried Bond. 'What's under that moustache, you Chinese bastard?'

007 made a lightning grab at the milkman's upper lip, misjudged the distance, and caught his forefinger in his opponent's mouth. The milkman closed his teeth on Bond's frail knuckle, and the agent fell back into the road. As he lay there, a bus-driver walked up, stood on him absently, and said to the milkman.

'These bleeding lights have gone green twice, sunshine.'

'Don't blame me,' said the milkman, 'this old bugger stuck his hand in my gob.'

The bus-driver glanced down.

'It's this ten pounds Christmas bonus they're getting,' he said. 'It's driving 'em all barmy. They've been smoking on the downstairs deck all morning.' He bent down, and hauled Bond upright. 'Come on, uncle, I'll see you across to the Whelk & Banjo.'

He took Bond into the public bar, and sat him on a stool, and went out again.

Bond took five pills. His hand was shaking, his heart was

pounding, there was a tic in his right eye, and his bronchitis was coming back. He ought to get on, it was four clear days to Naples, given that he refused to drive at night and wanted to pop into the clinic at Vitry-le-François for his monthly checkup.

But, then again, was it worth it? The KGB might hit him, the CIA might shout at him if he couldn't keep up, his surgical skis were as yet untested, and as for swimming the Bay of Naples, he had noticed in himself of late an unsettling tendency to sink. Added to all of which, his SMERSH counterpart was a big Balinese stripper fifty years his junior, and he doubted that his current sexual techniques would persuade her to defect, given that he preferred doing it in his herringbone overcoat these days, apart from the fact that he had last performed a mere eight months before and seriously doubted whether his forces were yet in a position to be remustered.

It wasn't a bad pub, all in all, thought Bond. He could write out a report from here, elaborating a bit. After all, what could they expect for fifty quid a week after stoppages?

The barman looked up at Bond's cough.

'What'll it be?' he said.

'I'll have a small Wincarnis,' said Bond. He took off his balaclava. 'Shaken, not stirred.'

29

Bottle Party

Boozers are being offered the bender of a lifetime: an alcoholiday in the sun. The special attraction is twelve hours' drinking a day, FREE! Tourists will pay £45 for the trip to the island of Majorca, and for their money they will get unlimited supplies of liquor at a three-star hotel. Tours manager Colin Woolf said: "Our clients will be able to drink until they fall down."

Daily Mirror

Hotel Borrachera
Playa de Palma
Majorca

38th July 1977

Dear Auntie Thing, Alice, tall woman, big yellow teeth, Well, here we are at the, oops, there's a blotty, hallo Blotty! Who's a pretty Blotty then? at the, you know, and we are all having a wonderful O God Almighty these bloody Spanish pens! THESE BLOODY SPANISH PENS! THESE STINKING BLOODY LONG–HAIRED GREASY SPANISH WOP CHEAP LOUSY ROTTEN

Expen the scusil. Thrown pen over balcony, whee goes pen, hope it sticks in Spanish head, ha–ha, serve them right throwing Norman out of El Wizzo Niteclub just because Norman sick on bongo, no business having bongo where people can be sick on it anyhow, how they expect Norman do Knees Up Mother Thing with six bottles of vino sloshing about in him?

Norman lucky didn't get run over, all mad drivers, also hate dogs, don't realise thing running out of El Wizzo on all fours is man doing brilliant impression of airedale, Norman now got tyre marks all over his nice El Wizzo tablecloth.

And what police doing banging on hotel door in small hours, anyone think it crime to borrow tablecloth, no business grabbing Norman either, man got perfect right to be on top of own wardrobe, paid for room didn't he? Only reasonable Norman lash out with Genuine Old Master showing Majorca at sunset. Man was desperate. As I informed magistrate, 'We did not splash three quid on priceless antique work of art just to have rotten fascist pig stick greasy head through it.'

Norman back now, got lice. Also had to share cell overnight with violent criminal, quantity surveyor from Wimbledon staying at posh place in Palma on fourteen-day gin excursion, went mad when barman tried to close bar, bit barman's ear off. Disgusting putting my Norman in with him, Norman never ate anyone in his life.

Glad I brought up food.

Oh God.

Here I am, Auntie, back again! Where was I, oh yes, glad I mentioned food, food quite good, really, except too much paiella, trouble with paiella is you get shrimps in hair when face falls in it after third bottle, steak days are best except when they overcook it and you bruise your cheek.

Went to see fullbight last Monday where is my cigarette and sat in the sun with these gourds Norman bought where you have to squirt the wine into I KNOW I PUT MY BLOODY CIGARETTE DOWN SOMEWHERE where you have to squirt the wine into your mouth, only after the first couple of gourds Norman squirted it into ear of woman sitting next to him, woman scream blue murders, Norman leap up, woman's husband leap up, sock Norman in his O JESUS AUNTIE PILLOW IS ON FIRE PILLOW IS BURNING, AUNTIE, AUNTIE, I MEAN NORMAN, NORMAN, PILLOW IS ON FIRE NORMAN.

O GOD AUNTIE NORMAN IS ASLEEP ON LOO WITH SOMBRERO ON MUST CLOSE NOW BACK LATER.

Back now, Auntie, it nearly dark, whole place smelling of foam. Not my fault, threw burning pillow off balcony, woman on balcony below leaning out drying hair in breeze, pillow land on head, hair flare up like chip-pan, woman shriek, people upstairs smell burning, call fire-brigade, fire-brigade come, no hydrant so attach pump to swimming pool supply, drain swimming-pool dry and find two English couples lying on bottom surrounded by bottles, police doctor say they dead two days. Funny thing, Norman wondered why conger line shorter than usual at El Wizzo last two nights.

Meanwhile man downstairs put wife's head out with fire-extinguisher, woman now not only burned bald but face all wrinkled up from chemicals and suntan fallen off, woman look like old golf ball. Husband ran upstairs, kicked in door, punched Norman in face, Norman fell off loo, now asleep in bath, so everything a bit calmer now.

Poor Norman, got black eye now to go with cauliflower ear received at bullfight after husband of woman with wine in ear sock Norman in his. Terrible blow, after that Norman see four bullfighters sticking four swords into four bulls every time he look.

Everybody know only two bulls and two bullfighters, clear as nose on thing. Two noses.

Anyway, Auntie, after bullfight met very nice English couple lying underneath charabanc, grocer from Birkenhead and lovely wife Arthur. All went out for dinner together, and Arthur danced in soup.

Arranged to meet on beach next day, and great fun burying Norman, falling down in sea, throwing ice cream at boring

Swede families, etcetera, until it was time for lunch. Invited couple back to our hotel for five or six bottles. Only when half-way through second course and Arthur asleep on butter dish that Birkenhead grocer suddenly start counting.

'What is it?' I ask him.

'What is two and one?' he reply.

We think for a bit.

'Three,' I say finally.

'Thought so,' he comment. 'We never dug up Norman.'

Rush back to beach, dragging Arthur by foot, Arthur's arms flailing about knocking things off tables as we cross diningroom, bloody lucky most diners asleep under tables, but one or two Germans, French, etcetera start kicking up fuss when chicken legs start falling in laps, screaming, shouting, terrible thing about foreigners, can't hold their drink.

O GOD AUNTIE I AM SOBERING UP. IF NORMAN COMES ROUND AND FINDS ME HE WILL GO SPARE, HOLIDAY COSTING HIM FORTUNE HE SAYS, MUST DRINK TWELVE BOTTLES A DAY JUST TO BREAK EVEN, WHERE TELEPHONE, WHERE ROOM SERVICE?

Hallo Mummie, Auntie, fat old cow, fancy giving us a wooden toast rack for a wedding present NO I DON'T BLEEDING FORGET EVEN IF IT IS TWELVE YEARS YOU FLY-BLOWN OLD RATBAG, feel a lot better now, nice bog bittle inside me, good idea having spiders walking all over the wallpaper, keep the flies off, especially green spiders, hallo green spiders wherever you are, I hope your troubles are few, all my good wishes go with you tonight, I was a spider, too, hee-hee-hee-hee-hee, O TOOTH ALMIGHTY I HAVE BROKEN A GOD ON THE BEDSIDE TABLE

hallo norman

Norman did not want me to wake him up Auntie he has hit me with the bidet HOW DID YOU GET THE BIDET OFF THE WALL AUNTIE, NORMAN, BELOVED, HOW DID YOU MANAGE TO why are my slippers floating past?

I have to close now Auntie, the manager has ordered a car to take us to the airport YES I AM REFERRING TO YOU YOU SWARTHY DAGO PIG I WOULDN'T STAY ANOTHER MINUTE IN YOUR BUG-RIDDEN RAT-HOLE FOR ALL THE TEA IN IN IN I DON'T KNOW WHERE SO STICK THAT UP YOUR CASTANET AND FLAP IT HAR HAR HAR.

You know what it is, Auntie, don't you, you know what it is all right, you know what it is with these bloody people, they're just a load of filthy anti-British bigots, that's what it is!

Hoping this finds you as it as it as it thing,

Your loving niece,

er,

30

The Unacknowledged Legislators of the World

The Poetry Society is falling apart. Rows about personalities, about money, about vanishing booze, fights over control and future plans, mass accusations and resignations have all played their part in what one of the poets has described as the war between poetry and bureaucracy: 'I can't remember when we last talked about poetry at a council meeting' he told the Guardian. *But wasn't it always like that?*

The meeting convened at 2.30 pm.

Mr William Wordsworth immediately rose to say, in his own defence, that there was a tree, of many, one, a single field which he had looked upon, both of them spoke of something that was gone; the pansy at his feet did the same tale repeat: whither was fled the visionary gleam? Where was it now, the glory and the dream?

Mr Andrew Marvell said that that was all very well, but it did not justify £28.40 return rail fare to Keswick, plus £14.26 overnight stay at the Come On Inne and £19.70 for a steak dinner for two, plus three bottles of Bulgarian Riesling. There were plenty of trees and fields within walking distance of the Society's premises perfectly capable of raising questions about the disappearance of visionary gleams and similar cod's wallop. Also, he would like to know why the steak dinner was for two people, and did it have anything to do with the pansy at Mr Wordsworth's feet?

Mr Wordsworth replied that he had found love in huts

where poor men lie, his daily teachers had been woods and rills, the silence that was in the starry sky, the sleep that was among the lonely hills, and you could not get that kind of thing in Camden Town. As to the steak dinner, he did not see what business it was of anybody else's who had joined him for it.

Mr Marvell said that had they but world enough and time, this coyness, Wordsworth, were no crime, but some of them weren't bloody paperback millionaires and couldn't muck about all day nattering, also this was taxpayers' money and not intended for filling Wordsworth's poofter shepherd oppos with foreign booze. His, Marvell's, mistresses never required more than a bottle of Mackeson's beforehand and a Vesta curry afterwards, never mind a night at the Come On Inne.

Mr Wordsworth said that if he must know, the gentleman referred to was Samuel Taylor Coleridge, exemplar of an imagination, which, in truth, was but another name for absolute power, and clearest insight, amplitude of mind, and Reason in her most exalted mood.

Mr Marvell asked Mr Wordsworth to pull this one, it had bells on. No offence to the Hon Member S.T. Coleridge, but he had recently seen him with an arm round a Chief Petty Officer outside a mission near Albert Dock.

Mr Coleridge replied that it was an ancient mariner and he had stopped one of three. If the other two were here today, he continued, they would corroborate his story. The sailor had an idea for a poem and was looking for someone to go halves with him. Anyway, he had a long grey beard and a glittering eye and was probably old enough to be his, Coleridge's, mother. Father.

Mr John Milton rose to enquire about the sailor's idea: did it have anything to do with Man's first disobedience, and the fruit of that forbidden tree whose mortal taste brought death into the world, and all our woe?

Mr Coleridge said no, he thought it was about a gull or something, why did Mr Milton want to know?

Mr Milton replied that the had paid good money for the idea about Man's first disobedience etc. and was buggered if he was going to see it come out in some tatty down-market form, such as rhyming bloody quatrains, before he had had a go at it. He was envisaging something in about twelve books, it could take weeks.

Mr Alexander Pope asked the Council if they intended subsidising Mr Milton's living expenses while he was knocking out twelve books on fruit. No slur intended, he went on, but he had always considered Mr Milton a bookful blockhead, ignorantly read, with loads of learned lumber in his head. Such laboured nothings, in so strange a style, amazed the unlearned, and made the learned smile. Pardon him, he said, but he spoke as he found.

Mr Milton said Mr Pope was a complicated monster, head and tail, scorpion and asp, and Amphisbaena dire, Cerastes horned, Hydrus and Ellops drear.

Mr Thomas Gray rose to say that this was all very well, but it wasn't getting the cracked pan in the Members' Gents repaired, which was why, so he understood it, the meeting had been convened in the first place. Only yesterday, he said, the caretaker had forbade the wade through water to the throne, and shut the gates of mercy on mankind.

Mr John Greenleaf Whittier enquired as to whether the crack was so wide, so deep, that no man living might this fissure weld?

Mr Milton replied that is was a gulf profound as that Serbonian bog betwixt Damiata and Mount Casius old, where armies whole have sunk.

Mr Pope said my God was he really going to go on like this for twelve bleeding books at public expense? Fixed like a plant on his peculiar spot, to draw nutrition, propagate, and rot?

Mr John Keats said that, as convenor of the Plumbing Sub-Committee, he was looking into the whole question of the refurbishment of the toilet facilities. It would not stop at a new pan and lilac seat; what he had in mind was a bower quiet for them, full of sweet dreams, and health, and quiet breathing.

Mr Pope asked Mr Shelley who his friend was.

Mr Shelley replied that he never was attached to that great sect whose doctrine was that each one should select out of the crowd a mistress or a friend, and all the rest, though fair and wise, commend to cold oblivion.

Mr Pope enquired whether Mr Shelley had met Mr Milton. It was his opinion that if they ever put their heads together, they would be able to come up with thirty-eight books on anything, Still, cold oblivion wasn't a bad phrase to describe the Members' Gents, if that was what he was talking about; better than a quiet bower full of people breathing, mind, though he couldn't, of course, answer for Mr Coleridge.

Mr William Shakespeare enquired of Mr Keats why they did pine within and suffer dearth, painting their outward walls so costly gay? Why so large cost, having so short a lease, did they upon their fading mansion spend?

Mr Keats replied that they required an unimaginable lodge for solitary thinkings; such as dodge conception to the very bourne of heaven, then leave the naked brain.

Mr Shakespeare said that if he understood correctly what Mr Keats had in mind, were the walls of the new khazi not going to end up covered in verse jottings, and would this not be an irritation to those wishing to lock themselves in cubicles the better to read the small print on their contracts so as not to end up with three bloody tragedies running simultaneously on Broadway and not even a percentage of the gross after producer's profits?

Mr Keats said he couldn't help it, the stuff just poured out of him. He informed them that he had been taught in Paradise to ease his breast of melodies.

Sir Edmund Spenser reminded them that at the last meeting, he had sought an undertaking that the new lavatory would be painted in goodly colours gloriously arrayed, but had as yet received no word from the committee as to what these colours might be. Three months had now passed.

Replying, Mr Shelley said he rather fancied azure, black, and streaked with gold, fairer than any wakened eyes behold.

Mr Marvell said what about orange bright, like golden lamps in a green night?'

Or, interjected Mr Shakespeare, what about having the majestical roof fretted with golden fire? It might cost a bob or two, he added, but it would not half impress publishers.

Mr Gerard Manley Hopkins said that he personally had always rather gone for dappled thing.

Green, said Mr Walt Whitman, green, green, green, green, green.

The committee looked at him.

Mr Milton expressed the opinion, after a short silence, that they were not getting anywhere. Chaos umpire sat, he continued, and by decision more embroiled the fray by which he reigned.

Mr Pope asked God to help him.

Mr Wordsworth said that as he had opened the proceedings, it was only fitting, not to say nicely constructed, that he should sum up. He then invited the committee to remember that dust as they were, the immortal spirit grew, like harmony in music; there was a dark inscrutable workmanship that reconciled discordant elements, made them cling together in one Society.

Mr Pope said ho ho ho.

The meeting rose at 4.26 pm.

31

The Hounds Of Spring Are On Winter's Traces, So That's Thirty-Eight-Pounds-Forty, Plus Making Good, Say, Fifty Quid

This is the week, according to my much-thumbed copy of *Milly-Molly-Mandy Slips A Disc*, when winter officially knocks off for a few days, the swallows return from Africa to foul the greenhouse roof, and you and I be a-diggin' and a-stretchin' and a-sweatin' as we work away with that most indispensable of gardening tools, the wallet.

And, as no newspaper or magazine is currently worth its salt without a few inches of pithy advice to the dehibernating gardener, it has fallen to my lot to deliver this year's handy hints. And if you think a sentence containing both salt and lot has been cobbled together as a subtle augury of the doom lying just beyond the french windows, then you might as well stop reading immediately: anyone who has time to work out textual cruces of that convoluted order clearly has nothing more effortful to bother about than a window box with a plastic begonia cemented to it. This piece is for committed gardeners only; although those who have not yet been committed may, of course, read it while waiting for the ambulance.

FENCES

This is the time of year to get together with your neighbour over the question of repairs to fences, trellises, and so on, that have deteriorated or even collapsed during the winter. I have always found that the best implement for dealing with this problem is a small hammer. If you have a large neighbour, then take a large hammer.

BLACKWOOD

Similar to the above, and particularly satisfying for bridge-players. You creosote your fencing somewhat enthusiastically, with the result that your neighbour's herbaceous border drops dead. He then digs a large trench on his side, until light shows between the soil and your new fencing. This is known as the Small Spade Opening. The conventional reply is Two Clubs.

CORM, BULB, TUBER AND RHIZOME

Not, of course, the long-established firm of country solicitors they might appear to the uninitiated, but the business end of those perennial plants which we gardeners carefully took up at the first sign of winter. At the first sign of spring, take them carefully out of their boxes and throw them away.

Exactly why all perennial roots die during the winter is an issue on which botanical opinion has long been divided: many experts argue that those stored in garages have an adverse reaction to being run over, and that this, coupled with the frost coming through the window the sack fell off in October and that nobody's wife got around to putting back up, explains why so many bulbs go flat and black during the weeks immediately prior to replanting.

Many other things, however, can carry off the apparently healthy corm, e.g. dogs, children, dailies with empty tubs at home, but since the plants will be dead anyway, these do not call for the hammer treatment.

THINGS LIKE GERANIUMS

Now is the time to go and look at the things like geraniums which you left in the ground all winter, knowing that if you lifted them, potted them, and stored them the way the books recommend, they would all die of mould. Left in the ground, they die anyway but at least you don't break your nails. If they haven't died in the ground, they are not geraniums but merely things and your best bet is to burn them off with a blow-lamp (see below under BLOW-LAMP) because otherwise they will take over the entire garden by March 23.

BLOW-LAMP

Now is the time to take down your blow-lamp and run. Because of an extremely complicated chemical process it would take far too long to elaborate upon, much gets up blow-lamp spouts between Michaelmas and yesterday morning. When you attempt to prime and light the blow-lamp, it ignites your suit. The way to avoid this happening is called £3.95.

MOTOR MOWER

The motor mower is exactly similar to the blow-lamp in principle, but rather more sophisticated, which means that after it ignites your suit, it takes your fingers off at the knuckle as well. The best thing to do is call in an expert, but make sure you phone before April 3, 1948, as they get pretty booked up at this time of year. You can always use a HAND MOWER if you want to lose the entire hand. This comes about through trying to remove last year's long grass which has become wound round the axle and, by an extremely complicated chemical process it would take far too long to elaborate upon, turned to iron. Again, there is a traditional country remedy for both these problems and your bank manager would be pleased to advise you.

LAWNS

Now you have your new lawn-mower, you will want to get something to cut, since all lawns are annual. A few tufts here and there may have survived the winter, but upon closer inspection these will turn out to be clumps of clover, sawgrass, couch-grass, and the cat. What your lawn needs now is feeding and planting. Many people ask me how I achieve a lawn like a billiard-table, i.e. no grass anywhere and full of holes, and I usually recommend any one of a dozen products now on the market in which various chemicals have been carefully blended to ensure that you will be back next year to try again. If you read the labels on these products, you will see that they may not be used either after it has rained or before it is due to rain, thus protecting the manufacturers from complaints lodged by anyone other than an astrologer with his eye in. Sprinkle these on the grass, watch them blow onto the roses, dig up and burn the roses, wait two days for the grass to be eaten away, dig over, pave, and sell the mower back. You can, of course, avoid this costly process by using lawn sand, a preparation used by experts wishing to turn lawn into sand, and there is much to be said for having a nice stretch of beach between your fences: put up an umbrella, a couple of deckchairs, and an electric fire on a long lead, and you could be in Baffin Land.

MANURE

Now is the time of year when you will want to think about top-dressing your rose-beds, and why not? There's no harm in thinking. Many people, it seems to me, worry far too much about finding true horse manure, when the commercial preparations available are just as good, bearing in mind that by the time you get them off the shovel, the roses have already begun to succumb to rust, leaf-mould, white-spot, black-spot, and greenfly. There is little point, surely, in chasing up and down the country with a spade and bucket merely in order to give a few dead twigs a nice send-off.

SEEDS

Children, I find, are always amazed that everything in the garden was once a little seed; particularly so when the packet of Sweet William they have nurtured so painstakingly is soon burgeoning as an assortment of diseased hollyhocks, misshapen sunflowers, chickweed, and an evil-smelling ground-cover that spreads like lava and is almost certainly carnivorous.

In the garden, seeds fall into two categories (a) the cracks in the path, and (b) where starlings have breakfast. To avoid wastage, therefore, grow all seeds in a greenhouse where, if it is properly heated, they will die before they can do any damage.

WATER

No garden can possibly flourish without adequate supplies of water. Now is the time of year to cut off the split ends of hoses so that they fit snugly onto the tap, or would if the jubilee clip hadn't rusted solid during the winter with the drip that was coming out of the tap before the pipe burst during the cold snap. Having replaced the upstand pipe, tap, and jubilee clip, bandage the fingers and secure the neatly cut hose; which, as a result of having been neatly cut, will now be some nine inches too short to reach the one bed which requires permanent watering. Never mind, any nurseryman or ironmonger's will be able to supply you with an extra length of hose and a connecting-link with which you can easily fail to connect the new bit with the old, since the old is too thick to go into the end of the connecting-link. The best course is to buy an entirely new hose of the required length; there is no other method of finding out that the tap you have just soldered onto the upstand pipe (since you had no means to hand of threading the pipe to take a nut) is itself .05 of a millimetre wider than the hose.

While you're at the nursery/ironmonger's, be sure to buy a sprinkler: there are two main varieties, the one that fails to spin round, and the one that fails to sweep from left to right and back again. Personally, I prefer the latter: at least you get half the garden sodden and know which side the shrubs are going to rot. The other variety sets up little oases at random, and it is all too easy, when strolling across a recently watered stretch, to find oneself sinking up to the shin in a tiny local quicksand.

GARDENING ADVICE ARTICLES

Now is the time of year to stop writing gardening advice articles and move into a tower block.

Appendix

The Bulletins of Idi Amin

32

All O' De People, All De Time

'General Amin is to sell off the two thousand motor
cars left behind by exiled Ugandan Asians.'

Daily Telegraph

Good morning, I see you is lookin' at de famous
Humber Super Snipe 1959 what only done 2,000
miles, all that on gravel drive by dis ole lady what is
using it fo' going down to de gate to git de milk, a bargain
at fifteen hunnerd poun', also you helpin' de economy no
end. What you lookin' at there, boy?

It lookin' like de treacherous rust to me.

Yeah, well you is an ignorant bugger, you go on like dat
you is li'ble to wine up wid a spanner in de head, de price
jus' went up to eighteen hunnerd an' fifty. What you got to
say to that, boy?

*Dis brown coachwork is damn elegant. What de fuel consummertion
like?*

Gittin' aroun' two hunnerd mile per gallon, cheapest fuel.
Dis car designed to run on anything. Conk out in de middle
of nowhere, jus' piss in de tank, you is good for another fifty
mile. Also note de fine upholstery.

*Hum. It all depending whether you a fan of de plastic. Pussonally,
I find it stick to de bum, but . . .*

Look, it my normal opinion de customer is always right,
but that don't mean I ain't gonna git a coupla colonels down
here to walk about on your face if you give me any more of

this kinda lip. You is looking at genuine pigskin there, boy. It bin treated to look like plastic on account of dis car bin built for gennelmen who ain't in the habit of bein' flash and goin' on about de three-piece suite. Dis also account for de lack of windows, what gets specially knocked out at de factory. Look at cheap cars, fust thing you notice is they all got windows.

Ain't no carpet on de floors.

Yeah, well you prob'ly noticing where there ain't no dining table neither, with lace cloff and wine bucket. This is on account of you ain't lookin' at a whorehouse parlour, son; it got a wheel on each corner, and we calls it a car. Take no notice of de price-tag, we knockin' dis one out at two grand, special offer, including free dog.

Can I have a run roun' de block?

Sure you can, it a free country, boy, you run where you likes, I ain't promisin' de car gonna be here when you gits back, this here automobile is a hot bargain at twennyfive hunnerd, no cheques.

Hum. What kind of guarantee you givin'?

Normal guarantee. Anything you find you don't like about dis top-class car, jus' give us a ring and we'll come roun' and kick your teef in. Where de money?

Hold on here, I don't have to buy it.

True, son, true. Don't have to spend de nex' ten years gittin' about on crutches, neither. Remember, you is doin' dis for de good of your country.

You sure about that?

Lissen, boy, would I lie to you?

33

A Word F'om De Sponsor

You prob'ly seen de well-known David Frost on *De Amin Programme* de other night, just show you de strides Uganda makin' under de new management, never got no David Frost comin' out here for *De Milton Obote Show*.

Pussonally, I got a lot of time for D. Frost, also for anybody what gittin' to de top, irrespectable of de talent an' de qualifications, no use havin' de four O-levels includin' Eng. Lit. if you ain't got de drive to go wid it, all very well bein' able to explain in your own words wot Macduff sayin' to Banquo in Act V, also how many times anyone usin' a oxymoron, but it ain't much help when de Opposition want to know wot you bin doin' wid de Oxfam money. Only thing you need then is a big stick wid a nail in de end, an' bugger de plot of de well-known *Sense an' Prejudice*, dat James Austin spendin' too much time hangin' about wid ole women to know wot life all about.

Anyhow, after de consid'able success of my tee vee show, I bin plannin' de summer schedules, an' I reckon we got a pretty good season lined up. Kickin' off mose evenin's wid *It A Knockout*, where we got two teams of Asians competing for de famous one-way economy ticket, got to shin up a greasy pole wid their families, winner gittin' de ticket an' a chance to go on de Treasure Trail for de val'able bus-ride to Kampala Airport. Dat shapin' up as a chart-topper, look like beatin' public executionin' in de ratings. Close second we got *Dis Your Life*, where people comin' on an' sayin' how they bin at school wid me and I a fust-rate board monitor and a natural leader, also all my own teef, and then we got de *News* wot gonna be all about de boomin' economy and de footer results and how Nyerere keepin' pigs in de bath. Also runnin' *Git Out*, dat de programme for de foreign residents, explainin' in their own language about where to leave de stamp colleckertions an' de gole fillins etcetera and where to stand for de next bus. Big one for Sat'day nights is *Sale Of De Century*, got to shift these damn cars somehow, got de rust showin' now, an' de upperholstery full o' rats, followed by *De Source Of De Nile* where you get me tracin' de history of Africa in song, doin' such famous nummers as *Swanee, Sonny Boy*, an' de ever-pop'lar *Shine On Harvest Moon* immortalised by T.S. Elliot and his Quartet.

Also got an entire new line in de Late Night chat show. Amazin' how people in England an' America bin puttin' up wid de crap all these years, nothin' goin' on but three people gettin' asked questions under de spotlight, an' if they don't feel like answerin' they goin' 'Har, har, har!' or similar an' Morris Parkinson sayin' 'Okay, now we gittin' a song from Lord Wigg's latest LP', an' that way people slidin' out from de awkward questions all de time. Ain't gonna be dat way in Uganda. People comin' on my Late Night show, I gonna say 'Right, Mbibi, what happenin' to de Annual Outin' Fund?' and if Mbibi start goin' 'Har, har, har!' he gonna git a kick in de mouf, jus' for openers. If dat ain't workin', he gonna be hangin' by his thumbs for de rest of de programme, an' if dat ain't de best way to git de rest of de guests shapin' up, I don't know what is.

De worl still got a hell of a lot to learn about tee vee, if you asks me.

34

De Whitehall Snub

It happenin' again dis week, world. Gittin' another snub on top o' de infamous occasion o' de Gowon visit, dis time it de matter o' Sir Alec Douglas-Home's birfday party at Number Ten. You no doubt bin readin' where Edward Heath layin' on de top-class binge on account o' de Foreign Seckertery reachin' seventy an' still in one piece. Heath openin' up de back room, I unnerstand, also gittin' in de draught Worthington an' layin' on them sticks wid bits o' pineapple an' Cracker Barrel on 'em, not to mention har' boil eggs where they minces de yolks up wid onions prior to stuffin' 'em back in de whites, no expense spared. Also openin' a nummer o' tins wid anchovies in, altho' it beatin' me why people goin' for marinated worms.

Whole lotta nob guests turnin' up, also; lotta peers an' women where you look down de front of de little Paris number, you can see de knees. No doubt he gonna have de Andre Previn Banjo Band an' his wife Mia Sparrow, de well-known warden of All Souls, plus other famous stars o' de dipperlomatic circuit, all gonna be doin' de ole knees-up an' puttin' de Boofs Dry Gin away wid both hands until four in de mornin', Sir Anthony Barber bangin' on de wall an' shoutin' 'Stop dat bleedin' row, some people tryin' to git a bit o' sleep!'

Only thing they ain't got is me. Bin sittin' by de door, jus' like last week, waitin' for one o' dem cards wid Winnie de

Pooh on an' Piggerlet where you open it an' it say *We're havin'*
a party an' we'd like you to come please, lotta pitchers o' balloons
an' funny hats an' stuff an' all de animals clearly havin' a damn
fine time. Nothin' comin', though.

I wun't mind, only I already bought de present. It a typical
piece o' de native folk art wot bin made up special by de
local craftsmen, a combined paperweight an' table-lamp,
lookin' jolly good on de ole Whitehall desk. Also, it a singularly
appropriate present fo' a Foreign Seckertary, on account of it
bin made out o' my last one.

The truth is, Sir Alec too damn busy wid worl' affairs to
git de guest-list right: pussonally, it gittin' on my wick where
he sendin' Sir Dennis Greenhill plus two other top Foreign
Office torpedoes down to Salisbury fo' de well-pubberlicised
secret talks wid Ian Smith. It beatin' me where de FO prepared
to go pissin' roun' de worl' on ten minutes notice every time
Rhodesia feel like havin' a secret talk wid someone flash.
Why de hell ain't no-one tryin' to woo *me* back? Why de hell
ain't I havin' a bit o' de secret talkin' prior to de unfreezin'
o' Uganda funds in London, includin' forty-eight-poun'-seven-
an'-six I got comin' from de British Home Stores Chrissermas
club, plus interest? Why de hell ain't no-one lookin' fo' a
honourable settlement wid *me*?

I prepared to be as honourable as de nex' man provided de
settlement comin' in used notes, pref'bly oncers, an' anyone
can come to my birfday party anytime they likes. I'd like a
cowboy suit, if you wonderin'.

35

A Star Gittin' Born

I damn glad to see where de Fleet Street hacks pickin' up de worl' scoop I givin' 'em considerin' de Uganda Fillum Industry! De fust thing you got to git when you cobblin' a fillum epic together is de pubberlicity, doan matter a pig's burp if you ain't got de script or de loot or de chrome Brownie wid de zoon lens provided de leadin' lady havin' it away wid de leadin' man an' Nyerere de Wonder Dog stickin' de paw in de wet concrete an' sim'lar.

Jus' fo' de record, Amin Studios doin' a bit o' de fishin' aroun' at present, ain't too certain what we gonna kick off wid: when you got de entire cinematic worl' at de feet, de only difficulty is choosin'. Pussonally, I goin' fo' de giant spectackerler, wid all de colossal an' stupendous trimmin's, I gonna be de noo Cecil Hur an' Dr. W.G. Griffiths rolled into one, wid a touch o' de famous Alfred Ballcock suspenders. De plot I got in mind fo' de fust production startin' off wid de American Civil War in which I takin' de part o' Rat de Butler, walkin' about wid de ten-gallon hat an' de smile playin' about de lips an' droppin' a nummer o' de minor characters wid de Colt .45. After that, we goin' into de famous chariot race bit, where I drivin' a worl'-famous team includin' such pop'lar favourites as Mickey de Mouse, Goofy, Yogi Duck an' de Andrews Sisters; soon as I winnin' de race, we switchin' to de Souf Pole where I waitin' wid de hot

221

Bovril for Captain Scott, played by de famous brudder-in-law Ngaga Mbibi.

Soon after that, it time fo' de comedy, I comin' on wid de baggy pants an' eatin' a shoe, which takin' de plot natcherly into de sequence where I suddenly fallin' down in de High Street at de top o' de cello-playin' career on account of I got de Unknown Wastin' Disease wot bafflin' wart specialists de worl' over, an' not only havin' to pack up sawin' de ole cat's innards but also takin' to de bed an' finally snuffin' it wid a lot o' de big-name stars weepin' all over de quilt an' de full treatment f'om de Entebbe Pubberlic Hygiene Department Tin Band whackin' out de *Dead March F'om Saul*.

'Course, it a well known fac' dat you can't have de lead star kickin' de jam jar after only four hours o' de film, so we got to do a bit o' de resurrectin', which is where we flashin' across to de super-colossal car'board castle wot goin' by de name o' Chez Frankenstein, an' befo' we knowin' it there's dis great big bolt o' lightnin' wot strikin' a item under a sheet, an' wow! Who dis but Idi Amin agen, only dis time he got de bolt in de neck an de stitchin' all over de worl'-famous bonce, lookin' like nuthin' so much as a Finance Minister wot bin helpin' de Uganda Special Branch wid de enquiries, an' soon as he off de operatin' table he start walkin' about an' knockin' down de doors etcetera, gonna scare de loyal subberjecks witless, also doin' 'em a lotta good, seein' de front door kicked down in de middle o' de night an' de famous Pres stompin' in wid de dander up!

Got a intermission at dis point, an' after we makin' a few bob on de lollies, wot we findin' but de Battle o' Britain, wid de young golden-haired Wing Commander Idi Amin Esq., DFC an' nine Bars, zoomin' about on de two tin feet an' knockin' de Messerschmitts out o' de sky like coconuts on Hammersmif Heath, prior to gittin' de wings knocked off of de Spit over France an' windin' up in de Jap POW camp due to de strong headwins, where I escapin' by diggin' a tunnel under de River Kwai an' swimmin' to nearby Broadway to change de entire course o' de fillum musical wid de revolutionary *Amin Git Yo' Gun*, LPs on sale in de foyer.

Dat de natcherl end, an' everyone goin' out hummin' an' dancin' an' weepin', an' sayin' (like de whole worl' sayin'): 'Wow! Dat Idi Amin gonna be de noo King Kong!'

The Golden Age
1980–1989

CLIVE JAMES

Introduction

Writers of humour often have a bag of tricks, and one day the tricks become recognisable. Eventually even S.J. Perelman could be caught in the act of copying ideas that he had been the first to have. But Alan Coren was so inventive that the new ideas – not just the dazzle on the surface, but the structures underneath – kept on coming, with the seeming ease which invites belittlement from the less blessed. The great Australian swimmer Dawn Fraser's achievements were often taken for granted by the local press, on the grounds that she was 'a natural athlete'. In the same way, Coren was naturally funny. Nevertheless even he had his peak period for minting new coin. He was never better than in the 1980s, when the first flush of youth had been tempered by wisdom and learning.

The learning showed up brilliantly in a piece like '£10.66 And All That', which can be taken as the pioneering instance in any medium of a modern humorist exploiting the probability that the yeomen of Olde England, while they waded through the mud, exhibited all the whining venality and warped entrepreneurial ambition that we so admire today. As we join the action, the estate agency William & Bastards is about to be 'dragged into the 11th Century'. While we read of how the agency strives to flog a 'property with relatively scum-free well', we can see how Coren was unmatched at the conceit of showing up the delusional sales vocabulary of Now by exporting it to the inappropriate context of Then. Almost every humorist has tried it but Coren could actually do it, at a level of ventriloquism which had been equalled, before him, only by Beachcomber.

Like Michael Frayn in his *Guardian* 'Miscellany' column at the turn of the 1960s, Coren always knew that the only way to keep up with Beachcomber's ghost was to cock an ear to the new, yet instantly tarnished, linguistic counterfeit of the present. This is the secret of Coren's extraordinary feat of mimicry in 'One Is One And All Alone', the story of what happened when our current queen accidentally found herself at a loose end for a whole day. She kept a diary, in which we find that she played I-Spy with Fusebox Poursuivant. ('One won.') At the end of the day (the kind of dud phrase that Coren always hijacked at the very moment of its ponderously sprightly arrival into the language) Her Majesty is in prison, and obviously grateful for the change of scene.

Nowadays, Google makes it easier to write a catalogue piece that sounds as if it has been researched in a library, but the list of phobias in 'No Bloody Fear' sounds like the inside job of someone who had done a lot of delving in his own head. With Coren it's always important to realise that his vast range of particular knowledge almost certainly included a deep insight into himself. He just never let on. Of all the great British comic writers – among whose number, we must surely see now, he stands high – he is the one whose flights of fancy tell you least about the agonies within. Probably, rather than being defensive, he was just too fascinated with the limitless extravagance of the follies in the outside world: to take them personally would have seemed, to him, disproportionate.

His consolation for a world whose cruelties mocked his mockery – Coren's Idi Amin was a talking doll that spoke from the puppeteer's sense of pity, not from his frivolity – was that the universal madness would always be there, if only because it had been there throughout history. Hence the enchanted insanity of 'Tax Brittanica', my personal candidate for the title of Coren Piece for the Time Capsule. The scene, once again, is ancient Britain, but this time very ancient. The Romans are here. A sniffling tax collector called Glutinus Sinus? Of course. But when I learned that the tax collector's assistant was called Miscellaneous Onus, I was helpless with admiration as well as laughter, because the name is so exact. *Miscellaneous onus* equals various jobs, get it? Or, as the skiving Briton in the piece would say, 'Narmean?' Coren was first with that, too: transcribing the tormented demotic with phonetic exactitude. Novelists got famous for doing the same. Coren just did it, from week to week, working so far within his abilities that he was the walking, laughing and dancing (he was a wickedly good Lindy Hop dancer) exemplar of a principle: the secret of success in the popular arts is to have power in reserve.

The worst a critic could say of him was that he didn't seem to be trying. There were critics who said the same of Gene Kelly. But although Coren never had to practise a knee-slide that would finish exactly on the mark that the cameraman's assistant had put down on the studio floor, he still had to do an awful lot of technical calculation in his head before he got his effects. He did it so quickly that he could go on radio programmes like *The News Quiz* and unreel impromptu lines which were so neatly compressed they sounded as if they had been written. They had been: written instantly, a nanosecond before he said them. Somebody with that kind of gift is always going to be underrated. Coren didn't care. He preferred to make the English language the hero. So generous a writer forms a conspiracy with the reader, as they both revel in the splendour of the tongue they speak. For as long as the spell lasts – and Coren could make it last for a thousand words at a time – the reader can almost persuade himself that he, too, knows how it's done. But it's a secret. Writers who convince you that you share their sense of humour are pulling a fast one. They are celestial con-men. Alan Coren was one of them, and one of the best.

36

Tax Britannica

Archaeologists have unearthed what they believe to be the first Roman tax collecting depot to be found in Britain, at Claydon Pike in the Upper Thames Valley. The depot was built around 70 AD, and probably remained in use until the Romans finally left Britain in 408

Observer

Glutinus Sinus, Tax Inspector 126 (Upper Thames Valley Collection), drew the parchment-piled in-tray towards him, removed the curling stack, carefully and neatly squared it off, pared a stylus with the small dagger issued for that exclusive purpose by Inland Revenue Stores (Silchester), straightened his little skirt, and nodded.

'Send him in,' he said.

Miscellaneous Onus, his clerk, scuttled sniffing to the fruitwood door, and opened it. An odour of goat and feet and orifice wafted horribly in; through the gap, Glutinus Sinus caught a brief collage of mud-caked beards and hovering flies and khaki teeth, heard, as always, the distinctive colonial undercurrent of scratching, spasmodically punctuated by the plop of targeting spittle. The inspector shuddered. He had been out here too long. They all had.

'Mr Cooper!' called Miscellaneous Onus, into the miasma.

A squat and patchily hirsute figure detached itself from a cackling group who had been engaged in a curious contest from which the clerk had been forced to avert his eyes, adjusted his mangy wolfskin, and loped into the tax inspector's office.

'Shut the door,' said Glutinus Sinus.

'The what?' said the Briton.

Glutinus Sinus set his jaw, and pointed.

'Oh,' said Mr Cooper, 'it's even got its own name, has it? I thought it was just a bit of wall that came open, bloody clever, you Romans, I will say that for you. Door,' he murmured, shutting it with somewhat melodramatic respect, 'door, door, door, well I never!'

Glutinus Sinus sighed.

'Don't butter me up, Mr Cooper,' he said.

'Me?' cried Cooper. '*Me?*'

'Please sit down.'

'I built a room, once, up my place,' said the Briton, dropping to his haunches, 'only we had to climb over the walls to get in and out.'

'Mr Cooper, about your tax-return for the current—'

'We had not cracked the secret of the door,' said Cooper. 'It was beyond our wossname. It must be wonderful, civilization.'

'Mr Cooper, you are a maker of casks and barrels?'

'Correct. Definitely.'

'And yet,' here Glutinus Sinus riffled through the pile of parchment, selected one, flourished it, 'you have entered a large deduction against last year's income for the purchase of new industrial plant, to wit millstones, four, nether and upper. Can you explain this?'

'I have branched out,' said Cooper. 'I do a bit of grinding on the side. Mind you, don't we all, ha-ha, catch my drift, all men of the world, narmean?'

'Branched out?' said the tax inspector, icily.

'Bit slack these days, coopering,' replied the Briton, 'due to introduction of the glass bottle and carboy. Do not get me wrong, I am not saying glass is not dead clever, probably miraculous even, it is what comes of having a god for everything, the Roman god of glass has come up with a real winner, I am not denying that for a minute. All I am saying is, it has knocked the bottom out of the cask business, having a container what does not leak on your foot when you are carrying it out over the bedroom wall of a morning. I have therefore diversified into flour.'

'Then you ought to be called Miller,' interrupted Miscellaneous Onus irritably. 'All this is cocking up the ledgers.'

'How about Cooper-Miller?' enquired the Briton. 'Due to following two professions? It's got a bit of tone, that, my old woman'd fancy being Mrs Cooper-Miller, she would be invited to open the Upper Thames Valley Jumble Fight, she would be asked to judge the Humorous Bum Contest, it could put us right at the top of the social tree.' He smiled oleaginously. 'We could be almost Roman. Uglier, mind.'

'So,' said Glutinus Sinus, 'you are engaged in the manufacture of flour for profit? Why, then, have you made no relevant return for—'

'Who said anything about profit?' replied Cooper. 'Cooper Flour plc is a registered charity, due to where it is distributed to the needy, gratis. It is a good word, *gratis*, we are all very pleased with it, what a spot-on language Latin is, got a word for everything.'

Glutinus Sinus put his fingertips together.

'True,' he murmured. '*Gratis*, however, does not translate as receiving chickens in return for flour.'

'Ah,' said Cooper. 'You heard about that, then?'

'Mr Fletcher entered them as outgoings,' said the tax inspector levelly.

'Yes,' said Mr Cooper bitterly, 'he would. You got to watch him, squire. The plain fact is, them chickens are definitely not income. We do not eat them. They are pets. You cannot count a household pet as income.'

'How many have you got?' enquired Miscellaneous Onus, licking his nib.

'I don't know,' replied Cooper, 'I can't count higher than XLVI. I have not had everyone's educational advantages, have I?'

'With all those chickens,' said the tax inspector, 'you must be getting hundreds of eggs a week. Surely you eat those?'

The Briton narrowed his already imperceptible brows.

'Eggs?' he repeated. 'What are eggs?'

Glutinus Sinus stared at him for a while. The Briton stared innocently back. Eventually, Glutinus Sinus snatched up his stylus, and drew an egg on the back of a tax-form.

'Oh,' said Cooper, nodding, 'chickens' doings.'

'No, no, no!' cried Miscellaneous Onus. 'They're delicious! You fry them!'

'Get off!' exclaimed the Briton. 'Pull this one. I've seen 'em coming out.'

'In that case,' snapped Miscellaneous Onus triumphantly, 'how is it that Mr The Other Cooper is buying them at eighteen denarii a dozen?'

'Search me,' replied the Briton. 'He is probably putting them on his roses.'

Miscellaneous Onus sprang from his stool, waving a document.

'This invoice carries your address!' he shrieked. 'How do you explain that?'

The Briton squinted at it.

'That's not me,' he said. 'You will notice it is signed Mickey Mus. Come to think of it, I've noticed our yard looks remarkably neat of a morning. Clearly this bloke is nipping in at night, nicking our chickens' doings, and flogging them on the side. What a liberty! Imagine anyone stooping low enough to steal droppings. Mind you, you'd have to, wouldn't you, ha-ha-ha, sorry, just my little joke, where would we be without a laugh now and then, that's what I always say.'

Glutinus Sinus grabbed the paper from his aide, and threw it in a wastebin.

'All right,' he cried, 'but how,' and here he plunged a trembling hand into the sheaf, 'do you explain *this*? It happens to be your list of deductible expenses for the year ending April 5, 408, in which you have not only put down the cost of enough protective clothing to dress an entire legion, but also some score of expensive items described as "professional gifts, disbursements, tips considerations, etcetera" which I cannot but—'

'What a marvellous word, *etcetera*,' murmured Mr Cooper, rolling his eyes and shaking his head, 'nearly as good as *gratis*, I do not know how you lot keep on coming up with 'em, no wonder your beneficent and gracious authority stretches from—'

'—take to be the most gross and transparent attempt to evade your dues, not only all this, I say, but also an enormous sum attributed to, where is it, here we are, "the entertainment of foreign buyers". Mr Cooper, do you really expect me to—'

'It is clear,' said the Briton, holding up one massive hairy hand, 'that you have never been up the sharp end when it comes to coopering and/or milling. On the one hand snagging your professional habiliments on splinters, nails, sharp reeds and I do not know what else, on the other coming home of an evening absolutely *covered* and looking like sunnink ritual cut out of a chalk bleeding hillside, you cannot wash self-raising out of a wolf pelt, sunshine, it turns to paste, try drying it by the fire and what you end up with is a flea–infested giant loaf.'

Glutinus Sinus's favourite stylus snapped between his fingers.

'Very well, but what is this entry: "VII formal III-piece gents' goatskin suits"?'

'Nor,' continued Mr Cooper, not pausing for breath, 'can you turn up with your casks at a smart brewer's premises with your backside hanging out. I am, after all, a director of the company. Similarly, going about the countryside upon my unpaid charitable works and doling out flour left, right and centre, I cannot look needier than the bleeding needy, can I?'

Glutinus Sinus licked dry lips, and glanced at Miscellaneous Onus.

'These professional gifts,' whispered the aide hoarsely, 'who exactly is receiving them?'

'You name it,' replied Cooper. 'It is dog eat dog in the barrel game. You got to grease palms, especially with foreign customers.'

'Aha!' cried Glutinus Sinus. 'At last we approach the nub, Mr Cooper, or would you prefer I called you Mr Mus? Just exactly who are these foreign customers of yours to whom you are so generous with bribes and entertainment?'

The Briton smiled.

'As a matter of fact,' he said, 'he is a Roman gentleman, one of my most esteemed business associates, a person of great probity and standing. I am sure you would be the first to appreciate that you cannot fob off such a man with a couple of bags of stone-ground wholemeal to stick under his toga and a ferret kebab up the takeaway.' Cooper picked a dead wasp from his beard, carefully. 'He is my accountant, Dubious Abacus. I understand he is a big gun. If you care to re-examine my files, I think you will discover that he has authorized my tax-returns personally. I do not know how he finds the time, what with constantly running back to Rome to do the Emperor's books.'

After a long silence, Glutinus Sinus said:

'We would appear to owe you a not inconsiderable refund, Mr Cooper-Miller.'

The Briton rose slowly from his haunches.

'I'll see the bloke on my way out,' he said.

After the door had closed, Glutinus Sinus stared at it for a long time.

'What year is it, Miscellaneous Onus?' he said.
'408, Glutinus Sinus.'
The tax inspector sighed.
'Get our suitcases down,' he said.

37

Blue Flics

Six English bobbies are off on a cycling tour of France.
They hope to meet the ordinary Frenchman in the street
and put across some idea of what life as an English
policeman is like.

Daily Express

Monday at 11.42 am, a time which will be corroborated by my colleague PC Garsmold although I did not, of course, consult with him prior to taking down these notes in writing, we disembarked with our regulation machines from the ferry *Sylvia Blagrove II* and proceeded in single file in an easterly direction along the Rue Maritime, in so doing passing several bollards.

After approx. six hundred yards, we come to a roundabout: pausing to ascertain it was safe to proceed, we had just pedalled off when this van came round it the wrong way, hurling PC Chatterjee from his machine, causing severe damage to his left-hand pannier with the result that a mutton vindaloo prepared special by his wife as a safeguard against trots etcetera brought on by, e.g. snails legs and so forth, got scattered all over the road, rice becoming all gritty and dogs jumping on the larger lumps.

The driver of the van then brought his vehicle to the halt position, and descended from it via the passenger door, this detail spotted by PC Wisley and took down by him at the time, 11.53.

The following conversation then ensued:

Driver: Gabble, gabble, gabble, etcetera . . .

PC Garsmold: Excuse me, sunshine, is this your vehicle?

Driver: Gabble, gabble, gabble, plus arms waving about.

PC Garsmold: Leave it out, you was on the wrong side of the road, we have got you bang to rights, also sitting in the passenger seat, definitely.

PC Garsmold: Do you reckon he might be intoxicated, PC Wisley?

PC Wisely: I think it is a line of enquiry worth pursuing, PC Rimmer, due to where he is a Frog and they are all piss-artists, if I may use the vernacular, get him to blow in the wossname.

PC Garsmold then extracted his breathalyser kit. The suspect then became agitated and, clearly refusing to blow in the bag as laid down in paragraph nine, subsection fourteen, seemed about to offer actual violence. We then employed reasonable force to restrain him, and while he was distracted by the action of picking up his teeth, PC Chatterjee stuck the tube in his mouth.

The test proved negative. We informed the suspect that he was a lucky bastard, and instructed him to mind how he went in future. As we pedalled off, PC Rimmer noticed that the steering-wheel was on the passenger side, and offered the opinion that the vehicle had probably been botched up after some major accident and would undoubtedly not pass its MOT. PC Chatterjee was all for going back and bunging chummy a 703/14b, but the rest of us reckoned he had probably learned his lesson, and anyway time was getting on.

It was now 12.27.

Proceeding through Boulogne, we became aware that everybody was on the wrong side of the road, also using hooters immoderately, but decided to take no further action due to reinforcements not being available.

Reached outskirts of Etaples at 2.07 pm, stopped at roadside to consume sandwich rations. We was on the last of the Marmite when a vehicle drew up, and an occupant dismounted, smiled at us in what might be described as a cordial manner, exposed himself and began widdling in the ditch. He was immediately apprehended by PCs Garsmold and Wisley, and charged with an act of gross indecency. He thereupon twisted himself free, adjusted his dress, and drew a revolver. Since we had not come tooled up, we were forced to lie face down on the verge while the flasher gabbled into a pocket transceiver.

At 2.09 (approx., due to watch-hand clasped behind neck), a vehicle with blue flashing light come up wailing, disembarking a number of uniformed men carrying sub-machine guns. Fortunately, one of these spoke English.

He immediately charged PCs Garsmold and Wisley with importuning.

I then produced my warrant card, and explained the confusion. This decision immediately regretted by our party, since our original suspect then grasped PC Garsmold and kissed him on both cheeks, instantly confirming our first suspicions. We did not take further action, however, due to where they was all armed to the teeth, but it was useful experience. In a country where the poofs go round mobhanded carrying automatic weapons, you have to watch your step.

Tuesday Spent the night at the Hotel les Deux Souris, and came downstairs at 8.00 am for cooked breakfast, just in time to spot landlord pouring large brandy for customer in blue vest.

Two blasts on whistle brought PCs Garsmold and Wisley

out of khazi on double to act as back-up while I charged landlord with Dispensing Alcoholic Beverages Contrary to the Stipulations of the Licensing (Hours) Act 1947.

The customer thereupon threatened me with a long cudgel he had clearly brought along for this purpose, and I had no other recourse than to truncheon him. As it fell to the ground, his cudgel split open to reveal several slices of salami and a thing with holes in which I originally took to be a house-breaking implement of some kind but which upon further forensic examination by PC Chatterjee turned out to be cheese.

The following conversation then ensued:

PC Wisely: I charge you with taking away a lavatory with the intention of permanently depriving the rightful owner. You are nicked, son!

Customer: Groan, gabble.

Me: To what are you referring, PC Wisley? It is my intention to nail him for assault with a deadly loaf.

PC Garsmold: PC Wisley is correct. When we was in the khazi just now, we noted that the pan had been nicked, due to where there was only a hole in the ground. It is clear to us that while chummy here was engaging the landlord in conversation over an illicit drink, his accomplice was out back half-inching the toilet. He is probably halfway to Paris by now, wherever that is.

At this point (8.06), the landlord's wife come in to see what the altercation concerned. She was able to reassure me that our friend in the blue vest was above board, also no licensing infringements, so it all passed off amicably enough, us chipping in for bottle of brandy (*see attached chitty*) for customer, plus small sum in compensation for beret. Upon being complimented on her grasp of English, landlord's wife explained she had sheltered escaping English prisoners, which very nearly upset the apple-cart again, due to where PC Chatterjee attempted to do her on a harbouring and abetting charge, since he had spotted someone in the room next door to his who bore a striking resemblance to a notice we'd had pinned up in our section house concerning a bloke wanted for the Lewisham payroll job. He can be a bit dim, PC Chatterjee, but we got to have one or two of them about, these days.

Pushed on towards Abbeville without further major incident, although PC Rimmer, when we were about halfway there down the N40, paused outside a small town and attempted to collar a bloke with a paintbrush for defacing a public sign. Turned out the place was actually *called* Berck.

Wednesday Further to our enquiries, and pursuing our investigations to the fullest extent, we have now formed the firm conclusion that this is a country populated entirely by the bent. At the same time, it is impossible to get a single charge, however reasonable, to stick.

At 9.47 this morning, proceeding down what was clearly High Road, Abbeville, in broad daylight, we come on a couple of wrong 'uns unloading a truck outside a butcher's, to wit, Gaston Dubois. We knew they was wrong right off, on account of they was both smoking during the unloading of fresh carcases, in direct contravention of the Health & Public Hygiene (1953) Act, but we did not know how wrong until PC Wisley drew his notebook and approached said offenders with a view to a sight of their Licence to Convey, which is a technicality you usually nick these buggers on due to invariably being out of date.

The following conversation then ensued:

PC Wisely (*sniffing*): Hang about, PC Rimmer, does that smell
        like normal decent tobacco to you?
PC Rimmer (*sniffing*): No, PC Wisley, that is definitely a
        substance. These men are smoking a substance.
        That is two cast-iron charges already, and you
        have not even got your pencil out yet!
PC Garsmold: Were we to find a half-brick in their apron,
        that would be . . .
PC Wisely, Rimmer & Garsmold: ONE HUNDRED AND
        EIGHTY!
PC Garsmold: I'll see if I can find a half-brick anywhere.

At this crucial juncture, however, an even more major crime
was detected. PC Chatterjee, who spent some time in the
Mounted Division until resigning upon the discovery that the
mucking-out was always down to him for some strange reason,
suddenly grasped my arm and informed me that the carcase
being carried into said Gaston Dubois was that of a horse! I
come over dizzy at the horror of this, but quickly recovered
due to years of training, and we launched ourselves upon the
miscreants firm-handed in the full assurance that there was a
Queen's Commendation in this, at the very least.

    As for coming out of it with three stripes up . . .

Thursday They finally let us out of Abbeville nick this morning,
but only after impounding our bicycles in lieu of surety. It is
clear to us that the Abbeville force is unquestionably on the
take, probably half a dozen fillet steaks per day per man from
Mr Bleeding Dubois, but it is not our intention to stay around
long enough to get an A10 investigation going. Sooner we
are out of this bloody country, the better.

    In accordance with this decision, and machines being in a

non–available situation as outlined hereinabove, we was away on our toes double-quick with a view to hitch–hiking back to Boulogne.

It was the first stroke of luck we'd had in four days. At 11.14 am, this big truck stops, swarthy occupant in dark glasses, on his way to Boulogne. We got in the back, and he was off like the clappers.

The following conversation then ensued:

PC Garsmold: What's in them crates, PC Wisley?

PC Wisely: *Tinned Fruit*, it says on the side. *Export to Mexico*. I'll have a shufti. Could be stolen blouses, anything.

PC Wisley then opened a crate.

PC Wisely: False alarm. Great long pointed tins with EXOCET on the side. God knows what that is. Probably the vegetable equivalent of horsemeat.

PC Rimmer: They'll eat anything, the Frogs.

Upon arrival at the Boulogne docks at 2.18 pm, we were at pains to thank said driver for his assistance and informed him he was the first straight Frenchman we had met. He replied that he was an Argentinian.

That explains it, we said.

38

Smiling Through

Computer scientists in California believe they have evidence that the Mona Lisa was originally wearing a necklace.

Dr John Asmus, who headed a team which investigated the picture using computer image analysis techniques, told yesterday's annual meeting of the American Association for the Advancement of Science that Leonardo da Vinci probably changed his mind about the portrait and painted over the necklace.

Independent

'Hallo!' shouted Leonardo da Vinci, into the cocoa tin. 'Is that Florence 2?'

He put the tin to his ear.

From somewhere deep inside came a sound not unlike a cockroach running through iron filings. He took his ear out of the tin again.

'Speak up!' he shouted.

The tin squawked, unintelligibly.

He pulled on the string. Beyond his attic dormer, it tautened above the umber roofscape, scattering sparrows. He was about to put the tin to his ear again, when the string went suddenly slack.

'Sod it,' said Leonardo.

He put the cocoa tin back on his desk, and ran out of his studio, slamming the door. Caught in the slipstream of his flying cloak, a preliminary cartoon for *The Battle of Anghiari* trembled on his easel, floated to the floor, and came to rest face up. The moted sunlight fell across two battered Medici grenadiers crouching in a muddy crater. '*If you knows of a better 'ole . . .*' the caption began; but, like so much else these days, it was unfinished, and would in all likelihood remain so.

On the landing, Leonardo sprang into the lift, plummeted, screamed, and was hurled off his feet as it stopped without warning between floors. He rang the emergency handbell, and was winched slowly down by a bloomered pupil.

'Up the spout,' muttered Leonardo.

'*Up the spout*, Master?' murmured the pupil.

'It is a technical phrase I have invented,' replied Leonardo da Vinci, straightening his plume, 'to describe lifts.'

'Is it like *on the blink*, Master?' enquired the pupil.

'No,' said Leonardo. '*On the blink* describes telephones.'

'Is Florence 1 on the blink again, then?'

'Yes. There is a fault on the line. It is my opinion the knot has come out of Florence 2.'

'It is nevertheless,' said the pupil, simpering warmly, 'a wonderful invention, and a boon to man!'

'Inventing the cocoa tin was the hard part,' said Leonardo. He sniffed, bitterly. 'You would think that once you'd come up with the cocoa tin, it would all be downhill after that. You would think the string would be a doddle. It's a bugger, science. Half the time, it makes no bloody sense at all.' He pushed into the new revolving door which led to his workshop, and the pupil pushed in behind him. After about ten minutes of banging and shrieking, the pupil came out in front.

'Up the blink, Master?' murmured the pupil, gloomily watching Leonardo's shredded cloak smouldering in the door's boiler. 'On the spout?'

'Down the tubes,' muttered Leonardo. He dusted himself off, and peered into the bustling workshop, on the far side of which a tiny buskinned man was throwing vegetables into a large glass cylinder. 'Hallo, what's that little twerp Giovanni up to now?'

The pupil examined his clipboard.

'Where are we?' he said. 'Tuesday, Tuesday, yes, Tuesday he is supposed to be on rotary-wing research. He is down here as developing the Leonardo Gnat.'

Cursing, Leonardo ran across and snatched an imminent cucumber from Giovanni's little hands; in the confusion, a chicken scrambled out of the glass cylinder and fled, clucking.

'That's never a helicopter!' cried Leonardo.

'Insofar as you would have a job getting to Pisa in it,' replied the pupil, 'that is true. However, Master, it works on the same principle. It is what we call a spin-off. If I may be permitted?'

Leonardo prodded the cylinder with his patent umbrella. The ferrule droped off.

'Two minutes,' he said. 'But God help you if it turns out to be another bloody toaster. They'll never send the fire brigade out four days in a row.'

Giovanni, who had meanwhile been turning a large key protruding from the base of the cylinder, now took a deep breath, and flicked a switch. Inside the cylinder, blades whirled, howling; a white lumpy mass spread across the ceiling. Leonardo lookcd slowly up, as the substance coalesced into soft stalactites; a blob fell into his beard, and he licked it off.

'Vichyssoise, is it?' he enquired, levelly.

'Leek and turnip, actually,' said Giovanni. He spooned a quantity from Leonardo's hat, and tasted it. 'Could do with a bit more garlic?'

Leonardo swung his umbrella. It turned, naturally enough, inside out, but the residual sturdiness was still enough to fell Giovanni where he stood. Slowly, his ear swelled, glowing.

'I want this one,' said Leonardo to the pupil-foreman, 'on the next train to Santa Maria della Grazie.'

'*The Last Supper*, Master?' cried the pupil-foreman, aghast. 'Are you sure he's up to it?'

'I'm a dab hand with apostles,' retorted Giovanni, struggling to his feet, 'also glassware. You could drink out of my goblets.'

'He will not be painting the wall,' said Leonardo, 'he will be plastering it prior to undercoat, as per ours of the 14th ultimo, plus removing all rubbish from site and making good.'

'Bloody hell!' cried Giovanni. 'All I forgot was the lid! I have not even mentioned the fact that the amazing new Vincimix comes with a range of attachments which chop, shred, slice, and whip the pips out of a quince before you can say Jack Robinson.'

At which point, all the windows blew in.

Slowly, Leonardo da Vinci walked through the settling dust, and looked out. A blackened face looked back at him. Neither spoke. Leonardo turned and walked back through the room.

'You'll have to go by horse,' he said to Giovanni.

'Do not be downcast, Master,' said the pupil-foreman. 'Nobody said trains were easy.'

Leonardo stared at the floor.

'Funny,' he said, 'the lid hops up and down all right on the kettle.'

The clock struck ten. Absently, Leonardo picked up the fallen cuckoo, walked out of the workshop, into the sunlit street, climbed on his bicycle, and began pedalling slowly towards Fiesole, scattering nuts and spokes. By the time he reached the house of Zanoki del Giocondo, he was carrying a wheel and a saddlebag, and sweating.

He tugged the bell-rope.

'I phoned,' he gasped, when she answered the door.

'The knot came out,' she replied.

'I thought so,' he said. He cleared his throat. 'Is he in?'

'He's out in his tank.'

'I thought he'd like that,' said Leonardo. 'I thought it might get him out of the house.' He walked into the hall. 'I hope he doesn't suspect anything, mind.'

'No. He thinks you're a faggot. Nobody else gives him presents.' A neighbour passed, and peered, and smiled. La Gioconda nodded, and closed the front door. 'How long is he likely to stay out?' she said. 'I don't know anything about tanks.'

'Days, possibly,' said Leonardo. 'We haven't cracked this business of the tracks. It tends to go round in circles until the engine seizes up. Even if he manages to get the lid open again, he won't have the faintest idea where he is.'

'But we ought to do a bit more of the painting, first?'

'You can't be too careful,' said Leonardo da Vinci. He propped his wheel against the dado, and opened his saddlebag, and took out his palette and his easel; but as he was following her through the house and out into the garden – not simply for the light but for the assuaging of neighbourly curiosity – he could not help noticing the way a sunbeam fell across her plump shoulder, and the way her hips rolled.

So they decided to do a bit more of the painting afterwards, instead.

And when they were in the garden, finally, he put the necklace around her neck, and fastened the clasp, and she cried aloud:

'Diamonds!'

'What else?' he said.

So she sat in her chair, with her hands folded and a broad smile on her tawny face, and Leonardo da Vinci's brushes flicked back and forth, and the neighbours peered from between the mullions, and were satisfied.

And then it began to rain.

Not seriously enough to drive them in; just a warm summer blob or two. But one such, unfortunately, fell on her necklace, and, after a few moments, she looked down, and stared; and then she said, carefully:

'The diamonds appear to be going grey.'

'Ah,' said Leonardo.

'Is that usual?'

Leonardo came out from behind his easel, and looked at them.

'It could be,' he said, 'With this new process.'

'I'm sorry?'

'It's a bit technical,' said Leonardo.

'Try me.'

'You start off with coal,' said Leonardo.

'I see.'

She stared at him for a long while after that, until Leonardo went back behind his easel. He picked up his brush.

He looked at her.

Her lip curled.

He put the brush down again.

'It isn't much of a smile,' said Leonardo da Vinci.

'It isn't much of a necklace,' said Mona Lisa.

39

The Gospel According to St Durham

. . . and Jesus went forth, and saw a great multitude, and was moved by compassion toward them, and he healed the sick with the blue mould that he had scraped off the five loaves that he had brought.

15 And when it was evening, his disciples came to him, saying, Shut the surgery, none of these people has an appointment anyhow, send them away that they may go into the villages and buy themselves some victuals.

16 But Jesus said unto them, They need not depart; give ye them to eat.

17 And they said unto him, We have here but two loaves and five fishes.

18 And Jesus said, It is *five* loaves and *two* fishes, for the umpteenth time, why does everyone always get that wrong, two loaves and five fishes would be tricky, but five loaves and two fishes is a doddle, we could even cut off the crusts.

19 And he took the two fishes, and he hung them over the fire a little while.

20 And his disciples marvelled, saying, What is this miracle that thou art performing now?

21 And he said unto them, It is called smoked salmon, you slice it very thin and you put it on titchy pieces of bread, you would not credit the number of people you can cater for, it will change the face of bar mitzvahs as we know them.

22 And lo! The miracle of the canapé was done, and the disciples went around with twelve trays, and the multitude said, Terrific, but what about the little slices of lemon?

23 And Jesus said unto them, Look up into the trees, and the people were amazed, for they had never realised that the things in the trees were lemons, they had only ever seen lemons in slices at catered functions.

24 And they that had eaten were about five thousand men, beside women and children and gatecrashers who had pretended to be distant relatives on the bride's side.

25 And straightaway Jesus constrained his disciples to get into a ship, and to go before him unto the other side, while he sent the multitudes away, and he went up into a mountain apart to pray.

26 But the ship was now in the midst of the sea, tossed with waves; for the wind was contrary.

27 And in the fourth watch of the

night Jesus went unto them, walking on the sea.

28 And when the disciples saw him, they were troubled, saying, It is a spirit; and they cried out for fear.

29 But straightway Jesus spake unto them, saying, Be of good cheer; it is I and this is the breast-stroke, be not afraid.

30 And Peter answered him and said, Lord, if it be thou, bid me come unto thee on the water.

31 And Jesus said, You do your legs like a frog and you push with your hands, but the main thing is not to panic.

32 And Peter was come down out of the ship, and walked on the water, to go to Jesus. But when he saw the wind boisterous, he was afraid; and beginning to sink, he cried, saying, Lord save me.

33 And immediately Jesus stretched forth his hand and caught him, and said unto him, O thou of little faith, if thou hadst merely turned upon thy back and not panicked, thou wouldst have floated, it is simple hydrodynamics, one day all Jews will swim, personally I blame Moses, parting the Red Sea was just molly-coddling people.

34 And the disciples gazed upward, fearing that the clouds would part and a great finger would come down and poke their boat, because the Red Sea plan had been God's idea in the first place.

35 But that did not happen; instead, the wind ceased, probably because God had conceded the point. And they that were in the ship came and worshipped Jesus, saying, Of a truth thou art the Son of God.

14 And after the miracle of the smoked salmon, Jesus was much in demand at big affairs.

2 And the third day thereafter, there was a marriage in Cana of Galilee; and the mother of Jesus was there.

3 And both Jesus was called, and his disciples, to the marriage. And the disciples murmured amongst themselves, saying, Wonder what it'll be this time, five cocktail sticks and two little sausages? The miracle of the croquette potato?

4 But it was the wine, this time, and when they wanted wine, the mother of Jesus said unto him, They have no wine.

5 Jesus said unto her, Woman, what have I to do with thee? Mine hour is not yet come.

6 But his mother replied in this wise, saying, Who is talking about hours being come, this is no big deal, this is just one of your smart tricks with the wine, so that I am not ashamed of the son that I have borne, his catering is already a house-hold word all over.

7 And Jesus said, Trick?

8 And his mother said, All right, miracle. And she said unto the servants, Whatsoever he saith unto you, do it.

9 And there were set there six water-pots of stone, after the manner of the purifying of the Jews, containing two or three firkins apiece.

10 Jesus said unto the servants, Fill the water-pots with water. And they filled them up to the brim.

11 And he turned to his disciples and he said, What kind of people throw a big function but do not lay on wine?

12 And Simon Peter said, How about people who never drink wine, Lord?
13 And Jesus said, Right in one, verily are there no flies on thee, Simon Peter, brother of Andrew. Thus shall the water be drawn from these water-pots and we shall pass among the guests with the cups, saying in this wise, It is a naive domestic Burgundy without any breeding, but I think you'll be amused by its presumption.
14 And he said unto the servants, Draw out now, and bear unto the governor of the feast. And they bore it.
15 And his disciples moved among the multitude, and very soon vast numbers in that multitude were saying, No more for me, it goeth straight to my head, and Good colour, lasts well, a plucky little wine, if a trifle farmyard, and Perhaps not quite forward enough yet, but well worth laying down a case or two.

15 After this there was a feast of the Jews: and Jesus went up to Jerusalem.
2 Now there is at Jerusalem by the sheep market a pool, which is called in the Hebrew tongue Bethesda, having five porches.
3 And a certain man was there, which had an infirmity, waiting for the waters of the pool to be moved by an angel so that he might step in and be made whole.
4 Because that was the kind of crackpot superstition Jesus had to put up with all his working life.
5 When Jesus saw the man lie, and knew that he had been a long time *in that case*, he said unto him, Wilt thou be made whole?

6 Because Jesus had been around, and he had learned a thing or two about psychosomasis; and he knew that *wilt* was half the battle.
7 And the man answered him, Sir, I was at this wedding at Cana a few days back, and they had this really good stuff there, I must have put away a firkin and I have this mother and father of all hangovers, my legs are like unto rubber, plus shooting pains all over.
8 And Simon Peter said unto Jesus, You were not wrong about the psycho-somatic stuff, Lord. Wilt thou tell him, or shall I?
9 And Jesus said, You are only my registrar, this is a job for the consultant.
10 And straightaway he told the man about the water at Cana.
11 And the man said unto him Art thou serious?
12 Jesus said unto him, Rise, take up thy bed, and walk.
13 And immediately the man was made whole, and took up his bed, and walked: and on the same day was the Sabbath.
14 Therefore the Jews said unto him that was cured, It is the sabbath day: it is not lawful for thee to carry thy . *bed*.
15 He answered them, He that made me whole, the same said unto me, Take up thy bed, and walk.
16 Then asked they him, What man is that which said unto thee take up thy bed and walk on the Sabbath?
17 And he answered them, saying: A doctor.
18 And the Jews said, A qualified man? That's different.

40

O Little Town of Cricklewood

I do not expect you to remember it, but I have mentioned our new neighbours before. It is one of the small perks of being a hack that one can very occasionally vent publicly things that cannot otherwise be de-chested. I am not proud of it, but sometimes it is the only alternative to roping the throat to an RSJ and kicking away the bentwood chair. I hope you'll understand.

Not that the imminent occasion is anywhere near as dire as the last, when the thirteen children of, let us call him Chief Paramount, all came home from Stowe and Roedean for the summer hols and, slipping out of their First XI blazers and navy knickers and into initially rather fetching ethnic clobber, threw a party which went on next door for six days and nights and employed a good eighty per cent of all the steel bands east of Tobago. No shortage of instruments for late-arriving guests to have an amateur bang on, either, doubtless because Chief Paramount owns a sizeable whack of the Nigerian oil industry, and the drums just keep on coming.

He also enjoys diplomatic status. Indeed, it would be hard to find anyone who enjoyed it more. The family hobby is parking on zebra crossings, sideways, and building peculiar baroque extensions to their house which would not only require planning permission but also a Special Royal Commission on Suburban Blight if they were perpetrated by anyone not in a position to torpedo the next Commonwealth Games if he's not allowed to build a lighthouse where his coalshed used to be.

Thus, we do not complain. It would be un-neighbourly as well as futureless to do so formally, and it is difficult to do so informally because not only is Chief Paramount in Nigeria all the time, but there are three Mrs Paramounts. I learned this when I called to enquire which of their thirteen heirs had flattened the party-fence, and had a long and interesting conversation with what I had taken to be the lad's mother, only to discover that I had picked the wrong mother. I assume the Chief to be a Muslim, or perhaps just careless.

Anyway, this multispousal situation lies at the root of my present little difficulty. We have occasionally dropped a note in next door, inviting the Chief to a gin and Twiglet, but he has always been abroad; he will, however, be home for Christmas, we learned from his manciple (now living in a tasty Gothic folly which appeared at the end of the garden only quite recently), and since we throw an annual Boxing Day party for our neighbours, we have decided to invite him in.

Them in.

You see the problem immediately, I know. It occurred to *me* of course, only after, milliseconds after, their letterbox-flap had snapped over my note: *I do not know how to entertain a man with three wives.*

They will come in. The room will be jovial, hot, mistletoe-hung, and full of guests mulled into a sense of false bonhomie. Do I say: 'May I introduce Chief and Mrs Paramount and Mrs Paramount and Mrs Paramount? Or simply 'This is Chief and the Mrs Paramounts'? In that case, other guests would naturally start attempting to establish which was his wife, which his mother, which his sister-in-law, to be followed by all kinds of embarrassments about who looked too young to be what, and so forth. Should I, therefore, take a positive, nonosense approach: 'This is Chief Paramount and his wife. The lovely lady in the long puce number is his other wife, ha–ha–ha, and that's his third wife over by the bookcase, in the green silk suit.'

I know these silences that open up at parties. Some prat is bound to step into the vacuum and start wittering on about how civilised it is to get on socially with one's ex, oh you all *live* together next door, do you, how extremely sophisticated, you people can still teach us primitive honkies a thing or two, ha–ha–ha, would you care for a prawn cracker, tell me, is it true, don't be offended, that . . .

Worse (probably), is there a pecking order in a three-wife situation? Does the tall one in the puce, having brought the largest number of heifers to the marriage, get to be introduced first? Or is that the prerogative of the green silk suit, who happens to be the seventh daughter of the seventh son of a Witch Consultant? Maybe the one next to him is Top Wife, having borne him the first of the thirteen, who can tell?

Tread on the wrong corn, and they'll all be off next door again in unscalable dudgeon, on the blower to Geoffrey Howe and making plans to build an unpermitted heliport on the roof of the unpermitted Gothic butlerdome.

Which brings me to the Saudis on the corner. Moved in last August when the hitherto resident shirt manufacturer retired to Marbella, but not a lot of social contact since, couple of curt nods in September, a brief smile in October, I think it was, when a cat got run over and everybody came out to wonder which of us ought to peel it off the road (guess who drew the short straw), but that was only with *him*. Nothing from his wife, if that's what he keeps inside the black sheet I occasionally spot nipping in and out of his Mercedes. Just a pair of eyes over the veil, could be anybody in there, they might be gay for all I know.

Anyway, we've asked them in for Boxing Day, too.

How are they going to get on with the Paramounts? I suppose they're all Muslim, so there's an ice-breaker, but is that going to be enough, I ask myself? 'Welcome, Mr and is it Mrs Ibn Ben Cornerhouse, I don't think you know the four Paramounts, did you realize you're all Muslims, there's a turnup for the book, ha-ha-ha, what a small world, do you have sprouts with the turkey in your country to commemorate the birth of the Prophet, I've always wondered, haven't I, darling, I don't think you know Mrs Coren, by the way. No, Chief, just the one, ha-ha-ha . . .'

The thing is, there are clearly different varieties of Mohammedan. Especially when it comes to wives. The Mrs Paramounts are all voluptuous, cheery, extrovert, whereas Mrs Ibn Ben Cornerhouse goes out in a shroud and avoids any eye-contact. There may even be half a dozen of *her* across the road, no way of telling, one length of black lagging is much like another, what do I do if six Mrs Ibn Ben Cornerhouses turn up and refuse to be distinguished, let alone introduced?

I bet none of them eats prawn dip, either. We shall have to watch the dietary strictures, or there could well be bloodshed. You know Arabs, very short fuses, plus great store set by social protocols and host-incumbency, my house is your house, all that: we shall probably have to get in sheep's eyes or something to pass round, and how can you tell if they're any good or not, I'm not tasting them, that's for sure, we shall just have to rely on the good name of Sainsbury's, they couldn't afford to put duff optics on their shelves, keeping the Arabs sweet is the only edge they've got over Marks and Sparks.

It's just occurred to me that Muslims don't drink. I think. There can be no other excuse for mint tea. I bet the Paramounts knock it back, mind, I still remember that week-long summer party, they had people laid out three-deep on their gravel drive, you don't get that way on Tizer, it's definitely a different branch, I was right. I hope to God they're not incompatible, I seem to recall something about Sunnis and Shi-ites, that's all I need on Boxing Day, big Muslim punch-up in the front room and the Ibn Ben Cornerhouses sprinting home to start lobbing mortars on the house next door.

I've just remembered dancing. Not that we plan it, it is simply that there is a gramophone, all right musicentre, we like to have a bit of background Albinoni to start off with, but after the first few bottles of Old Sporran have gone about their eviscerating business, someone or other of the regulars fishes out some warped Dixieland relic of my *jeunesse d'Ory*, lurches the pick-up arm onto it, and grabs someone else's better, or occasionally worse, half in that desperate Yuletide bid for a seasonally-endorsed grope, until, before very long, those unpartnered may stand quietly by the window, tactfully ignoring the Saturnalia at their backs, and watch the tiles coming off the roof.

I do not know how this will go down with Mrs Ibn Ben Cornerhouse.

Yes I do.

God knows how they order these things at the Foreign and Commonwealth Office. They probably have a book. In The Event Of A Dusky Husband Turning Up Mob-handed, The First Wife Receives A Cheese Football From The Host's Elder Unmarried Son, The Second Wife Has The First Dance With The Hostess's Youngest Brother From Lowestoft (Except During Ramadan), The Third Wife Is Shown The Host's Collection Of Great British Beermats, The Fourth . . . They must be up to their eyes in small etiquettular print, no wonder they didn't notice Galtieri's lads trundling their boats out. Put an inadvertent hand on a shapely bum at the annual FO tea-dance and you could be looking down the wrong end of an oil embargo in less time than it takes to tell.

Thinking of which, it occurs to me that I do not know

Ibn Ben Cornerhouse's line of country, but it must, surely, be oil, too, in which case he and Paramount could well be at extremely nasty loggerheads. How do Saudi Arabia and Nigeria get on? Did they meet in the qualifying round of the World Cup, and if so, who won? Do they even recognize one another? Am I letting myself in for some fearful United Nations scene, all the wives snapping their reticules shut on a single pre-arranged signal, chucking their crisps in the air, and storming out *en masse* to draft Stern Notes to the premises across the road?

Words cannot adequately encompass (I have tried Roget, but he obviously lived in a different street) the bleak apprehension with which I face the season of goodwill currently rumbling towards me. I don't even have room left, fortunately, to tell you about the gown manufacturers, on the other side of us from the Paramounts, who think that Menachem Begin is an appeaser. They haven't met the Ibn Ben Cornerhouses yet.

They will on the 26th, though. I suppose there is nothing for it but to keep the fingers crossed and hope against hope for the best.

It is, after all, Christmas.

41

Just a Gasp at Twilight

Joseph Califano Jr., the U.S. Secretary of Health, yesterday called for a global campaign to end cigarette smoking by the year 2015.

Daily Telegraph

It was December 31, 2014; and it was nearly time. My companion and I hobbled out onto the roof terrace, fetched up wheezing against the low balcony wall, and gazed silently out over winter-black London. A mile or so away, the trusty old face of Digital Ben read 11:36.

'Twenty-four minutes,' I said.

'The fags are going out all over Europe,' murmured Watson. He coughed for a while, and I watched the dislodged tiles detach themselves from the nearby roofs and slide into the chill darkness. 'We shall not see them lit again in our lifetime.'

'True, old friend,' I said.

'There is a clean fresh wind blowing across the world,' said Watson, 'sod it.'

I took out a kitchen-roll tube stuffed with Admiral's Greasy Black Shag, and turned it lovingly in my ochre fingers. Watson stared at it for a minute or two, rocking back and forth on his frail heels as he struggled for breath.

'What's a nice chap like you doing with a joint like that?' he said, at last.

'Ah, the old jokes, Watson!' I cried, with such atypical energy that I swear my lungs twanged. 'When shall we look upon their like again?' I hefted the giant fag, and the cold starlight caught the maker's hand-set monogram. 'It was the last one my little man underneath St James's made for me before they took him away. It was his *coup d'adieu*, cobbled cunningly from ten thousand dog-ends, bonded with vintage dottle, the final defiant gesture of a genius, made even as the Health Police hobnails clattered on his cellar steps! I have been saving it for the big occasion. Have you a Vesta?'

Watson reached into his waistcoat pocket, sweating from the effort.

'It could kill us both,' he said.

'Something has to, old friend,' I replied.

'God knows, that's true,' nodded Watson. 'It has long been my philosophy. I once gave up, you know; in 1988. For almost thirty-two minutes. And during all that time, the only thing I could think of was: Suppose I were to be knocked down by a bus? The sacrifice would have been utterly in vain. I am, I think, a connoisseur of irony.'

'I, too,' I said. 'I have toyed with abstinence myself, and felt: Suppose a rabid fox were to fix his fangs in my shin?'

'Suppose thermonuclear war were to break out?'

'Suppose some errant meteorite . . .'

'Exactly,' said Watson.

He lit up, and we choked for a while.

'There aren't many of us left, you know,' hawked Watson, after a bit.

'Tubby Stitchling's wife went last week,' I said.

'Really?'

'Emphysema.'

'Ah. I'd only known her as Mrs Stitchling, I'm afraid. I had a sister-in-law called Pondicherry once, though.'

I stared at him through the encircling fug. It was always possible that smoking induced brain-rot. Over the years, research had indicated that it induced everything, despite some intermittently heartening reports from various tobacco companies that it cured baldness, enhanced virility, prevented foot odour and made you taller.

'I think it must have been a joke of her father's,' continued Watson, after his fit had subsided. 'He was in the FCO, you know. He was a smoker's smoker. Put in for a posting to India solely on account of the stogies.'

'Amazing!'

'They were the world's most advanced smoke. Dark green, as I recall. If you left them out in the sun too long, they could blow your hand off. He was dead in six months.'

'Lungs, eh?'

Watson shook his head.

'Dizzy spell. Got up one morning, lit his first of the day, inhaled, and fell on his borzoi.'

'They're sensitive animals,' I said. 'Easily startled.'

'Had his throat out in a trice,' said Watson. 'A fearfully messy business.'

'I can well imagine,' I said.

'There was tar everywhere.'

'Ah.'

'Smoking tragedies always dogged Tubby's family,' gasped Watson. He watched fallen ash burn through his dickie, waving a thin hand feebly at the spreading char. 'D'you suppose it was some kind of ancient curse?'

'What else could explain it?' I said. I stared into the empty night, and my eyes filled with tears. It was good shag, all right. 'So many dead. Do you remember the night old Bob Crondall bought it?'

'As if it were yesterday, old man. A chap with his experience, an eighty-a-day wallah, you wouldn't have thought he'd have been caught out like that, would you? Pottering down the M4, lights up, fag drops in lap, old Bob gropes frantically at the incinerating crotch, next thing you know he's jumped the reservation and swatted himself against an oncoming juggernaut. They found him in the glove compartment, you know.'

'Fate,' I said. 'If it's got your number on it, old man, there's no point trying to duck.'

'Just a matter of luck,' nodded Watson. 'My wife died peacefully in bed. Went to sleep, never woke up.'

'Wincyette nightie, wasn't it?'

'Right. Went up in a flash. Roman bloody candle.' He laughed, a short wry laugh, and went into spasm. When he'd recovered, he said: 'The ironic thing was, she was trying to give up at the time. She was using one of those filter jobs designed to wean you off the weed. The holder was still clenched between her teeth when they found her. It took three morticians to prise it loose.'

I blew a thick grey doughnut, and watched it dissolve.

'The risks in giving up are enormous.' I said. 'I don't think you ever knew Maurice Arbuckle?'

'Only by reputation,' said Watson.

'He used to get through a hundred a day. Gave up just like that, one morning, and was dead an hour later. Choked to death on a Polo.'

'Good God!'

'Tried to inhale.'

We fell relatively silent; only the faint crepitations beneath our vests, like the sound of distant mopeds, disturbed the night. The far clock said 11:50.

'They never tried to ban Polos,' muttered Watson bitterly, at last. 'You never hear the figures for tooth cancer.'

'Conspiracies,' I said. 'Big business interests, powerful dental lobby, all that.'

Watson sighed; then, faintly, smiled.

'I wonder if old Sam Wellbeloved is looking down and laughing, now,' he murmured.

'Bound to be. Anyone who takes a pinch of snuff and blows himself through a plate glass window on the 8.14 has to be able to see the funny side of things.'

Watson sighed again, a sort of low sad rattle, and leaned over the balcony.

'It was all such fun, old chap,' I said, sensing his mood, 'wasn't it? The cheery smoke-filled parties, the first deep drag of the new dawn, those happy post-coital puffs in the days when we still had the wind? The new brands, the bright ads, the racing-cars and free-fall parachute teams, the vouchers, the gifts? And what shall we do now, old friend?'

There was no reply.

'Watson?' I said.

And then, far off, the great clock struck midnight. I reached out, and prised the smouldering stub from my old companion's rigidifying fingers, and took my final drag. It was what he would have wanted. In my place, he would have done the same.

Sentiment is sentiment; but waste is waste.

42

For Fear of Finding Something Worse

Eccentric, yes, emotionally repressed, possibly, yet courageous, resilient, cunning, ruthless and tender by turns, both passionate and aloof, fiercely loyal, sometimes funny, sometimes maudlin, religious, the English nanny did more to forge the influential men of England than any other single factor. It will be a generation before we truly discover exactly what we have lost with her passing.

The Lady

My first nanny was just Nanny. I never knew her real name. Perhaps none of us did.

She joined our household in that soft autumn of 1939, when I was scarce fifteen months old, an engaging toddler, I am told, much given to projectile vomiting and opening frogs with a rusty hacksaw blade to get at their hopping mechanism, a practice from which nanny very soon weaned me by the cunning little trick of batting me with a fence-post whenever the gin was on her.

My parents never interfered. My father was just Father. I never knew his real name. All I knew was that he was something in the City. Every morning he would go off in his silk top hat, his astrakhan coat, his high button boots, and the white stick he had purchased as a hedge against conscription. My mother, the younger daughter of the Earl – he was just Earl, I never knew his real name – would then, having thrown his pyjamas after him and slammed the door, retire to her boudoir and address herself to the needlepoint which was her passion. I hardly ever saw her, but from time to time, during the day, one would catch sight of the little embroidered *toiles* she would slide under the boudoir door, showing men in various stages of amputation.

My early upbringing was left to Nanny. Nanny doted on me. She had, I later learned, like so many of her generation lost her only true love in the Great War, a nursing sister who had run off at Mons with a Prussian dragoon who had broken into her tent in search of something to wipe his bayonet on. After the Armistice, they opened a delicatessen in Bremen, from where, every Christmas, Nanny would receive a small ochre *knackwurst*, tied with a pink ribbon, but no message. With the outbreak of World War Two, this *tendresse* not unnaturally ceased, and Nanny's first Christmas with us was, in consequence, a very dark time. She drank heavily, and brought home the worst kind of waitress from a number of ABCs.

Doubtless, it was from her that I caught my deep and abiding hatred of the Hun. Every morning, for example, as she walked my perambulator in Hyde Park, she would suddenly jam on the brake and hurl herself into the ack-ack gunpits, laying about her with a small yet weighty cosh and frequently rendering several gunners senseless, on the grounds that they had shot nothing down the previous night. The Military Police never pressed charges, however, preferring to incorporate Nanny's forays into the Royal Artillery's training schedules, since there was no greater test of the men's alertness. Eventually, the battery was compelled to set up a Lewis gun beneath the Achilles statue, in the hope of bringing Nanny down before she crossed Park Lane, but she could jink faster than a wing three-quarter and the closest they ever came was to blow off my rear wheel and put three rounds into Panda.

By now it was the spring of 1941, and we were unhappily

forced to leave London, partly because of the Blitz (our house was struck on three consecutive nights by shells from Hyde Park), but mainly because the military authorities had grown suspicious of my father's disability since, whenever a siren sounded, he would take off at top speed, dragging his unfortunate guide-dog behind him, and threshing his way to the head of the shelter-queue with his luminous cane. So, in early May, with my father now in a ginger beard and his two legs enclosed in lengths of guttering which he would tap fiercely with his pipe, crying, 'My God, I'd teach those Nazi swine a thing or two if only I had my pins!', we left for the peace of rural Hampshire.

Nanny did not accompany us, preferring to bivouack on Hampstead Heath with a pitchfork in earnest hope of a German invasion, so, at the age of three, I was introduced to Nanny Phipps.

Nanny Phipps was what I believe is termed 'the salt of the earth', a bucolic Catholic fundamentalist who considered Pius XIII a Lutheran bolshevik. It was she who inculcated me into religion by waiting for me in dark corners of our rambling rented parsonage and sandbagging me with a four-pound crucifix. She would then drag me to the bathroom and baptize me by total immersion in a tub of fresh blood, recounting as she did so, in an undulating Wessex chant, the parting noises of some of the more mutilated martyrs. This took place every night during our first three months of residence, only coming to an abrupt end when two inspectors from the Ministry of Food, spotting the mound of slaughtered lambs which by this time had risen above the encircling privet, called at the house on suspicion of black marketeering.

Unfortunately, upon hearing the bell and spotting the official van through the lancet of his attic bolt-hole, my father, fearing the press-gang, panicked, knotted his sheets together, abseiled down the rear face of the house, and set off on his rigid gutter-pipes across the fields in a terrible clanking lurch. I watched him go from the wall opposite my nursery window on which Nanny Phipps had hung me by my wrists for mortification, powerless to help or follow. Crows rose, cawing, as he hurtled jerkily across the dwindling furrows. I never saw him again.

A load seemed immediately to lift from my mother's shoulders. Freed from the nightly trudge up the let-down ladder to the fortified eyrie where my father, according to Nanny Phipps, waited, crouching on the wardrobe, to pierce her with the forked tail common to his infernal kind, my mother now tripped about the premises, singing. Nanny Phipps herself, having been thrown into Holloway on several counts ranging from treasonable butchery to maliciously wounding a health official with a sharp instrument, to wit, a censer, she was replaced by Nanny Widdershins, a great, plump, apple-cheeked, rosy-nosed, white-haired, cottage-loaf of a woman, always smiling, always with a joke on her lips, even when force-feeding me tapioca down a rubber tube or shaking me awake in the small hours to see whether or not I had wet the bed. To this day, I cannot see a chicken crossing the road without either throwing up or ruining my trouser-leg.

Since my mother had always wanted a daughter, and Nanny Widdershins had always wanted an airedale, these two, freed from the constraints which my vanished father might otherwise have put upon their fancy, now had their way with me. Dressed in a velvet frock and false ringlets, I was led around the house on a leash; when other four-year-old boys were learning fretwork and football, I was taught how to crochet and retrieve. Indeed, at the 1943 Cruft's, only a technicality (spotted at the last minute, and in a fashion I shall carry with me to the grave, by a large borzoi) cost me Best Of Show. But Mother and Nanny Widdershins were good sports; they laughed all the way back to Hampshire.

All good things, however, as one learned so often in the nursery, come to an end. In the bleak midwinter of 1944, even as Patton and von Runstedt hurled themselves upon one another in the Ardennes Forest, so Mother and Nanny Widdershins locked wills in a no less bitter battle. I fell sick, and could not crawl out of my basket: Mother diagnosed chicken-pox; Nanny Widdershins insisted it was distemper. Doctors and vets fought it out with bare knuckles on the gravel drive; times were hard, fees were few. How it might have ended, who can say? For, as the altercation reached its height, a camouflaged Hillman Minx swung suddenly into the drive, disgorging four burly redcaps who flung themselves upon Nanny Widdershins, manacled her to the front bumper, and charged her with desertion.

She protested in vain; the more hysterical her shrieks, the more convinced the MPs became that here was but one more pusillanimous metamorphosis of the notorious blind cripple who had eluded them for close on five years. Even the ultimate appeal to reason, at the sight of which even the older vets blenched, was summarily dismissed on the grounds that there were no lengths to which a treacherous swine like that would not go to avoid serving his King. The khaki Hillman shot out of the drive; the medical practitioners sheepishly gathered up their scattered bags and bottles, and slunk quietly away.

As for Mother, she thenceforth gave up the parental ghost. Unable, on her own, to cope with a growing boy given to singing 'The Good Ship Lollipop' in a breaking falsetto and biting postmen on the ankle, she promptly answered an advertisement in a Salisbury tobacconist's window and despatched me to Miss Sadie Himmler's Academy For Strict Discipline, at which I presented myself the following Monday with my tin trunk and jumbo packet of Spiller's Shapes. Miss Himmler, though initially somewhat surprised, took me in, since I had brought a term's fees in advance, in folding money.

A kindly soul when she was not thrashing middle-aged businessmen with her rhino whip, she was good to me, even if I did not fall precisely within her professional remit, and I was happy there, learning much at her fishnet knee. Indeed, as a middle-aged businessman myself now, I still travel down to Salisbury to visit her, though just for old time's sake, now that arthritis has sadly sapped her magnificent right arm.

And what of those early years themselves, and the proud procession of magnificent female authorities that moved so memorably through them? Did they indeed make me what I am today? Who, at such distance, can categorically say?

I know only that when I step into my polling booth next time around, there will, for me, be no alternative.

43

Mr Noon

A Novel by D.H. Lawrence is to be published by Cambridge University Press next month, 54 years after his death. Researchers found the MS. among papers at the Humanities Research Centre of the University of Texas, Austin.

The new book is called 'Mr Noon.' Lawrence wrote it in two parts and hoped they would be published as separate novels, but the publishers found them too short.

Daily Telegraph.

M r Noon lived up to his name.

He did not get up with the cock.

He did not get up with the sun.

He did not get up and collect the nice fat heavy eggs, still warm from squeezing out of the plump chicken loins.

He did not get up and tug the long rubbery-flubbery teats of Daisy the Cow so that the bright hot milk spurted ringingly into the big dark depths of the bucket.

He did not get up and take Roger the Ram down to the bleating sheep to let Roger the Ram go humpity-humpity and make the sheep feel as if great big waves were crashing on the shore time and time and time again.

Mr Noon did not get up in the morning at all.

He stayed in his bed until noon.

Mr Noon would stay in his bed in case a visitor turned up.

Many visitors *did* turn up at the little cottage, but Mr Noon would send them away again.

Every day, the Postman would call up to the little open window of Mr Noon's bedroom.

'Good morning, Mr Noon!'

And every day, Mr Noon would call out:

'Eff off, Postman!'

Every day, the Jehovah's Witness would call up to the little open window of Mr Noon's bedroom.

'Good morning, Mr Noon!'

And every day, Mr Noon would call out:

'Eff off, Jehovah's Witness!'

And so on.

Mr Noon liked using naughty words. He did not think they were naughty at all, and he was right. People who object to naughty words are guilty of hypocrisy and cant. Mr Noon hated cant.

'Silly cant!' said Mr Noon, lying in his bed.

He would look at the ceiling all morning, and make pictures in his head. Don't you do that, too?

Mr Noon would see trains rushing into long dark tunnels.

'Whoosh!' went the trains.

'Wheeee!' went their whistles, inside the tunnels.

Mr Noon would see his Dad going to work.

His Dad was a miner. Every day, his Dad went down a long dark hole. When he got to the bottom, he would take out his big shovel.

Dig, dig, dig, went Dad Noon!

Mr Noon would see all this, lying on his bed.

He would also see his Mum. Mum Noon was a school-teacher. But most of all, she liked riding horses. He would see her, on the ceiling, riding a big black stallion, with her skirt tucked into her knickers, and her nostrils flaring. The stallion's nostrils flared, too. Sometimes they would ride into a tunnel, if there wasn't a train coming.

When they got home, they were all sweaty! So Mum Noon would get out a great big tin bath, and put it in front of the fire, and put the horse in it, and scrub its back.

Mr Noon liked that picture best of all.

By mid-day, when no visitors had called, except the Gasman, and the Man About The Rates, and the Double Glazing Man, and the Reader's Digest Man, and the Tally Man, Mr Noon would at last get out of bed, grind his big yellow teeth, and say:

'Boogger! Boogger! Boogger!'

Then he would clump down the little creaky staircase in his big honest clogs and out into the smelly old farmyard and try to find something nice to worm.

On a good day, it might be Sharon the Sow. But on a bad day, it might only be Corky the Cat.

Then, one fine, ripening, spring morning, with the fat fuzzy pussy-willow catkins jiggling up and down outside his bedroom window and making his throat go all dry and funny, Mr Noon heard an unfamiliar voice call up from below.

'I say!' it trilled. 'Is anyone at home?'

Slowly, the image of tall dark beetling industrial chimneys raping innocent verdant hills faded from Mr Noon's ceiling. The voice was not a Postman's voice or, indeed, anything remotely like it.

'Aye,' grunted Mr Noon cautiously, from the bed (for it was still only ten-fifteen). 'Aye, appen there be.'

'Oh, ripping!' cried the voice. 'Oh, top-hole! Oh, super!'

Slowly Mr Noon broke the habit of a lifetime and, well before mid-day, swung his big hairy feet out of bed and onto the linoleum, and walked, squeak-squeak-squeak, to the little window and looked out.

Mr Noon found himself staring down into the upturned smiling face and almost equally upturned open blouse of a very pretty lady. Mr Noon gripped the little window ledge with his big hairy hands to stop them trembling: it was a Visitor!

'Can ah elp thee, miss?' croaked Mr Noon

'Oh, would you?' cried the young lady. 'I was just driving past in my motor and I could not help noticing your little chickens. I have a teensy-weensy dinner-party tonight, just a few ripping top-hole chums from the upper classes, and a couple of plump pullets would be absolutely tickety-boo!'

Mr Noon closed his eyes. Then he opened them again, struggled to ungrip his hands from the little window ledge, and retreated, lurching, into the room.

Mr Noon pulled on his thick corduroy trousers.

Mr Noon pulled on his coarse linen shirt.

Mr Noon spat on his big hairy hands and smoothed down his big hairy head.

Then he went downstairs. Clump, clump, clump, went his clogs.

Mr Noon stepped into the unfamiliar morning.

'Pullet?' he said, hoarsely.

'Definitely!' trilled the young lady.

The breeze blew her thin cotton skirt against her legs. Her huge eyes were the deep blue of a faceworker's scars. The sun caught her soft forearm down, reminding Mr Noon of the lioness's belly at Nottingham Zoo.

Mr Noon licked his lips.

'Appen ah'll ketch thee a couple,' he murmured, fighting a sudden dizzy spell. 'Tha'll want plump 'uns, ah tek it?'

The young lady nodded, and winked, and clapped her hands, and giggled.

Mr Noon lunged suddenly, his huge corded muscles bulging, and hurled himself at the squawking chickens.

Scuttle! went the chickens.

Grab! went Mr Noon.

Kof-kof-kof! went the chickens.

Oh! went the young lady.

Mr Noon brought them to her, one in each hand. They were still warm. They were still wriggling, slightly. She touched the plump little bodies with her long slim white fingers.

'So many feathers!' she murmured. 'And I'm late already.' She turned her big blue eyes up to Mr Noon's strong dark face. 'I suppose a pluck would be out of the question?' she said.

Mr Noon fainted.

When he came round, he found the Postman, the Double Glazing Man, the Tally Man, the Reader's Digest Man, and the Man About The Rates standing over him. They had been watching, the way folk do in those parts.

Only the Jehovah's Witness had made an excuse and left.

'Where be er?' enquired Mr Noon.

'Er be gone,' replied the Postman.

'Funny to see you up and about so early,' said the Tally Man. 'Reckon as how we won't be able to call you Mr Noon no more.'

The Double Glazing Man nudged him in the ribs, and winked.

'Mister Bloody Good Opportunity, more like!' he said.

How everybody laughed!

All except Mr Noon, of course.

44

No Bloody Fear

HOTEL FOR PHOBICS
Britain's first hotel for phobics has opened in Firbeck Avenue, Skegness, helped by £42,000 from the Government's small firm guarantee loan. Mr Tony Elliott, founder of Nottinghamshire Phobics Association, said: 'People may have all sorts of psychological problems and we will try to look after them at the seaside.'

Daily Telegraph

Dear Sylvia,

Well here we all are, safe and sound if you do not count Norman's hairpiece blowing off coming from the station, that is one of the little penalties of having to keep your head stuck out of cab windows, I am always on at him to get his claustrophobia looked at but it is not easy to find a doctor who will see him in the middle of a field. We would have stopped to retrieve it, but a gull was on it like a bloody bullet, it is probably halfway up a cliff by now with three eggs in it.

Sorry, Sylve, I had to break off there for a minute, it was writing *cliff* did it, one of my little turns come on, I had to put my head between my knees and suck an Extra Strong, I do not have to tell *you* why, I know; remember that time before we was married and you and me went to the Locarno, Streatham, and that ginger bloke sitting by the spot-prize display asked me to dance, and when he got on his feet he was about six feet nine and I brought my Guinness up?

Anyway, we got to the hotel all right, apart from Norman's bloody mother trying to avoid stepping on the pavement cracks between the cab and the gate and walking into a gravel bin, she come down a hell of a wallop and her case burst open and her collection of bottle tops was bouncing all over the place, it took us near on two hours to get her into her room in the cellar on account of no lift below ground floor, so the management had to bag her up and winch her down through the coal chute, all on account of she can't get to sleep unless she hears rats running about. Still, one consolation is that that's the last we'll see of the old bat for two weeks, due to where Norman will not go inside, Tracy comes out in blackheads if there's no windows, big Kevin is allergic to hot water pipes, little Barry gets diarrhoea in the presence of rodents, and me, well, you know about me and bottle tops!

The landlady was ever so nice about Norman. They had a bed all made up for him in the shrubbery, no plants so big he couldn't see over them if he began to panic in the night, and a very nice man near him, but not *too* near, who sleeps in the middle of the lawn with his foot roped to a sundial in the event of gravity suddenly stopping and him falling off into space. Turned out they had a lot of army experience in common: they both had boots as pets, during National Service.

My room is quite nice, too, lots of things to arrange: you can stand the coffee table on the tallboy and put the hearthrug on it with the potty on top, and if you turn the potty upside down you'll find it's large enough to stand a hairspray aerosol on it. Of course, it's all getting a bit high by then, but it looks lower if you stand on the bed, so I'm quite happy really, even if I can't have Tracy sharing with me due to bees figuring prominently in the wallpaper, and I can't visit her, either, on account of they've put her on the top floor. It's all expense, Sylve, isn't it? Still, we managed to get big Kevin and little Barry to share: the management found them a triangular room, so they've got a corner each to stand in, leaving only one for them to keep an eye on; they can get quite a lot of sleep, in turns.

Mealtimes are great fun, everybody is ever so sociable, there's a very nice man from Norwich I think it is, who comes round to every table just after we've all sat down and touches every single piece of cutlery, and two charming sisters from Doncaster who eat standing on their chairs due to the possibility of mice turning up sudden, and a former postmaster who sings 'Nola' whenever there's oxtail soup. My Norman has been a great hit, due to not coming in for meals: everybody takes it in turns to go to the window and feed him, also give him little titbits to carry over to his friend tied to the sundial, because the waitress has agoraphobia and can't even look at the forecourt without going green.

Not that there aren't little squabbles from time to time: Sunday, we had plums and custard, and little Barry likes to arrange the stones on the side of his dish. What he did not realize was that this makes Mr Noles from Gants Hill, who is on our table, punch people in the mouth. Big Kevin, as you know, is not called big Kevin for nothing and has had to learn to look after himself from an early age, due to where his father is unable to come inside and help him, big Kevin took hold of Mr Noles by his collar and chucked him out into the corridor, which was a terrible thing to do, it turned out, because Mr Noles has a horrible fear of narrow places and pays £2 per day extra to enter the dining-room via the fire-escape, but big Kevin was not to know this, he is only a boy, though getting enormous enough for me to feel queasy every time I stretch up to make sure he's brushed his teeth. The upshot of it was, Mr Noles was hurling himself about in the corridor for close on twenty minutes before Mrs Noles could get a net over him. He broke eighteen plaster ducks, three barometers, and put his elbow straight through 'The Monarch of the Glen', though doing less damage than you might think since its face had already been painted out on account of the night porter having a morbid fear of antlers.

And all the time my Norman is shouting '*What's going on? What's bloody going on?*' from the garden, deeply distressing his friend tied to the sundial who can hear all this breakage and shrieking and reckons gravity is beginning to pack up and bring things off the walls.

Still, it turned out all right, Mr Noles and big Kevin made it up, they have a lot in common, basically, both being unable to walk down a street without picking bits off hedges, and he asked big Kevin to join him on the beach because Mrs Noles never went there on account of her terror of being buried alive. She likes to spend her afternoons standing on the concrete forecourt with a big bell in her hand and a whistle between her teeth in case of emergencies, so her husband and big Kevin and little Barry and Tracy and Norman and me all went off to the beach. Trouble was, it would all have been all right if Norman's new friend hadn't been unsettled by the false alarm over gravity: he did not want to be left alone, so the porter found a huge coil of rope so that Norman's new friend could come down to the beach without untying himself from the sundial, but it was nearly three hundred yards and you have to go round two corners, so you can't see what's going on behind, and what happened was the rope got caught in a car bumper and one moment Norman's new friend was cautiously creeping along beside us, and the next he was suddenly plucked from our midst.

We visited him in the cottage hospital, but even our presence (minus, of course, Norman, also Tracy, who faints in the vicinity of linoleum) could not persuade him that he had not fallen off Earth and hurt himself dropping onto some alien planet. His argument was that we had fallen with him but, being unencumbered by rope or sundials, had managed to land on our feet, unhurt, and were keeping the truth from him so as not to alarm an injured man.

There was no convincing him, so we just left him there and collected Norman and Tracy and went down to the beach to find big Kevin and Mr Noles. But all we could find was big Kevin, he was huddled under a stack of deck-chairs and sobbing: we ran up to him (all except little Barry, who was terrified in case the shadow of the deck-chairs fell on his foot), and asked him what was wrong, and he said he had been getting on fine, he had buried Mr Noles in the sand, because Mr Noles had been told by his psychiatrist that this was a very good way to overcome his fear of narrow spaces, and he was just about to stick a little windmill over where he had buried him when a crab come out of the sea and started running towards him sideways.

We all gasped!

'It is my own fault,' shouted Norman, from a nice open space he had found in between the airbeds, 'I knew the lad was an arachnophobe, it never occurred to me that he would associate crabs with spiders, that is not the sort of thing what occurs to a claustrophobe on account of you never get near enough to anything to distinguish it.'

'So what happened, big Kevin?' I said, aghast.

'I run off, Mum,' he sobbed. 'I must have run miles.'

A cold chill shot down my spine, as if I'd just seen the Eiffel Tower or something.

'Where is Mr Noles buried?' I enquired, gently.

I think you probably know the answer to that, Sylve. I tell you, we prodded lolly-sticks all over that beach for five hours, i.e. well after it was too late anyway, and no luck. It was getting dark before I knew I would have to be the one to break the news to Mrs Noles. Her of all people.

She was still standing on the forecourt when we got back to the hotel. I put my hand on her arm.

'How are you, Mrs Noles?' I murmured.

'Nicely, thank you,' she replied. 'I got a bit worried around half-past four. The sun was very hot, and I thought: any minute, this asphalt is going to melt and swallow me up. But it didn't.'

Quick is best, I said to myself, Sylve. So I come right out and told her that Mr Noles had been buried alive. And do you know what she said?

'Serves him right, the stingy bastard,' she said. 'I always told him we ought to have bought a bell each.'

That's the best thing about holidays, Sylve, I always say: you meet so many interesting people.

It takes you right out of yourself.

Your loving friend, Sharon.

45

Getting the Hump

A suit of armour sold last week for £1,850 is believed to have been worn by King Richard III. It had been tailor-made for a man 5ft 4ins tall with a curvature of the spine and one shoulder lower than the other.

Sunday Express

Although, on the morning of April 6, 1471, the bright spring sun may have been warming the narrow London streets and cheering the spirits of the teeming citizens, its heartening rays unfortunately penetrated neither the dank and tatty premises of Master Sam Rappaport (Bespoke Metal Tailoring Since 1216) Ltd, nor the sunken soul of its hapless proprietor.

Master Rappaport had staff shortages. True, Rappaport's had had staff shortages ever since that fateful day in 1290, but this week was particularly bad: his vambrace cutter was off sick, his hauberk finisher was in labour, and the heads of his two best riveters were currently shrivelling on the north gate of London Bridge for dishonestly handling a church roof which they had hoped to turn into a natty spring range of lead leisurewear.

'So ask me where I'm getting gauntlets from!' he demanded bitterly of his senior assistant, as he walked through the door.

The senior assistant sighed; but it was what he was paid for, mainly, so he said:

'Okay, Sam, so where are you getting gauntlets from?'

'Don't ask!' snapped his master.

The senior assistant summoned his dutiful laugh, for the thousandth time.

'Gauntlets I'm buying off the peg, thank God my poor father never lived to see it,' muttered Master Rappaport. 'A man walks out of here in what he thinks are genuine hand-forged Rappaport gauntlets, he goes into a tavern for a glass of sherry wine, he bangs his fist on the table, and what is he looking at?'

'What?'

'Flat fingers, is what he's looking at. A webbed hand, is what he's looking at. Tin is all they are. Time was, a man in a Rappaport gauntlet, he wanted to shake hands, he needed two other people to help him lift.'

The shop-bell jangled.

A tall good-looking young man filled the doorway.

'Good morrow,' he said. 'I am the Duke of Gloucester.'

Master Rappaport turned bitterly to his senior assistant.

'See?' he snapped. 'I ask for underpressers, they send me dukes!'

'I think he's a customer, Sam,' murmured the senior assistant.

The grey preoccupation ebbed from Master Rappaport's face. He smacked his forehead. He banged his breast. He bowed.

'Forgive me, Your Grace!' he cried. 'How may we assist you?'

'I should like,' said the Duke of Gloucester, 'a suit of armour. Nothing flash, and plenty of room in the seat.'

The master tailor beamed.

'Wonderful!' he said. 'Formal, but also informal, smart for day wear, but if God forbid you should suddenly have to kill somebody at night, you don't want to be embarrassed, am I right?'

'You read my mind, sir!' cried the young Duke.

'I have been in this game a long time,' said Master Rappaport. 'Nat, the swatches!'

The senior assistant bustled across with a number of clanking plates gathered on a loop of chain. Master Rappaport flicked over them.

'Not the toledo,' he murmured, mostly to himself, 'toledo is all right on an older man, it's a heavyweight, it's fine if you don't have to run around too much, also the sheffield, personally I got nothing against sheffield, it has a smart glint, but you have to be short, there's nothing worse than a long glint, believe me; likewise, the cast-iron, a tall man in cast-iron, he can look like a walking stove. For my money, I see you in the non-iron.'

'Non-iron?'

'It's a synthetic, 20% copper, a bit of this, a bit of that; a lightweight, wonderful for summer battles. A lot of people couldn't get away with it, but you're young, you got broad shoulders, a nice figure, you can carry a thinner metal. It's flexible, it's cool, it don't creak suddenly when you're with – hem! hem! – a young lady, you should forgive my presumption. Also got a lightweight fly, just a little snap catch, very convenient; the cast-iron, for example, it's got a big bolt it can take you all day, first thing you know you're rusting from the inside, am I right, Nat?'

'Absolutely,' said the senior assistant.

The young nobleman smiled generously.

'I shall be guided entirely by you,' he said. 'I have just returned from exile with His Majesty Edward IV, and have in consequence little notion of current fashion trends.'

'With Edward IV you've been?' cried Master Rappaport. 'So Saturday week you're fighting at Barnet?'

The Duke nodded.

'Problems, Sam?' enquired Nat, catching his master's sudden furrow.

'Eight days,' murmured his master. 'It's not long. At least three fittings he'll need.'

'Perhaps, in that case,' said the Duke, 'I ought to try—'

'We'll manage!' cried Sam Rappaport hastily, 'We'll manage! Nat, the tape!'

And, lowering his eyes respectfully, the master tailor, tape in hand, approached the comely crotch.

The senior assistant looked at the morning delivery. He shook his head.

'We shouldn't send the greaves out for making,' he said. 'They're a good two inches short. Also the cuisses.'

Master Rappaport stared dismally out of the little window.

'Maybe he'll agree to crouch a bit,' he said, at last. 'Look, Nat, he's been abroad, you heard him say he was out of touch. So we'll tell him all the smart crowd are crouching a bit this season. Who knows, maybe we could set a whole new—'

The bell jangled. The two tailors bowed.

'I can't get on the leg pieces without crouching,' said the young Duke, after a while, panting.

'Wonderful!' cried Sam Rappaport. 'Look at His Grace, Nat!'

'Perfect!' shouted the senior assistant. 'It fits you like the paper on the wall. This year, everybody's crouching.'

'You're sure?' enquired the anxious young man, hobbling uncomfortably before the pier-glass.

'Would I lie?' said Sam Rappaport. 'Tuesday, please God, we'll have the breastplate and pauldrons.'

'Tuesdays,' muttered the senior assistant, 'I never liked.'

They stared at the breastplate, for the tenth time. Then they measured the two shoulder pieces again.

'So we'll tell him everybody's wearing one shoulder lower this year,' said the master tailor. 'He's young, he's green, what does he know?'

'Here he is,' said Nat.

'It hurts my shoulder,' complained the Duke of Gloucester, after a minute or two. His left hand hung six inches lower than his right, his neck was strangely twisted, his legs crouched in the agonizing constrictions of the ill-made greaves and cuisses.

'Listen,' said Master Rappaport gently. 'To be fashionable, you have to suffer a bit. Is His Grace smart, Nat, or is he smart!'

'Fantastic!' cried the senior assistant, looking at the wall. 'Take my word for it, he'll be the envy of the Court.'

'When will the backplate and gorget be ready?' gasped the Duke.

'Friday,' said Master Rappaport. 'On Friday, you get the whole deal.'

'On second thoughts,' murmured the senior assistant, 'Tuesdays are a lot better than Fridays.'

'We're working under pressure!' shouted his master. 'Miracles you expect suddenly?'

He held up the backplate. It was strangely bowed, like a turtle's carapace.

'Well, gentlemen?'

They spun around. The door having been open, they had not heard the Duke come in.

'We were just admiring the backplate!' cried Master Rappaport. 'What cutting! What burnishing!'

'And what a wonderful curvature!' exclaimed Nat.

'Curvature?' enquired the Duke of Gloucester.

'It's what everybody's talking about,' said Sam.

'This time next month,' said Nat, 'everybody will be bent. I promise.'

The Duke took the finished suit to the fitting room.

Time passed. The two tailors looked at their shoes, arranged their patterns silently, cleared their throats, looked at the ceiling.

After a few minutes, the fitting-room curtains parted, and the Duke of Gloucester slouched through, dragging his leg, swinging his long left arm, his head screwed round and pointing diagonally up.

'It looks – as though – I have – a – hump,' he managed to croak, at last, through his tortured neck.

'Thank God for that!' cried Master Rappaport. 'We were worrying, weren't we, Nat?'

'Definitely,' said the senior assistant. 'We said to ourselves: suppose the suit comes out without a fashionable hump?'

'It's killing me!' cried the Duke.

'Good!' shouted Sam.

'Wonderful!' shouted Nat.

'You're sure it's fashionable?' gasped the Duke.

'You could be a—a—a *king*!' cried Master Rappaport.

So the young Duke of Gloucester paid his bill, and, wearing his new armour, lurched horribly out into the street. And, as he walked, so the pain burned through his body; and, before very long, an unfamiliar darkness spread across his sunny face, and a new sourness entered his disposition, and angers he had never known, and rages he had never believed possible, racked the flesh beneath the steel.

And, suddenly, strangely, the world began to look a different place altogether; until, penetrating to the very innermost recesses of his soul, there fell across him on that soft spring day, a deep, black discontent, like winter.

46

True Snails Read (anag., 8,6)

Squire **Walt Reeny**, Dr **Yesvile**, and the rest of these gentlemen having asked me to write down the whole particulars about **True Snails Read** from the beginning to the end, keeping nothing back but the answers to 14 across and 23 down, and that only because there is treasure still to be lifted, I take up my pen in the year of grace 17—, and go back to the time when my father kept the Admiral Benbow inn, and the brown old seaman with the terrible nib-scar first took up his lodging under our roof.

I remember him as if it were yesterday, as he came plodding to the inn door, his twenty-four salt-caked volumes of the *Oxford English Dictionary* following behind him in a hand-barrow, his high reedy voice breaking out in that old sea-song that was to haunt my dreams:

'Corpse at bottom of scrum! We hear
He's worth more than one small bier!'

I opened the door to him, and he threw himself into a chair, crying:

'A palindrome? Yes, but this one's not for kids, me hearties! It's peculiar.'

I stared at him.

'I beg your pardon, sir?' I said.

'I think,' said my father, from the dark recess of the bar, 'he wants a tot. Of, if I am not mistaken, rum.'

The stranger smote the table.

'Be 'ee a crosswordin' man?' he cried joyously.

My father smiled.

'4, 4, 1, 4,' he replied, 'according to the best fairy stories. Not these days, though.'

The old sailor nodded, and, when my father went out for the bottle, drew me to him with an inky claw, so close that I could see the flecks of chewed quill stuck upon his lip, and smell the indiarubber on his nails.

'Yonder,' he whispered excitedly, nodding towards the bar-window and the broad bay beyond, 'lies the S.S. *Canberra*. I ships aboard 'er on the morrow tide.'

'You are bound for the Crossword Cruise, sir?' I exclaimed. 'You go in search of the Grand Prize? May I wish you the very best of luck?'

'Luck?' cried the old man in a terrible voice. **'Luck's a chance, but ——'s sure (*Housman*) (7).** I makes my own luck, lad! See this 'ere diddy-box 'o mine?'

I nodded. It was a battered, brassbound thing, with **FLAT CAP, INNIT?** engraved upon the lid.

'Yes,' I said, proud of myself, 'I noticed it immediately. It seemed such a queer shape for a hatbox.'

The old blood-threaded eyes gazed at me as if I were deranged.

'Hatbox?' he muttered. 'That be no hatbox, lad. That be the personal property o' the late –' and here his voice dropped to a cracked whisper '– *Captain Flint!*'

Letters swam in my head. Truth dawned.

'It be why I doan need luck, see?' said the old sailor. His eyes grew moist with more than rheum. 'Flint were the smartest puzzle dog I ever shipped with, lad. Flint knew the Latin handle of every plant that ever were, 'e 'ad the entire *Oxford Dictionary o' Quotes* to heart, 'e could spell backwards in fourteen lingos, 'e knew eight 'undred words wi' two letters in 'em! He dreamed in anagrams, did Flint, he saw acrostics in the stars. I remember one time we was becalmed off the Dry Tortegas, half-mad from heat and thirst and not a man among us capable o' getting 1 across in the *Sun* – **It sat on the mat (3)** – and there were Flint on the after-deck doing the *Telegraph* with 'is left hand and *The Times* with 'is right, while 'is parrot read him the *Guardian* so's he could do it in 'is head simultaneous!'

'Remarkable!' I cried.

'This rare genus had one eye (6),' murmured the old man, blowing his nose fiercely on a red bandanna, 'but has now **gone up to meet his dog (3)**.'

'What, then, is in his box?' I enquired.

A dry hand closed over my own, so firmly that I could feel the sharp callus on a forefinger flattened by a million clues.

'Ye seems a lad who would **look after his short mother (4,3)**,' murmured the ancient. 'A year or two back, just after Flint 'ung up 'is sextant, the P&O come to 'im wi' a proposition. Not a sea-dog from Maracaibo to the Cape as 'adn't 'eard tell o' Flint's magic powers, see, an' it were only a matter o' course afore—'

'No need to go on, sir!' I cried. 'I may be a stranger to the cryptic force, but I can divine a drift as well as any! You are telling me that Flint became the brains behind the Crossword Cruise! You are intimating that the incalculable treasure which awaits one brilliant, albeit peculiar, passenger comes with the solution to a Grand Prize Jumbo Puzzle set by—'

My companion spread his hands, nodding.

'Did the good doctor fail to diagnose his digestive problem? Sounds as though his friend Sherlock has! (10),' he said.

I pointed excitedly at the diddy-box.

'And this can only mean,' I exclaimed, 'that you have Captain Flint's papers, and therefore the answer to the Canberra's Prize Jum—'

The finger was across my lips. Its tremble was so stricken that my ear-ring shook.

'*What is that strange tapping?*' he croaked.

I searched for the true meaning hidden in this cryptogram, knowing by now that *strange,* like *disturbed, confused, upset,* and so forth, betokened some anagrammatic interference. But what could I make from **tapping**? Was *gnippat* some rare Sumatran weevil, *pantpig* a Jacobean pervert, *I gnappt* the early working-title of something by that drunk Robert Louis Stevenson who lived in our small back room? It was while I was pondering this that I became aware of a noise beyond the window, as of a stick banging rhythmically against the wall.

I glanced at my companion, who had begun to gasp horribly.

'**We see nothing on this church bench! (5,3),**' he managed, finally, to sob.

I swivelled as the inn door burst open; and caught my breath. At first, I saw naught but the white stick that had thrust it wide: but soon thereafter, a squat, malign figure entered the room, a dreadful leer playing beneath the sightless eyes. He tapped his way to our table, and, reaching out a clammy hand, touched my face.

'Pew,' he said. 'I am confused.'

Wep? I thought, *ewp?*

'I had been expecting an old friend but – ah!' he cried, as his hand groped on and suddenly found my companion, cringing in his chair, 'I was not wrong.'

Whereupon he removed a folded scrap of paper from his smock, placed it carefully on the table between us, turned, and made his echoing way out again.

Since my companion seemed too stricken to move, I took the liberty of picking up the scrap and unfolding it. The eyes in the rigid face opposite now flickered in resigned enquiry.

'Negro Topsy upside down? Don't say why! (5,4),' I read.

He groaned horribly. A further, deeper shudder racked his ancient frame. His eyes rolled to white. As a drowning man throws up one sinking hand, he beckoned me close.

'Skin –' he wheezed, but the rest of the sentence ebbed.

'Go on!' I urged. 'I could not hear!'

He made a supreme and dreadful effort.

'Skin game – for Cricket Cup?' he gasped, finally. **'(4,3).'**

I racked such brain as I could muster. The ruin opposite, tongue lolling noiselessly behind cracked lips, could be no help.

And then, clouds parted, light burst through.

'Hide box!' I shouted.

He nodded, just perceptibly.

I snatched up Flint's precious bequest, wrapped it quickly in a tablecloth, rose, and would have left forthwith to seek a spot of suitable impenetrability, had not the dying unfortunate clutched at my urgent sleeve in one last desperate bid.

He pulled, with terminal strength, my ear towards his lip.

'Beware!'

His voice was like an on-shore breeze against the dry grass of the dunes.

'Beware of what?' I said.

The tongue laid a last bead of moisture on the lip.

'Of a seafaring man with one backward gel!' he gasped.

And died.

Next Week's Episode. **Hallmarked underwear? (4,4,6) Why not, if the parrot's good as gold! (6,2,5)**

47

One is One and All Alone

The last-minute cancellation of the Canadian visit does of course leave a large gap in the diary which probably cannot be filled at this late date. The Queen will be at something of a loose end.

Palace spokesman

MONDAY

Got up, finally.

Sat at escritoire. Filled in all o's on front page of one's *Telegraph*. Put paperclips in long line. Pushed paperclips into little pile. Straightened paperclip and cleaned old bits of soap out of engagement ring. Bent paperclip back to original shape. Put paperclip back in little pile and tried to identify it with eyes shut.

Noticed tiny flap of wallpaper curled back from skirting just behind escritoire. Took one's Bostik out of escritoire drawer, put little smear on wall, little smear on wallpaper, pressed down wallpaper.

Picked old dried crusty bits off one's Bostik nozzle.

Read Bostik label. It is good for glass, wood, ceramics, light metal, leather, and plastic, whatever that is. If one gets it in one's eyes, one should wash it out immediately.

Saw fly go past.

Saw fly come back.

Watched wallpaper curl off wall again.

Turned on *Play School*. Noticed flat head on presenter.

Summoned Lady Carinthia Noles-Fitzgibbon, who confirmed head not normally flat. She enquired if she should summon Master of the Queen's Ferguson. One told her no, one was perfectly capable of fiddling with one's apparatus oneself.

One was in fact quite grateful.

Took lift to West Loft. Keeper of the Queen's Smaller Gifts (West Loft Division) most helpful. One had, according to his inventory, been given a zircon-encrusted ratchet screwdriver by King Idris of Libya, following 1954 reciprocal trade agreement on depilatory soup. During Keeper's search for this item, put on alligator's head presented by Friends of Mbingele National Park on the occasion of one's Silver Wedding. A snug fit, but some tarnish on the molars.

Keeper rather taken aback upon return to find one in alligator's head and Mary Queen of Scots' execution frock, but recovered admirably. Having to suppress his distress at poor Professor Blunt's departure has matured him considerably; one may soon allow him to fondle the odd corgi.

Returned to one's apartment. *Play School* now finished, so put on one's husband's video recording of yesterday's *Postman Pat*. It is now Mrs Goggins the Postmistress who has a flat head.

Applied screwdriver to hole in back of one's apparatus. Blue flash. Zircons all blown off. One's husband burst in, ranting: apparently, one's husband's Hornby Dublo layout had fused itself to nursery floor.

One's husband now at worse loose end than ever, stormed off in foul mood to put up shelf in garage. Has been talking about putting up shelf in garage since Suez.

Lunch. First lunch alone since October, 1949.

Moulded mashed potatoes into Grampians, poured gravy in to stimulate Loch Rannoch, cut pea in half to make two ferries. Had ferry race by blowing down one's straw. Left-hand pea won.

Knighted it with fork.

After lunch, one's husband stormed in again, carrying gold claw-hammer (Ghana, 1962), diamanté pliers (Melbourne, 1968), set of inlaid mother-of-pearl ring-spanners (Tongan gift on occasion of PoW's first tooth), and shouting *Where one's bloody zircon-encrusted screwdriver?*

Stormed out again with rather nice Louis XV rosewood side-table, muttering *Soon chop up this tarty frog rubbish, make bloody good plank, this, rip a couple of brackets off that poncey Tompian clock upstairs, shelf up in two shakes of a CPO's whatsit.*

Fusebox Poursuivant arrived to repair apparatus. Commanded to remain and play I-Spy. One won.

Bed at 8.15, with ocelot-bound *Fifty Things To Do On A Wet Day* (New Zealand, 1978). Made flute out of old sceptre. Played *God Save One.*

TUESDAY

Woke early, made hat from *Telegraph.*

Drew up list of all one's acquaintances with spectacles. Compared it with list of all one's acquaintances with flat feet.

Watched one's husband rush in clutching bloodstained thumb, shouting *Where bloody Dettol, where bloody Elastoplast?* Watched him rush out again.

Sudden brilliant thought. Decided to make one's own breakfast. Cheered to find nursery kitchen empty. Recognised frying-pan. Put egg in frying-pan. Oddly, egg did not go yellow and white, egg just rolled around in frying-pan, went hot, then exploded.

Had bath.

Rang TIM, Weather, Cricket Scores, Puffin Storyline. Listened to Mrs Goggins story. Rang Starline: good day for throwing out old clothes, will meet interesting short man with financial proposition, a loved one will have exciting news in evening.

Threw out old clothes and waited for interesting short man.

Did not come, so got old clothes back. Put them into symmetrical heaps.

In evening, loved one stomped in with exciting news: Louis XV garage shelf had fallen on Rolls, dented bonnet, knocked off wing-mirror.

Bed at 9, with interesting book. There are 3, 786 Patels in it.

WEDNESDAY
Got up, put *Telegraph* in bucket of water. Added flour, as recommended by *Fifty Things To Do On A Wet Day*, made papier-mâché head of Mrs Goggins.

Removed old glove from pile waiting for interesting short man, put it on, poked forefinger into Mrs Goggins, did puppet-show for corgi.

Corgi passed out.

Rang 246 8000 again, but no further news of interesting short man or his financial proposition. Nothing about one's dog falling ever, either. However, it is a good day to go shopping. One leapt at this! Why had one not thought of it sooner?

One has never been shopping.

It being a fine day, one decided to slip out quietly in sensible shoes and headscarf, and walk up Constitution Hill to Knightsbridge. Most interesting. Sixty-two street lamps.

Several Japanese persons stared at one strangely. At Hyde Park Corner, a taxi-cab driver slowed, pushed down his window, and shouted 'I bet you wish you had her money!'

Quite incomprehensible.

One recognised Harrods at once, from their Christmas card.

One went inside. Most impressive. One selected a jar of Beluga caviare, a rather splendid musical beefeater cigarette-box with a calculator in its hat, a pair of moleskin slippers, a Webley air-pistol, and a number of other items one might never have thought of to help one while away the remainder of one's spare fortnight, and one was quite looking forward to strolling back to the Palace, putting one's mole-shod feet up, treating oneself to a spoonful or two of the old Royal fish roe while potting starlings through the window and totting up the toll on one's loyal Yeoman calculator to the stirring accompaniment of *Land of Hope and Glory*, when one suddenly felt one's elbow grasped with an uncustomarily disrespectful firmness.

'Excuse me, madam, but I wonder if you would mind accompanying me to the Assistant Manager's office?'

One was aware of a grey-suited person.

'Normally,' one replied, 'one allows it to be known that one is prepared to entertain a formal introduction. One then initiates the topic of conversation oneself. It is normally about saddles. However, one is prepared to overlook the protocol occasionally. One assumes the senior staff wishes to be presented?'

FRIDAY

Got up, slopped out.

One might, of course, have made a fuss. One might, for example, have pointed out to one's Assistant Manager – the entire place is, after all, By Appointment – that not only does one never carry money, but that money actually carries one, and would therefore serve as a convenient identification.

One chose, however, to retain one's headscarf, one's glasses, and one's silence; since something had suddenly dawned on one.

Thus, yesterday in Bow Street, being without visible means of support, one was not even given the option of seven days. One now has a rather engaging view of Holloway Road, albeit only from the upper bunk, a most engaging companion with a fund of excellent stories, and a mouse, and one is already through to the South Block ping-pong semi-finals.

Tonight, there is bingo, rug–making, cribbage, aerobics, bookbinding, squash, pottery, chiropody, raffia work, community singing, petit–point, judo, darts, and do–it–oneself. One can hardly wait to see what tomorrow may bring!

One is, in short, amused.

48

£10.66 And All That

A Dorset wood which was valued at £9 in the Domesday Book is now on the market at £120,000.

Daily Telegraph

Gloomily, the Shaftesbury branch-manager of William & Bastards rubbed a clear patch in the little mullioned window with his smocked elbow, and stared out.

'Cats and dogs,' he muttered.

'What?' said his assistant.

'The rain is coming down,' replied the manager, 'cats and dogs.'

'Bloody portent, that is,' said the assistant. 'There'll be bishops dead all over by tea-time.'

'Not *real* cats and dogs,' said the manager, irritably. 'It is just an expression.'

'It doesn't mean anything,' said his assistant.

The manager rolled his eyes, rooted in his hirsute ear, cracked a hidden nit.

'You cannot expect to know what everything means, these days,' he said. 'The language is in a state of flux. Cats and dogs is probably from the Norman.'

'Why not?' grumbled the assistant. 'Everything else bloody is. I never eat out any more. Time was, you found a maggot on your plate, you stuck an axe in the cook. These days it's more than likely simmered in a cream sauce with a bloody peppercorn on its head.'

The manager sighed.

'Nevertheless,' he said, 'estate agency is nothing if not adaptable to change. We are at the forefront, Egwyne. We have got to be perceived to be red-hot. Hence smart fashionable expressions, e.g. cats and dogs.'

'What is e.g. when it's at home?' enquired the assistant.

'It's another one,' replied the manager. 'You hear it everywhere.' He peered out again. 'Funny thing about this glass stuff,' he said, 'it makes people's legs go little. That woman from Number Four just went past, her feet were coming out of her knees. Her dog looked more like a bloody lizard.'

'If she finds out it's the glass what's doing it,' said the assistant, 'she could very likely sue us. I reckon we ought to have it took out again. God knows what it's doing to our eyes, they could start going little any minute, why did we have it put in in the first place?'

'It is what is called chic,' said the manager.

His assistant stared at him.

'Do not blame me, Egwyne,' said the manager, looking away, 'this stuff is coming straight down from head office. I am getting memos headed *From the Stool Of The Senior Bastard* informing me they are determined to drag estate agency into the eleventh century. You do not know the half of it, Egwyne. It is a whole new, er, ball game. It is where it's at.'

His assistant sniffed.

'I wouldn't care,' he said, 'we've hardly shifted nothing since we were set up. It may well be estate agency is not a British thing.'

'Concept.'

'What?'

'Never mind. Since you raise the point, Egwyne, the plain fact is it is all a matter of marketing.'

'What is marketing?'

'It is the name of the game. The old days of if you want somewhere to live you go round to the bloke with three chickens and if he doesn't reckon it's a fair price you knock him about a bit are over, Egwyne.'

The shop-bell tinkled. A young couple, entering, shrieked and ran out again. The manager hurried to the open doorway.

'What is it?' cried the young man, backing off. 'Leprosy? Boils? Ague?'

'Do not be alarmed!' replied the manager. 'It is only a concept. It rings when you open the door.'

His assistant appeared at his shoulder.

'Yes,' he said reassuringly, 'it is a ball game where it's at. Come on in out of the cats and dogs, it's bloody chic in here, e.g.'

Hesitantly, the young couple re-entered.

'We're after a hut,' said the man.

The manager beamed, drew up a pair of stools, flicked an unidentified dropping from one, and motioned his clients seated.

'And what sort of price range are we talking about?' he said.

'About eight bob,' said the husband, 'tops.'

The manager sucked his teeth.

'What have we got in the way of eight-bob huts, Egwyne?' he said.

'There's that rat-riddled old drum we've been trying to shift down by Aelfthryth's Swamp,' said his assistant, 'or possibly in it, by now; you know what it's like with bogs.'

'Rats?' enquired the young woman.

'Not large ones,' said the manager. 'Some of 'em are virtually mice. It's got a lot of roof.'

'It would have to have,' said the young man, 'for eight bob.'

'I'm not saying eight bob,' said the manager, quickly. 'We could certainly knock one-and-threepence off for cash. It's got a door up one end with a brand new string on it,' he added, 'it's got a ladder for climbing up to repair some of the roof it hasn't got, and a nice window without any of that glass what makes your legs shrink.'

'Has it got a floor?' enquired the young man.

'All right, six bob,' said the manager.

'Any land?' said the young man.

'Ah,' said the manager. 'It has got land, hasn't it, Egwyne?'

'No point denying it,' said his assistant. 'They'd notice it straight away, anyhow. You cannot miss it, bloody great forest out back, could be anything in there, goblins, bogeys, trolls, you name it, well, it wouldn't be five bob otherwise, would it?'

'Four and sevenpence,' said the manager. 'It's got a relatively scum-free well, mind.'

'I don't know,' said the young woman, 'we were rather set on . . .'

'Tell you what,' said the manager quickly, 'you could chop the trees down, anything nasty'd soon run out, call it four bob and I'll chuck in Egwyne to come round with his axe, he'll have that lot down in next to no—'

But the shop bell had tinkled again. Egwyne watched them go, from the window.

'She'll never fancy him now his legs have gone little,' he said. He grinned. 'Serve 'em right, it was a steal at four bob, some people don't know when they're lucky.'

The manager might well have responded, had not the door opened again.

It was a slim young man in a neatly tailored smock, flared, patch pockets, and polychrome embroidery at the scalloped neck. He was clean-shaven, save for a thread of ginger moustache, astonishingly symmetrical for the period, and his hair glinted with polished lard. He had at least four teeth.

'Good morning,' he said. 'Edward the Smart, from head office.'

The manager and his assistant cringed expertly backwards. 'Sir,' they murmured, 'sir.'

Edward the Smart waved the deference away with one heavily ringed hand, while the other raised a large leather-bound book it had been holding and laid it on their table.

'We have noticed up head office,' he said, 'that Shaftesbury is into a disappointing situation tradewise. In short, as of this moment in time, you have shifted sod-all.'

'It is always a bit quiet after a war, Edward the Smart, sir,' mumbled the manager. 'People want to be dead sure the pillaging etcetera has finished before rushing into property.'

'E.g.,' added his assistant, keenly.

'Yes, well, be that as it may,' said the man from head office, 'we have something we wish for you to run up the flagpole.'

The manager narrowed his imperceptible brows.

'Is it a concept?' he asked. 'Is it red-hot and chic?'

Edward the Smart looked at him, and knuckled his moustache smooth.

'It is called advertising,' he said. 'We have just invented it.'

'Is it like cream sauce?' enquired the assistant, eager to commend himself. 'Is it like snails' legs? Is it e.g.?'

Edward the Smart opened the big book. The page was blank.

'This is what we call the *Domesday Book*. It is a property guide. It goes free to everybody earning more than two pounds per annum.'

'The rich get everything,' muttered Egwyne.

'On each page,' continued the man from head office, 'William & Bastards will advertise a desirable property to the discerning buyer. Now, what can we put in from the Shaftesbury branch?'

'We got a four-bob rat-infested drum in the middle of a haunted wood,' said the manager. 'That's about it.'

'Better write down three-and-six,' said his assistant. 'No point misleading anybody.'

Edward the Smart looked at him for a very long time. Finally he said:

'Do you have a written specification of this item?'

The manager produced a crumpled note, licked a cheese-crumb off it, and handed it across. Edward the Smart considered it for a while, hummed a snatch or two of galliard, finally began to write.

'Just in the market,' he said aloud, quill darting, 'a bijou cottage-style residence in the midst of a fine wooded country estate, magnificently located beside a lush water-meadow supporting a truly rich profusion of wild life. The house itself is wholly original and constructed from local materials to blend perfectly with its environment, and requires only a touch of sympathetic decoration to create a magnificent rural retreat that is, nevertheless, being secluded but not isolated, within easy reach of all amenities. The superb woods which go with the property are rich in local legend, and offer a mature aspect from all windows. Due to bereavement, the present titled owners wish to dispose of the property quickly, a factor reflected by the realistic price of only nine pounds. An early inspection is advised.'

Edward the Smart put down his quill.

The manager was whimpering quietly in the corner.

The assistant licked dry lips.

'Nine pounds?' he croaked, finally, '*nine pounds?*'

Edward the Smart snapped shut his book.

'Yes, I know what you're going to say,' he said, 'but if it *does* turn out to be underpriced and we get a few nibbles, we can always withdraw it, bung it in at auction, and crank it up a bit on the day, could go as high as a tenner. I take it you have a false beard and something to wave?'

And with that, he was gone.

Slowly, the manager pulled himself together and hobbled to the window.

'Tell you a funny thing,' he said, 'his legs haven't gone little. What do you suppose that means?'

The assistant thought for a while.

'That he's Old Nick?' he said.

'E.g.,' replied the manager.

49

Red Sales in the Sunset

Sun Guiying, a middle-aged woman chicken farmer, was given the full propaganda treatment in China's Press yesterday as a heroine of the new peasant elite. This year she has sold more than 492,800 eggs.

Her family's profit was said to be £12,486 sterling and so she was entitled to the ultimate accolade − she was given permission to become Peking's first peasant to own a car.

Daily Telegraph

A saffron hangnail of moon rose gently over Dao Deng Hua, tinting the corrugated roofs of its serried coops. Inside, ten thousand chickens, ranked like feathered kebabs upon their alloy perches, let out one last staccato choral cluck, and settled, knackered, for the night.

In the village Hall Of Egg Norm Victory And Reciprocal Criticism, five hundred peasants packed the wooden benches no less formally, but far more excitedly: five hundred eager faces shone above the collars of their dropping-spattered smocks, a thousand rapt and gleaming eyes targeted in on the little raised platform, a thousand hands ignored the decadent speculation as to the sound of one of them clapping and set up a keen and rhythmic beat, as the dais party filed up the steps, and took their seats.

Sun Guiying was, naturally, the last. She did not sit. The applause rose to an echoing crescendo, bringing flakes of cheap eau-de-nil distemper fluttering down from the trembling ceiling so that, for a brief time-warped moment, she became a demure virgin in an old T'ang frieze, teased by encircling butterflies.

'We welcome,' said the Chairman, as the cheering at last died down, 'egg heroine Sun Guiying, who—'

'So sorry to be 47.9 seconds late,' interrupted the heroine, bowing slightly, first to the Chairman, then to the audience, 'but these Toyotas are buggers when it comes to cold starting. If throttle-pedal over-depressed, automatic choke flood carburettor. Soon I chop it in, get Merc 450 SEL, gimme that Stuttgart fuel injection every time!'

Below her, jaws dropped open, the bright eyes glazed. What hens were these, of which the heroine spake? What was the black smear on her nose? Why, above all, was she wearing string-backed gloves? Faster egg-handling? Antibeak protection? In the depths of the hall, a small man stood up, shyly, and took off his cap.

'Egg heroine Sun Guiying,' he said, 'we, the comrade-soldier-villagers of Dao Deng Hua, congratulate you on the triumphant sale of 492,800 eggs! What is your expert advice to all those who aspire, humbly, to achieve such figures? Is it a question of enriched grit, or perhaps—'

'Get them to throw in loose covers,' replied Sun Guiying briskly. 'That is my advice. Do not let them fob you off with standard PVC upholstery, you would not believe how your bum slides about when drifting through the Nu Hau Heng roundabout, I bloody nearly wrote her off, there was this yo-yo in a clapped-out Su Shiu 205 tractor, fortunately I was able to take him on the inside, these people should not be allowed on road, also, since you raise question, do not take delivery before they have modified suspension, this is a factory job, the Toyota has tendency to rear-end lightness, at present I have compensated for this by sticking two hundredweight millet-sacks in boot, but this is only stop-gap measure since what you are doing is forcing weight down onto aft wishbone, this has knock-on drag effect on rear differential, plus sump banging on road, hence oil on nose, I have very likely shredded a gasket, the stuff is seeping from the bell-housing like loose bowel motion from broody pullet, next question?'

There was a long pause, punctuated by sporadic snores and the odd whimper. Several members of the audience had begun reading *Gizzard Parasite Leaflet Number 86*. In one of the darker corners, two elderly pluckers were huddled over a Mah Jong board, normally a hanging offence. At last, the Chairman himself said:

'Glorious poultry exemplar Sun Guiying, your dazzling achievement shames us all. I should like to begin tonight's dialectical proceedings by pointing the finger at myself. What have I been doing wrong?

'You have been cycling in the middle of the road,' replied Sun Guiying, 'you dozy old sod. What are you?'

'I am a dozy old sod,' muttered the Chairman.

'Do you think you own the road?'

'Yes I think I own the road.'

Sun Guiying turned from the Chairman to the audience.

'How many other cyclists here think they own the road?'

Gradually, some sixty per cent of the hall rose slowly and sheepishly to its feet.

'ALL CYCLISTS THINK THEY OWN THE ROAD!' shouted the heroine.

One by one, the rest of the audience stood up.

'ALL CYCLISTS THINK THEY OWN THE ROAD!' they shouted back, and sat down again.

'It may interest you to know,' said Sun Guiying, straightening her nylon rally-jacket and sending the highlights skating across her heavy bust, 'that it can take up to one hundred metres to stop car travelling at 100 kph *in normal conditions*, let alone eggs all over road, bloody chickens running off pavement without warning, droppings everywhere, it is like a skating rink, does anyone have any idea what I am driving on?'

An elderly lady, nudged to her feet by her front-row neighbours, stood up, hung her head, wept, banged her frail breast.

'No one has any idea what you are driving on, triumphant egg champion hero,' she sobbed. 'Forgive us.'

'Mixed radials and cross-ply is what I am driving on!' shrieked Sun Guiying. 'Also two with canvas showing, one with pork-pellet plug, due to no bloody stocks up distributor, car is damned death-trap, got no toe-in, got no down-line tracking, and suddenly road full of cycling nerds wandering all over shop, have you ever costed out wing-dent repair, beat out, rub down, apply four coats metallic to match in, replace chrome trim, mastic metal-to-metal edge, re-underseal wheel-arch, make good?'

'No!' cried the old lady, and ran from the hall, scattering feathers, to hurl herself into a freezing slipper-bath, shave her head, and begin her fast.

The Chairman watched her go.

'Are we to get rid of the bicycles, incredible egg-producing paragon?' he murmured.

'And the eggs,' said Sun Guiying.

'AND THE *EGGS?*' howled the audience.

'No question,' replied Sun Guiying.

The Chairman bit his knuckle. One did not incautiously oppose a Heroine Of The Peasant Elite, an Idol Of The Glorious Press, a Mega-Egg Producer upon whom the great sun of the Central Committee had specifically directed a major beam. He cleared his throat.

'And what, then, shall we produce?' he murmured.

'Droppings,' answered Sun Guiying.

'Chicken droppings?' croaked the Chairman.

'Are there any other kind?' said Sun Guiying. 'We shall sterilise the chickens and put them on a laxative diet, and from the droppings we shall manufacture methane, and on the methane we shall run the car. That is the way of the future! That is what progress is all about!'

The Chairman sank to his chair again, and dropped his head in his hands.

'You cannot have poached droppings on toast,' he muttered.

Sun Guiying looked at him and the audience looked at her; the dialectic had reached, surely, an insuperable crux? The heroine, however, merely smiled, strangely; and when she spoke, her voice was throaty, quivering, full of dreams.

'True,' she said. 'But then again, you cannot go round Silverstone on an egg.'

50

Cave Canem

Dog left to live alone in council house

By James O'Brien

Mick, a 15-year-old Labrador, has been sole occupant of a three-bedroom council house for three years. The house, described as 'the most luxurious dog kennel in Britain,' has recently been modernised by the council at a cost of £6,500.

The dog has had the run of the house since his master, George Chapman, 65, went to live with his daughter to recover from injuries received in a road accident.

Neighbours let Mick out for a run each day and take his two meals a day into the house in Langton Place, Hilston, Wolverhampton.

Daily Telegraph

I knocked on the tastefully pastelled door in Langton Place, and, after some scuffling, it opened.
'Good morning,' I said.
'It's these door handles,' said the dog. 'Take all bloody day, round knobs. You wouldn't credit how many times I been up the Public Works Department. All they say is, brassette spheres with satinette finish is standard. I told 'em they ought to come up Langton Place and try opening the bloody door with their teeth, never mind standard.' He sat down

suddenly in the hall, and truffled noisily for a flea. 'What I'm after,' he said, after his muzzle re-emerged from his greying groin, 'is a straightforward handle – up, down, catch my drift?'

'I can see your difficulty,' I said.

''Course you can, 'course you can,' said the dog. 'I can tell you're not Council. For one thing, you speak dog.'

'Just a smattering,' I said. 'Un petit peu.'

'Trouble is,' said the dog, 'they're mostly Pakis up the Council, know what I mean? Come over here, push people around, can't even speak the bloody language. Prob'ly never seen a dog, except on a plate, follow my meaning?'

'I really don't think they—'

'Or Irish. I don't know what's worse, sometimes.' He trotted past me, and cocked a leg against the footscraper, decorously. 'I got this file of bloody letters, all signed by Seamus something-or-other, file this high, about my post-war credits, I can't make head nor tail of 'em.'

'Post-war credits?' I said. 'But surely—'

'Don't stand on the mat,' said the dog. 'Come in.'

He trotted up the hall. I followed.

'Excuse the mess,' he said, 'I got the men in. About blooming time, I don't mind saying, you'd think they could take out a low-flush avocado suite in less than a fortnight, wouldn't you?'

'You didn't like it?'

'Like it? *Like* it? *Avocado?* Where are we, 1965? It's desert sand, this year. Or possibly apricot. You wouldn't catch me drinking out of an avocado bog, sunshine, there's such a thing as standards, or am I wrong?' He sat up suddenly on his hind legs. 'You wouldn't have a Jaffa cake on you?'

I felt in my pockets, for form's sake.

'Sorry,' I said.

He dropped to all fours again.

'I get sick of a tinned diet,' he said. 'Bloody neighbours, PDSA, old ladies, all they can think of is Fidochunks or Choochinosh or whatever it is, them tall wobbly cylinders, could be anything, jellied mule, extruded whale-gland, don't ask me. See this coat?'

'Very nice,' I said.

'Not what you'd call glossy, though, is it?' snapped the dog. 'Not what might be described as shining with inner health? Suffering from a serious lack of fillet steak, is my diagnosis. Advanced case of no bleeding lamb chops since I don't know when. Sometimes I wonder what this country's coming to, know what I mean? I been up the Council three times about my diet, all they offer is supplementary benefits, don't come to more'n couple of kidneys a week, half a pound of mince, it's not fit for a, for a—'

He broke off, wheeled suddenly on his own tail, rooted frenziedly, relaxed.

'You ought to go up them executive homes past the bus garage,' he growled, 'I seen poodles up there, chihuahuas, afghans, all kinds of foreign rubbish, you name it, bows in their hair, snouts down in a monogrammed dish of Vesta beef stroganoff, if you don't mind. Sometimes,' he muttered, baring a yellow fang, 'I wonder who won the war.'

There was the sound of hammering from the back garden. The dog trotted to the kitchen door. He nosed it open, and began barking furiously. The two workmen backed down the muddy lawn, bearing a blush-pink lavatory between them.

'So I should think,' said the dog, coming back. 'I never heard such a row. You'd think they could remove a seat without serious inconvenience to the householder. Rubbish, is what they employ up the Council these days. Micks, mainly.'

'That, I take it, is your new lavatory pan?'

'Right. But is it apricot? Is it buggery! Autumn rose, that is. They'll palm you off with anything.'

'Why,' I enquired, perhaps a little faintly, given the circumstances in which the interview now found itself, 'are they removing the lid?'

The tenant snorted.

'Easy to see you never been a dog,' he said. 'Get up in the night, raging thirst, nip out for a bit of a lap, last thing you want is the lid coming down on your head.'

'The Council,' I murmured, 'seem to have been fairly accommodating.'

The dog turned a terrible ochre eye on me.

'I had to bite the Clerk of Works twice before they'd even look at me,' he snarled. 'I don't call that accommo-dating. I was stuck in that waiting room a good twenty minutes. Also, they tried to palm me off with a quarter of Good Boy drops. Treat you like dirt,' said the dog, 'if you're unemployed.'

'Well, I hardly—'

'Course, if I was a *zebra*, werl!' said the dog, sourly. 'If I was a zebra, if I was an *antelope*, stuck up Rome airport, they'd all be running round like bloody lunatics trying to sort it out, am I right? Television, papers, questions in Parliament, you name it.' He dropped to his belly, put his head on his forepaws, stared across the lino. 'They look after their own, Pakis,' he muttered.

Since it was time, I felt, to change the subject, I said:

'You mentioned post-war credits, I don't *quite* see how you, er, qualify. I understand you're fifteen?'

The dreadful eyes glanced up from the floor.

'As a *dog*, I am fifteen,' he said. 'I never said I wasn't fifteen, and here's my point, *as a dog*. But what you are forgetting, what the Council is forgetting, is that in human terms that equals seventy-five, I am actually a poor old sod of seventy-five currently being screwed by the Thatcherite Nazis out of what is rightfully mine. I fought the war against that kind of thing. Or,' he added, 'I would have done.'

'You *were* born in 1964,' I pointed out, I thought, gently.

The dog sprang to his feet.

'Oh, excuse *me!*' he barked. 'I did not realise I was in the presence of Magnus bleeding Magnusson. I was not aware that an attempt to baffle an unfortunate geriatric in the twilight of his years was under way.' His mouth opened, and I realised, with sudden unease, that the serried incisors were between me and the door. 'You are not, by any chance, from the Council after all?' enquired the dog, with nasty sarcasm. 'You would not care to nip upstairs and have a little snoop as to whether I am living in sin or perhaps running a small manufacturing business in the back bedroom?'

'I apologise,' I replied quickly, 'it was honest curiosity, merely, I do assure— you watch *Mastermind*, then? How very inter—'

'Only,' muttered the dog, 'in black and white. Also, the vertical hold's up the spout. Picture's like a slot in a letterbox. Peter Woods looks like Chu Chin bloody Chow. Know how many times I been up the Council about that?'

'Well, I—'

'There's dogs in this town with *three* colour sets at their disposal,' snapped the tenant. 'We are two nations, as Disraeli so succinctly put it; for a Jew, anyway.'

'Nevertheless,' I said, taking my courage firmly in both hands, 'for an obviously deeply concerned social democrat—'

'Absolutely,' nodded the dog, 'definitely.'

'—you seem oddly unconcerned, if I might say so, about the fact that you have been living for three years in a three-bedroomed Council house, modernised for six-and-a-half thousand pounds, when the Council waiting-list contains the names of four thousand families, most of them with small children. Does that not, perhaps, leave you feeling somewhat uneasy?'

The tenant's teeth bared again, whether in a smile or a snarl it was impossible to say.

'In this world, sunshine,' he said, 'it's dog eat dog.'

The Cricklewood Years
1990–1999

A.A. GILL

Introduction

This isn't going to be funny. The first rule of comedy is: 'No, we're not to be funny.' Actually that's the second rule of comedy. The first rule is: 'Be funny.' No . . . as you were, that's the first footnote of comedy. The first rule is: 'Learn how to be funny.'

Whoever said that the first rule of comedy is timing was either an actor or a subeditor, a brace of callings that are Bell's palsy to humour. This isn't going to be funny because I know the rules; I know when not to compete. You don't want to follow Shakespeare in a sonnet karaoke, or Motley Crue into an orgy, and you really don't want to drop a stream of fey drollery into the collected works of Alan Coren. I know my limits, and I know my place. I'm here to introduce the next act, say something nice and get off.

The fourth, or perhaps the fifth, rule of comedy is: 'Always be funny for a reason.' There is nothing so happy-sapping as the unattached purposeless joke, and that was what always made Alan Coren's newspaper columns so readable, so insinuatingly, quietly memorable; they were never just comedy calories, there was always a context. Often – no, usually – the seed, the grit of the homily, was so small, so faint, that you barely noticed it. It would sit in your frontal lobe's in-tray for the rest of the day and grow a green shoot of an idea, or a pearl of wisdom, depending on whether you got the seed or the grit.

There is in this section a column that I reckon is an almost perfect example of the humorist's craft. Not least because it manages to get 'concatenation' into the first sentence without a 'by your leave' or 'excuse me'. It's about crisps and Gatling guns. How it gets from crisps to Gatling guns, by way of an Italian driving school, is a small master class in the long and classy tradition of the English humorous essay. It moves with an effortless nonchalance, a saunter, without apparent destination or point. And only when you get to the end can you look back and see that it is as finely constructed, as pristinely pleasing, as a wren's nest in an Elizabethan knot garden.

The first tradition of the tradition is that we all pretend there is absolutely nothing to humorous writing, that it's a negligible parlour trick, a piece of amateur patter, an effervescent sleight of mind. Well, let me just this once tell you that no tradition had ever been harder-honed, or more diligently practised, polished and delivered with a lethal accuracy, than Coren's. The sticky-palmed pianist cracking his knuckles as he faces the sheer precipice of Rachmaninov's Third needs no less technical skill and dexterity than the comic columnist staring at the glacier of the blank A4 on a Monday morning.

Coren was a craftsman, not an artist. Artists are excitable men with extempore facial hair who beat their mistresses, leave their children destitute and their agents millionaires. An artist makes a unique thing every so often, a craftsman produces things of the same quality over and over by 4.30 on press day. Alan wrote to a standard that rarely varied by the girth of a semi-colon. I could at this point tell you about the perfect pitch of his ear for a rhythm and the mouth-feel of words, his prestigious ability to hug-a-mug colloquialisms with baroque elucidation, the elegance with which he would cast a sentence to make it curl and curve in the air before dropping the feathered hook precisely where he wanted it. I could tell you about the eye for the absurd and the nose for irony – one of the most difficult things to pass off in print. I could dissect all that, but let's just continue with the traditional pretence that it's all an amateur hobby.

The 1990s were a foolish, cruel and boastful decade that was made for Alan Coren's particular view. Remember the idiotic fuss about the Millennium? The sugared dome of New Labour? It was all fields of corn for Coren. We might call these The Cricklewood Years, the low view through the letterbox from the suburbs. Of course it was a front, a conceit. Of course really it was Chaucer, Swift, Cobbett, Pepys, Jerome, McDonnell and Wodehouse, posing as Mr Pooter and Mr Polly. Alan's column in *The Times* was generally to be found in the Thunderer's comments and editorial page, and it would invariably have the startled look of a chap who's turned up in his tennis flannels at a white-tie dinner. Surrounded by the stentorian stuffed shirts, he would make his sideways discursive point with that characteristic tone of a man who finds a naked duchess in his garden, but notices that she's standing on the begonias. And then he'd cut along home for cheese on toast, because craftsmen are generally happily married and pass their trade on to their children.

It is a wry and blissful irony that you're holding Alan's humbly passed-off thoughts here; it is they that have been collected for posterity, while the louder spittle-flecked diatribes of strident opinion have long since been recycled as crisp packets and that chaff they annoyingly stuff into padded envelopes.

It's all here in this concatenation, that rare and very English parochially homespun ability to see the world in a grain of sand, and a universe in Cricklewood.

51

Here We Go Round the Prickly Pear

I have nothing against poetry. If it were not for poetry, Postman Pat would have a black-and-white dog.

Poets, however, are another matter. While I derive much joy from what they do for a living, primarily because of the manner in which they do it, when they deploy this manner where it has no business, I derive no joy at all. I go up the wall. I kick things about. For, though I relish the ellipsis and elusiveness of poetry, though I am more than happy to tangle with the ambiguity, the obliqueness, even the downright inaccessibility which poets needs must bring to their tricky trade, I abhor their apparent inability to talk straight when straight talking is required. Never ask a poet what a spade is; you will be there all night.

Oo-er, I hear you murmur, something has clearly upset him today, he is normally the most equable of men. His wick must have something major on it. We are entitled to an explanation.

Let us go then, you and I, to the works of T.S. Eliot. Not to the wondrous conundrums of his verse, but to a letter he wrote, on 26 April 1911, to his cousin Eleanor Hinkley in Boston. He was 22, and on his first trip to Europe; he had gone to stay in Paris, but decided to nip over to London for a few days, and it is this visit about which he is writing. Here is the nub, both of his letter and of my complaint:

'I was out of doors most of the time. I made a pilgrimage

to Cricklewood. "Where is Cricklewood?" said an austere Englishman at the hotel. I produced a map and pointed to the silent evidence that Cricklewood exists. He pondered. "But why go to Cricklewood?" he flashed out at length. Here I was triumphant. "There is no reason!" I said. He had no more to say. But he was relieved (I am sure) when he found out that I was American. He felt no longer responsible. But Cricklewood is mine. I discovered it. No one will go there again. It is like the sunken town in the fairy story, that rose just every May-day eve, and only one man saw it.'

Is it any wonder that as I stumbled upon that paragraph in my nice new *Letters of T.S. Eliot* yesterday I trembled with anticipation? Nor any less wonder that as I came to the end of that paragraph and found it was all that Eliot had to say about Cricklewood, I trembled, now, with rage? For God's sake, Tom, what did you *mean*? Why 'pilgrimage' – what did you know beforehand? More to the point, what did you know afterwards? Why is Cricklewood yours, what did you discover, why is it like the sunken town in the fairy story?

A terrible urge came on me to chuck the book in the bin; here was the century's greatest poet, certainly the greatest ever to fall for Cricklewood, offering me nothing of which I could make head or tail. Why could he not come right out and say what made my backyard so magical, so worth not merely a detour, but a pilgrimage? Why couldn't he have bunged Eleanor a simple postcard, *Here I am in fabulous Cricklewood, bloody ace, Guinness is tuppence a gallon, you never saw such big whelks, no bedbugs to speak of and I have to beat the women off with a stick, hoping this finds you as it leaves me, in the pink, T.S. Eliot?*

I did not, however, bin the book, I went instead to fetch another, for something had occurred to me; only two months after visiting Cricklewood, Eliot finished his first major work, *The Love Song of J. Alfred Prufrock.* Since he had fiddled and fussed with it for years, what might have spurred him, suddenly, past the post? I opened *Collected Poems*.

> Let us go, through certain half-deserted streets,
> The muttering retreats
> Of restless nights in one-night cheap hotels
> And sawdust restaurants with oyster shells:
> Streets that follow like a tedious argument
> Of insidious intent . . .

I closed the book again. I had hitherto believed that the squalid, unnamed town in which J. Alfred murmured his glum monologue was part Baudelaire's Paris, part Dante's Hell. Now, I looked at his letter again. It was as I feared: how had I beguiled myself into believing he had said what I thought he had meant? Why had I imagined it contained one single word to suggest Eliot had actually *liked* Cricklewood?

Between the idea and the reality, falls the Shadow.

52

Uneasy Lies the Head

If for nothing else, today's *feuilleton* will be remarkable for recording the smallest thing ever to go wrong with a house in its owners' absence. Indeed, so confident am I of this claim that if any reader writes to me with a smaller, he will receive, by return of post, a magnum of the finest Toblerone.

I spent the Bank Holiday weekend in Edinburgh, where it turned out not to be a Bank Holiday at all; so that I came home feeling oddly deprived. It was not for some time that I discovered the yet odder depths to which deprivation may plummet.

It was four hours, to be precise; which is precisely what I can be. I know that my key turned in the lock at 3 p.m., because I heard the cuckoo clock in the kitchen observe this; just as I know that it was 7 p.m. when I discovered what I discovered, because I was in the kitchen itself at the time, slicing the lemon for the yard-arm gin, and when the clock cuckooed, I looked up.

Owners of clocks of the order *cuculidae* will not need an explanation for this, but the rest of you might be thunderstruck to learn that that is what you do if you are in a room with one at any time after five o'clock. Up until five o'clock, the number of cries registers in the head, but after that time you have no idea how many it is, and you have to look up at the clock to see what hour it is.

I looked up just in time to see the little door shutting. And, in the nanosecond before it did, to note that what it was shutting on was not the cuckoo.

I walked across to the clock, prised open the door with my forefinger, and peered into the cuckoo's premises. It was not there. It had flown its tiny coop. To make doubly sure, I forefingered the minute-hand around to eight o'clock: the door burst open, the voice cried eight times, but what leapt out on each of these eight occasions was nought but a wobbling spring. The cuckoo was not on the end of it.

Where had it gone? And why? Had it, perhaps, in ecstasy at finding it had the house to itself, hurtled so joyously from its cavity that it had detached itself from its tiny umbilicus? Or heard, maybe, the rumour of a sparrow-clock somewhere, and gone off to lay an egg in it?

Unlikely. It is, in truth, only half a cuckoo. It is little more than a head on a spring. I cannot speak for more expensive clocks, it may well be that the Swiss houses of parliament sport a giant example which hourly lurches from its penthouse atop Big Bird intact in every particular, but mine, sadly, does not have the wherewithal to parturiate. It does not even have legs. It could not have gone far. I searched the kitchen floor. Nothing.

Had a clockwork cat got in?

I wondered if the head might have fallen off not forwards at all, but backwards. It could be lying on the floor of the works, struggling ventriloquially every time the spring sprang out. It dawned upon me that Wordsworth must have suffered similar horological shock; nothing else could explain so awful a line as 'O Cuckoo! Shall I call thee bird, or but a wandering voice?' It is exactly what the old fool would have cried upon walking into Dove Cottage to find himself confronted with a headless chime.

I took the clock from the wall, and removed the back,

appropriately enough, with my Swiss Army knife. Exactly, I'm sure, what the Swiss Army would have done in the circumstances. The head was not inside.

Three days have now passed, and some 50 phone calls. Can you believe that there is not a spare cuckoo head to be found anywhere in these islands? I tried this morning to fashion one from Plasticine, with a little matchstick beak, but it was too heavy, it lumbered out on the first cry, hung dangling over the clockface, and refused to go back until manhandled.

I do not know what to do. I may have to junk the clock. The kitchen is below my bedroom, I hear the cry in the small hours, and I would swear a derisory note has crept into it. They do change their tune, you know.

53

Salt in the Wound

I experienced a remarkable concatenation yesterday. I had
gone to the Italian Driving School in Clerkenwell Road
to make an enquiry on a friend's behalf (sensitively
refraining from making any on my own, despite burning to
know about the teaching of Italian driving, eg how to steer
with your chin so that you can simultaneously keep the hooter
depressed and leave both hands free, one to shake its fist, the
other to raise its central finger), and when I came out again,
I found myself a bit peckish, so I bought a packet of Smith's
potato crisps.

I strolled on, thinking of nothing in particular, when I
chanced to notice a blue plaque, high up on a redbrick wall
at the corner of Hatton Garden, attesting to the curious fact
that Sir Hiram Maxim (1840–1916), inventor of the machine-
gun, had lived there.

That is the kind of information which suddenly makes one
think of something in particular. While I already knew a bit
about the great man – including the tragedy wherein a
malicious Fate cruelly snatched him away in June, robbing
him by only a few short days of the chance to see his greatest
masterpiece, the First Battle of the Somme – I had no idea
that this was where he had hung his hat. How tolerant landladies
must have been, then! Not to mention the people in the flat
downstairs; but, then again, you might think twice, might you

not, before banging on the ceiling and thereby getting on the wrong side of a man who had just been practising at 500 rounds a minute?

These and similar woolgatherings having brought me to the end of the packet of crisps, I looked for a wastebin; and that I could not immediately spot one was what brought on the remarkable concatenation. I put the empty bag back in my pocket, where it remained until I got into the bus on Farringdon Road and dug for change. The bag was now in my hand again, where, by sheer chance, a word leapt off it and into my eye, the way this word, as I may have mentioned before, will. On the top right-hand corner of the packet, this legend ran: 'Frank Smith sold Britain's first crisps to the pubs of Cricklewood. The salt-cellars he provided vanished as fast as the crisps. The little blue twist of salt was his ingenious solution.'

Well I never. I mean, literally. Twenty years in Cricklewood, and I had never caught whiff nor whisper of our greatest son: for how else was one to describe a man who had invented not only the crisp, but also the little bag of salt to be a helpmeet for it? This was major genius. It was as if the Earl of Sandwich had come up with the pickled onion. Research was urgently called for. And when, an hour later, I rang Smith's (or as it now is, *eheu fugaces*, PepsiCo Foods International), one who still remembers the old days remembered them for me.

In 1920, Frank Smith was a young Cricklewood grocer, left to mind the shop while his employer holidayed in France. When the employer returned, he brought with him a wondrous tale of a little French restaurant where he had been served with thinly-sliced fried potatoes. He then got back to doing what employers do, leaving Frank to do what geniuses do. Geniuses have a bit of a think. After which, they remove their apron, politely hand in their notice, pop round to a bank manager whom they have circumspectly ensured never went short of a nice bit of gammon even in the darkest days of the recent hostilities, and buy the lease on a rundown Cricklewood garage which the instinct of genius tells them is just the place to begin manufacturing potato crisps.

How could it fail? It did not. The only commercial setback was that as Cricklewood's boozers fell upon Smith's delectable invention, they ungratefully nicked the saltpots he had loaned them. Smith, however, was up to that. Smith took fresh guard. The answer was in the bag.

I put the phone down, and dried my eyes, and drove to where the original garage used to be. It is now a B & Q superstore. I trekked its every wall, but there was nothing to show. What an odd world it is that reveres the machine-gun but not the crisp! Surely it is time to offer the honour of a small blue plaque? Preferably one with a twist in it.

54

Good God, That's Never The Time? (2)

Fifty-two? No age, they said. Fifty-two? *These* days? No age! They said it all day Wednesday. Rang up, dropped in, brought presents, popped corks, filled the premises with cheery cards (albeit mainly about impotence and coffins), shouted, through clouds of marzipan crumbs, what Gladstone did at 87, what Picasso did at 83, what Rubinstein did at 88.

Convinced me utterly. Despite what, after 50, has become the annual shock of seeing it written down, I did not feel what 52 sounded as if one should feel like. After tea, I went over to the club and played three sets without dying, and it was one of those good days when the Fate who handles the fortuity portfolio allows the ball to coincide with the racquet more often than not, and you think, *Bring me Ivan! Bring me Boris!*, and you jog home feeling good, despite the little bird trilling beside you to the effect that even if they were to bring you Fred Perry, you'd be going back on a stretcher.

And when what was lowered into the subsequent bath appeared to displace no more water than it had done when its digits were in reverse order, and when its glottis proved still competent to handle *Ol' Man River* without a quiver at either end of the register, and when its teeth stood up to the Extra Hard without the hint of a wobble, and especially when it sloshed on its new skin bracer, tautening each incipient wrinkle to the sleekness of a snare-drum, could it not be forgiven for murmuring to itself: '52? No age!'

So I skipped downstairs, and I decanted lunch's dissimilar dregs into a single tumbler with that nonchalance which springs from the conviction that 52 is no age for a liver, either, and I set about tearing wrappers from the rest of my presents with these amazingly youthful fingers I have, and, oh what fun!, someone had given me a video called *1938: A Year To Remember*.

I put it on. It was a compilation of Pathé newsreels. Black and white, of course. No colour newsreels, then. And who is this, stepping out of a piston-engined item at what the commentator, in his jovial cut-glass accent, tells me is an aerodrome? The chap is waving a piece of paper. He has a wing-collar on. He is surrounded by photographers in three-piece suits. They keep removing bulbs from what look like frying-pans. The commentator is very happy. 'This is the greatest diplomatic triumph of modern times!' he cries.

And what's this? The scene has changed. 'A new giant of the sky is floating into the mist on its maiden flight!' This is September 1938. I am already on strained solids. I am older than the Graf Zeppelin.

Oh, look, here comes sport. Wimbledon finals day. Men leaping about in long trousers. 'And so we say farewell to Bunny Austin!' Tonight, it will be Donald Budge leading Helen Wills Moody on to the parquet. What will they murmur, as they waltz decorously at arm's length? That they would be able to go home on the Queen Elizabeth, if only it had been launched? Oh, look, there it is being launched now. Not the QE2, of course. There wasn't anyone to name a QE2 after, yet, except that little girl running about.

That's her father, now, on a beach, surrounded by small boys. He is singing 'Ooja! Ooja! Rub A Dub A Dub!' It makes a change from trekking round council estates. 'Their majesties go into humble homes!' shrieks the commentator. 'This Hoxton house is 12 shillings a week!'

There is a child outside, in a pram. I crane: could it be? Too late, here is Hutton knocking up 364, here is a flying-boat inaugurating the England–Australia run, here is six-year-old Teddy Kennedy opening the Children's Zoo, here is Gracie, singing as we go, here is Englishman Dick Seaman winning the German grand prix in what appears to be a Mercedes soap-box car. Dick has a swastika round his neck.

The End. And, at that exact moment, a Lancaster thrums overhead, rattling the sashes, and I run outside just in time to see it, flanked by a Spitfire and a Hurricane. How nice of Tom King to lay it on, if a little *de trop*. It's not as if I'm 90, or anything, like the Queen Mother.

Just 52. No age, these days. Hardly older than a Lancaster.

55

Japanese Sandmen

I have returned to Cricklewood to find that our local futon centre has closed down. I realize that, in the great roster of homecoming trauma, this ranks somewhere below Odysseus's dog dropping dead or Scarlett's discovery that Tara is going to need a bob or two spent on fixtures and fittings, but nevertheless it has come as a considerable shock.

Not because the closure spells, I suspect, the end of some sort of era, nor even because, in the nine years during which I have driven past it every day, the futon centre has become a much-loved feature of the landscape, but because I never once, in all those thousands of days, stopped and walked into it to find out what a futon was. I shall never walk into it now, and I shall never know.

Mind you – were I to be utterly honest – I cannot be certain that I should ever have plucked up the courage to do it. The time for asking what a futon was passed some years ago. You have to be quick off the blocks with fad-enquiries, if you do not wish to sound like a high court judge looking up from his jotting quill to enquire of the clerk what a hula-hoop is when it's at home. Even in the matter of bedding: I asked what a duvet was as soon as I heard the word, and to this day I get cold shudders when I think of the ridicule a week's delay would have invited. As for futons, one morning they did not exist, and the next morning, it seemed, everyone except me was banging on about them with remarkable authority. Since I tended to sidle away from these conversations in case I was exposed, I never did discover what they were, and soon everyone had stopped discussing them and gone on to cellphones and gravad lax, and it was too late.

Now, lest you begin to think me so untouchable a nerd that the authority of this entire opus is undermined, I should quickly say that I know *roughly* what a futon is. I can drag the new *OED* from its shelf as deftly as the next Waterstone browser, and I can read that a futon is a Japanese bed-quilt. This of course tells me nothing at all. Nor do the two quotations the OUP has dug up to endorse this definition, although they go back an astonishing long way for a fad, to 1876 and 1886 respectively. The first, taken from the *Transactions of the Asiatic Society of Japan*, cites: 'Those who are tired of tinned meats and live futons', and the second, attributed to one E.S. Morse, says: 'The futons, or comforters, are hung over the balcony rail to air.'

I quote these arcana in their entirety. It is obvious that both Mr Morse and the Hon Sec of the ASJ were devout Nipponophiles attempting to curry face by showing that the round-eyes, too, are dab hands when it comes to banging out impenetrable *haikus*. I have little doubt that the latter gobbet does not mean what it superficially appears to say at all, and probably refers to the insolence of princes or something, and as for the former, it is a yen to a threepennybit that you could sit 50 structuralists in front of their decoders till Doomsday and they would never even come close.

No, when I say I do not know what futons are, I do not mean I do not know they are some kind of Japanese bedding (I have, after all, caught glimpses of them in the now-whitewashed window these nine years past); I mean that I do not know what is special about them. I have no idea what futonness comprises. What is the essence of its difference from a posture-sprung Slumberland, a chaise-longue, a hammock? Why, on that bright confident morning a decade ago, did everyone who was anyone, from Campden Hill to Tuscany, suddenly and simultaneously become excited by them?

I suppose it sprang from our peculiar conviction that Oreintals have cracked the secret of relaxation. They do go on about it rather a lot. Five minutes in the lotus position, a couple of mantras, a quick tot of ginseng, a pull or two on the old Zen bow, and then into the futon for a good night's kip and next morning you're fresh as a daisy.

That may be *onto* the futon, of course, or under it, or even between them, if they come in twos; I wouldn't know, and I very much doubt, now, that I ever shall.

56

Card Index

I have received a Christmas card from a dog.
When I first drew it from the envelope, I did not think
it had been sent by a dog, I thought it had been sent by
a human being who had bought a Christmas card with a dog
on it. I did not think it was much of a card, mind, because
the photograph of the dog was not much of a photograph.
The head of the dog was all right, but the far end of the dog
was a bit out of focus, and the house beyond the far end of
the dog was not only even more out of focus, it was wonky
as well. This was not a photograph at all, it was a snapshot.

None of which is to say that it mightn't have been a
professional Christmas card. It is quite hard to tell, these days,
with so many charities on the go; I have already received a
fair few cards with ill-drawn blobs on the outside and, on the
inside, information about dolphin shelters and acid rain and
the like, and this canine item might very well have been one
such. The dog looked relatively hale, but you never know, it
could have had some psychiatric ailment, and as to the quality
of the snapshot, perhaps it was the best that the Miserable
Dog Trust or whatever could afford. It would be irresponsible
to chuck good money away on Lord Snowdon if the Hon
Sec had an Instamatic.

But when I opened the card, it just said: *Merry Christmas
and a Happy New Year from Bruno* in type, with '. . . and his

humans, too!' added in green ink. No signature, no address. I closed it and looked at the dog again. It was a total stranger. Nor could I identify the fuzzy house. It has a fuzzy car outside it, possibly a Volvo, but it's only a guess.

This kind of thing has been getting worse, over the years. When I was young, people sent one another cards with robins on. They were not in aid of Robin Relief, nor was the bird a family pet whose turn it was to do the cards that year. You opened them, and they said 'Merry Christmas to you and yours from Jim and Millie Nugent, "Erzanmine", Walnut Crescent, Uxbridge'. You knew where you were with cards like that.

But then, instead of the robin, the personalised card came bob-bob-bobbing along. This had the senders on the front, generally two adults you recognised, surrounded by several infants and a cat. As a shorthand method of keeping abreast of events in households you never visited, it served, I suppose, its purpose. As Yules passed, you watched hair fall out, waists thicken, spectacles arrive, children lengthen, cats degenerate. Sometimes the family moved to the country, and a horse joined them. Sometimes they emigrated, and the Eiffel Tower or the Great Barrier Reef materialised behind them.

But, as Yeats used to scribble gloomily on his own cards, things fall apart, the centre cannot hold. A Christmas would come along when you noticed a new baby sitting by the car, and you thought, 'Hallo, they're a bit old for another kid,' and then you looked at the picture again, and it wasn't the same wife as last year. An extreme and deeply unsettling example of all this was the card we had a couple of years back from a man I didn't know at Oxford 30 years ago. He had married the ex-wife of a man I did know at Oxford, and, when she remarried, she was the one who carried on sending cards. These cards had her and her new husband on, plus a couple of new children standing next to her old ones. Then her second marriage broke up and her ex-husband married again, but hung on, apparently, to the old Christmas card list. We now get an annual card from two people we don't know standing next to a lot of big unfathomable children who could belong to almost anybody.

And now we have an unfathomable dog. Why the hell Bruno couldn't have had his surname or address printed, who can say? Might it be some kind of test? People with dogs, I find, expect you to recognise their pets, so it may well be that Bruno's humans have got him to sort out the wheat from the chaff. If they do not receive a card from me in return, my name will be mud.

I can think of only one solution to all this. I shall put a notice in the personal column of *The Times* to the effect that Mr Alan Coren wishes Bruno to know that he will not be sending any cards this year.

57

Brightly Shone The Rain That Night

Boxing Noon, and Hampstead Heath resembles nothing so much as the gale-scattered covers of all those comic annuals ripped yestermorn from their urgent stockings. So many bright new Mickey Mouse gloves! So many bright new Rupert Bear scarves! So many bright new Garfield earmuffs and Kermit boots and Peanuts pullovers! The world, new-laminated, is crying 'Hallo, Chums!' Cavorting gaily in the drizzled gloom, all this iridescent giftery – on adult and child alike – seems to bespeak not so much Christmas as some medieval Haberdasherie Fayre upon which the city's cordwainers and hosiers and mercers and drapers and hatters have descended to propitiate their diverse tutelary gods and flog their latest lines.

It is all so cartoon-jolly that I do not immediately notice that something is missing. What makes me finally notice it is the singularly poignant sight of a small boy sledding down the sodden East Heath slope, towards the Vale of Health. He has new yellow moonboots on, and a new Snoopy flying helmet. He has a new sled. He could be on the cover of the *Beano Annual*, were it not for the one thing he does not have. He does not have snow.

Poor little begger. He is making a valiant fist of it, shoving himself off from just beneath me, lurching down the wet grass, slaloming the bushes with expert toe and mitten, bumping to a halt after a dozen yards, then struggling up again, his mudcaked sled trailing erratically behind him on its sodden string. Had he snow, he would not stop at all, he would hurtle on, shrieking joyously, scattering the pirouetting skaters on Hampstead Pond and finally fetch up, breathless, in Gospel Oak. Because, if he had snow, there would be skaters on Hampstead Pond today, rather than the goosebumped madmen flaunting their traditional braggadocio in the unfrozen ooze.

Maybe, in his head, he has it. The imagination, at seven, is rich. Maybe he goes down the hill with six huskies in front and a pack of wolves behind. Maybe the unflagging effort is all about getting to Gospel Oak before Amundsen. My point (I have just decided) is that he shouldn't have to. He is forced to imagine only because he is forced to compensate for unnecessary disappointment. He should not have been led to expect snow. He should not have torn open his bedroom curtains, immediately after tearing open his sled-wrappings, to have his heart sunk by only drizzle specking the panes.

For two months now, cotton-wool has been his promissory note. He has stared through it at frosted toys, while Muzak jingled sleigh-bells at him. Tempted inside, he has sat on Santa's snow-booted knee, and heard how reindeer struggle through blizzards on behalf of good little boys. All his weekly reading has featured snow-capped mastheads, all the stuff within has occupied itself with snowball fights, thin ice, risible snowmen, and mad dogs happily frozen suddenly solid in the act of going for a newsboy's shin. Everything he has watched on television has ostensibly taken place in arctic conditions, and all anyone has talked about has been the prospect of the white Christmas of which he has been encouraged to dream.

No chance. We have not had a white yule in 20 years, and the odds on our warming globe ever offering one must be incalculably long. This isn't Lapland. Christmas snow is but one more EC standard to which we have let ourselves be hijacked. Is it not time to chuck this damaging delusion in?

What it does here at Christmas is rain. We should make this a meterological virtue. Let us have a British Santa in cheery yellow oilskins and sou'wester, ho-ho-ho-ing through the drizzle in a dory tugged by six big cod. Let fake raindrops twinkle down our shop windows from autumn on, let our cards show robins on floating logs and coaches in flying spray, and each display, advertisement and grotto anticipate the joys of snug dry firesides bonding happily families together against the cats and dogs beyond.

Sing *I'm Dreaming of a Wet Christmas*, Cliff, and let's be done with it.

58

Tuning Up

They came to take the piano on Friday. They brought it down the stairs from the landing where it had stood for 25 years, and it went bong as it hit every step, but not a bong any musician could have put his finger on, because it had been out of tune for 20 of those years, and if you put your finger on it, the notes that came out belonged to it alone.

After they had got it down the stairs, they heaved it on to a little cart to wheel it up the garden path to their van, and I walked behind, though lacking an old cock linnet, to see it off. It was a bit like a cortège. One or two neighbours watched – neighbours always watch a removal van – but they didn't say anything, because there is something about a piano leaving a house that begs discretion. Has the owner gone broke, has he gone deaf, are we watching divorce proceeds being distributed to the musical one?

It was none of these, it was simply that the piano was clapped-out. It had in truth never been very clapped-in; we had bought it for fifty quid in 1972 for the children to learn, but they learnt very little, except that you don't get much of a piano for fifty quid. It then stayed in the upstairs hall so that I could use it to tune my banjo, though as the piano was out of tune, the banjo was warped, and my ear is tin, I was never able to play anything that anybody could recognise, except parts of the slow movement of *Polly Wolly Doodle*.

Musicologists among you may be surprised to learn that *Polly Wolly Doodle* has a slow movement, but that is only because you have not seen my fingering technique. I have to stop after each chord to have a cigarette and work out where to put my fingers for the next one. So, a few days back, I asked a man round to tune the piano, and he said it wasn't worth tuning, let it go.

I came indoors again after they had driven away with my quarter of a century, feeling a bit glum because it seemed as though the piano had been delivered only about five minutes earlier, and I went up to look at the spot where the piano had stood, and there was this amazingly thick oblong of untrodden carpet with a lot of stuff on it which had, over the years, fallen off and behind the piano, snapshots, bits of Lego, marbles, Christmas cards, wizened toffees, an Action Man's head, three light-bulbs, an arrow, what might once have been the newt that climbed out of Victoria's aquarium in, I think, 1980 – and a book.

The book was the fitness manual of the Royal Canadian Air Force. I had never seen it before. I do not know anyone in the RCAF, I hardly even know anyone who is fit, and I could come to no other conclusion than that Giles, at about 10, had decided either to escape piano lessons by running away to Toronto and becoming a fighter pilot, or to get himself fit enough to knock his piano teacher about. And then I opened the book. It was a revelation. It was the fitness book I had been looking for all my life. It said you did not have to go to gyms, jog for miles, buy exercise bikes or rowing machines or weights, you could get fit by answering the telephone or putting your hat on.

Thanks to isometrics. Isometrics was a muscle-stress technique whereby every physical action you took was done with total effort: you lifted a phone as if it weighed a ton, you put your hat on as if Arnold Schwarzenegger were trying to lift it off, with the result that you not only drove blood oxygenated to Bollinger effervescence throughout your body, you also transformed that body into a rippling powerhouse able to see off Canada's enemies without even getting into your plane.

Drawbacks? Social only. I was on the phone when my wife got home, and she was haggard with concern by the time I rang off (what's happened, your knuckles were white, your veins were standing out, you're covered in sweat) and when friends came for bridge on Sunday and I went out between rubbers to get drinks, I could hear their fraught mutters (is he all right, he closed that door as if 2 Para were trying to push it open, he's gripping his cards like a madman, his face went purple during that last contract), but you ignore such things if you're turning yourself into a titan. Any day now, I shall buy another piano, just so the neighbours can watch me carry it indoors.

59

The Queen, My Lord, is Quite Herself, I Fear

The only time I lunched with the Queen, the first words she said to me were, 'Have you any idea what a trial it is to own a golf course?'

I do not remember what I mumbled, but I do remember reflecting that when it came to pre-emptive strikes, my sovereign left Admiral Yamamoto at the post. I had turned up at her palace with my conversational fleet dressed overall, there was not a potential topic I had not buffed to shimmering nick, there was not a drollery unprimed, but she had dived on me out of the sun, and her first wave had devastated me; my battleships were going down by the stern, my carriers were ablaze, and where my submarines had once lurked there were now but pitiable patches of flotsam-dotted oil.

She then launched, while the prawn hung trembling on my fork, into a hilarious account of the shenanigans at her Windsor links, where a demarcation dispute between groundsmen and gardeners had left the fairways unmown. When she had finished, she asked my advice as to her best course of action. I put the prawn down and mumbled something else, drawn this time from my vast experience of owning golf courses, whereupon she said. 'Was there an exact date when workmen stopped wearing boots? You never see boots on workmen any more.'

The whole of, let us call it our conversation, followed this bizarre unpattern, the monarch unfalteringly displaying a surreal penchant so relentlessly nimble it left the clodhopper winded. It was like going ten rounds against a class flyweight trained by René Magritte and managed by P.G. Wodehouse. By the end of three hours, I had pledged my life to her. Here was wackiness of an order so incomparable it must have been hers by divine right. She was barking regal.

Her husband? I had first met him some years before, when as Rector of St Andrews I attended the investiture of Magnus Magnusson as Rector of Edinburgh, where Prince Philip was Chancellor. We were all in the robing room, struggling into our floor-length velvet numbers, when the Consort suddenly cried: 'If we were stark naked under these, nobody would be any the wiser!' He then laughed for a very long time.

It thus came as no surprise to me when, soon after, their son stopped doing Bluebottle impressions and began confiding in flora, leaving me with a conviction rendered all the more unshakeable by the Princess Royal, who when I invited her to a *Punch* lunch and apologised for limping on a swollen knee, said: 'Yes, it's been a ghastly year for equine VD. Did you know it can cause rheumatoid arthritis in jockeys? Everyone's taking phenylbutazone.'

What am I trying to tell you here? Merely that I have been growing daily more irritated by demands for the Royal Family to shape up, remember who they are, and behave accordingly, because my view is that is precisely what they are doing. They are a very odd lot, and they stand in a long and remarkably impressive line of highly peculiar figures of whom this country ought never to cease for one instant to be proud.

Hitherto, we have cherished them for this astonishing distinction, Edward II, Richard III, Henry VIII, Elizabeth I, Charles II, George III and IV, Edward VII and VIII – and I pick only the royal tree's fruitier plums, the ones we relish most for their egregious lusts and vagaries and misdemeanours, for even the dullest have had their moments, be it George V's terminal injunction to bugger Bognor, or that exercise of Victoria's remarkable libido which, indulging itself at Windsor, could rattle windows in Cardiff.

So why are we distressed now at what delighted us before? Whence this nonsense requiring the current lot to be moral exemplars and behavioural models, because if they won't, then it is all up with them? They have never been anything of the sort; what they have been is a collection of flaky English eccentrics beyond the dreams of Ealing Studios, as thankfully unlike their subjects as it is possible to be. Oh, yes, we may rightly tremble at the thought that we might find ourselves married to one, but candidates have had a thousand years to be warned, and if in doubt, Sellar and Yeatman are a quick and easy read.

60

The Green Hills of Cricklewood

You know how it is early in the morning, after you have done the thing with the toothbrush and the razor and you look out the window and it is not raining any more the way it was raining before it stopped, and there is just this mist coming off the sidewalk, now?

I squinted up at the sun which was making the mist do what mists do, and I thought: this is one of the days when you do not start work right away, this is one of the days when you walk up the street, past the old one who is bringing the milk and the young one who is carrying the mail and the tiny one who is pushing newspapers through those holes they have in the doors for pushing newspapers through, and you walk on up to where your street joins the big wide one called Finchley Road, because that is where the place is that is cleaning your trousers, and it is a good day to collect your trousers, before you start work.

But when I got to the big wide one, I noticed that something was not the way it had been before. I noticed this because I had to wait to cross to where the trousers were, on account of the big red buses and the heavy trucks that were driving between me and the place with the trousers and I knew it was not a good time to do the running with the traffic. You could get a wound, down there. These are things you learn. I remembered the time in Pamplona, when I was younger than I am now and had not learned those things, and a cab ran over my suitcase, and the suitcase was never the same, after that. So I waited, which was how I noticed what it was that wasn't the way it was before. There was a new café there, where there used to be a greengrocery.

The café was called Papa's.

When I finally crossed over to the place where the trousers were I said to the cleaning one: 'I see there is a new café here.'

'Yes,' he said. 'It has been here a week, now. They could not get this stain out. They have done a note. They say it is oil.'

'They are right,' I said. 'It is the oil of the mower. If I ask for the Special Treatment they offer in the window, will it come out?'

The cleaning one shrugged. 'Who can say?' he said.

I left the trousers with him anyway, and I crossed the road again, and I looked through the window into Papa's. It had a red tiled floor and round white marble-topped tables and black iron chairs and an electric fan in the ceiling, and I thought: I know why they have called it Papa's, and I went in and sat down.

A waitress came up. She was one of the slim ones, with the big dark eyes they have, if you are lucky.

'Welcome to Cricklewood,' I said. It is the kind of thing you say, if you have known a lot of women, over the years. 'It is good to see a café dedicated to Hemingway.'

'I'm sorry?' she said.

I smiled. She was very young.

'The owner of this café would understand,' I said, but gently. 'Ernest Hemingway was a writer. He was one of the best writers there was. People called him Papa. He used to sit in cafés just like this, in the days before Paris was the way it is now. The cafés were called the Dome and Les Deux Magots and stuff like that, and they had red tiled floors, too, and white marble tables and black iron chairs and electric fans, and Papa would sit there writing in this ring-backed notebook he had, while the little saucers piled up in front of him.'

'Does he still do it?' she said.

I looked away. I did not want to tell her it was thirty years since he had put the shotgun in his mouth.

'Ask your boss,' I said. 'He knows about all that.'

She did the thing with the cloth that makes tables shine.

'My boss is my dad,' she said. 'That is why we called it Papa's.'

I picked up the menu, after that. There were a lot of breakfasts on it.

'I'll have the one with the eggs and the bacon and the tomatoes,' I said. 'The Number Four.'

'Is that the one with the fried bread as well?' she said.

'Yes,' I said, 'that is the one it is.'

61

Making Old Bones

In my younger days, I used to wonder what my skeleton looked like. I can even pinpoint the spark which detonated this speculation: I was studying *Hamlet* at the time, or at least hitting Gerald Finch over the head with it, because he sat in front of me for O-level English, and Mr Hoskins, to whom Lady Luck had dealt Finch and me from the bottom of her deck, enquired why I had struck my colleague with a cornerstone of our culture, and rather than bring up a girl's name, for these were gallant days, I replied that we had been having an argument about the play. Oh really, he said, because he had not been born yesterday, what kind of argument, and I said I wanted to know how Hamlet knew the skull was Yorick's, all skulls look the same, and Finch said the clown told him, sir, and I said why would Hamlet believe a clown if he told me how much water got poured into the average trouser, but would you believe anything a clown said to you in a cemetery sir, and Mr Hoskins said not necessarily, and that is an interesting point, Coren, well, fairly interesting, I shall try to find out whether skulls look different from one another, Mrs Gibson might know, her brother was in the RAMC.

He never got back to me, and it was *Guy Mannering* the week after that, but the question of what skulls looked like remained inside mine for some years. Nor only skulls, but

354

the entire osseous sub-frame: it bothered me that I should never see mine, except in X-rays, where it always appeared hilarious: there were all these little grey bones, apparently not joined together, one serious sneeze and your entire infrastructure would fall to the bottom of your legs, leaving you to spread across the floor like a deflating blimp. I don't know why skeletons should be funny, perhaps it is nature's way of palliating *timor mortis*; a few years ago I fell off a horse and the osteopath I went to see had a skeleton dangling from his ceiling, pretty comical in itself, but when he hit it with a stick to indicate which vertebra I had damaged it started dancing, I laughed till it hurt, i.e. immediately, and the poor quack said to my wife, is he always like this or could it be concussion?

He said it because she's a doctor, which brings me to last week's issue of the *British Medical Journal*, a comic she regularly passes on to me in the forlorn hope of bridging the marital gap, but for once it contained an article worth the unequal struggle. Entitled 'A prospective study of alcohol consumption and bone mineral density', by Troy Holbrook and Elizabeth Barrett-Connor of the University of California, it concluded that heavy drinkers had stronger skeletons than teetotallers. Even better, while drinking strengthened bones, exercise weakened them; i.e. provided you eschewed jogging in favour of slumping in front of *Cheers* with a large Scotch, you could advance happily into old age knowing you contained a skeleton on which Eiffel himself could not have improved.

Not surprisingly, this lifted the spirits no end (oh, please, today's is a scientific treatise, if you want puns come back next Wednesday), especially since I could not remember the last time my lifestyle had received anything but an admonitory caning from the medical establishment: it is normally impossible for me to open a paper without reading that everything I do is lopping years off my life, unless I start fell-walking and eating a daily stone of bran I shall not see Christmas, so you may imagine my joy at learning that tipsy inertia was good for you.

And my wretchedness at subsequently discovering that it was not. For Troy and Elizabeth, canny as any hack, had saved the twist for the tail; arriving at their closing paragrahs and poised for statistical evidence that these strong bones of ours were proof against geriatric breakage, I found all hope summarily dashed. Can you guess why? Of course. 'Studies of fractures and alcohol consumption are confounded by other risk factors, including increased likelihood of impaired vision and falling.'

Alas, poor Yorrick! A' may have pour'd a flagon of Rhenish on your head once, he always liked a drop, he had bones like pike-staffs, but a fat lot of good they did him the night he walked right off the Elsinore battlements. Thought he saw a ghost, they say.

62

Osric the Hedgehog

There could well be a knighthood in this. For is not my voice broken, my wind short, my chin double, my wit single and every part of me blasted with antiquity, and will I yet call myself young? Add to this the fact that I was born about three o'clock in the afternoon, with a white head and something of a round belly (both of which, interestingly, I seem to be getting back), and you will, I am sure, be hard put to come up with a candidate better qualified to hurtle down to his local job-centre this very minute and offer himself for the position of drinking companion to the Prince of Wales, specialist subject the works of William Shakespeare 1591–1613.

Is there a vacancy? Is there ever. Because, despite the fact that our beloved heir is girt round with all manner of advisers, mentors, boffins, coaches, gurus, tutors and other consultant sycophants ever on the *qui vive* at the end of a cellphone should HRH's brow begin to furrow, he appears to have nowhere to turn when it comes to solving the problem of his offspring's indifference to the Bard. I learned this from the speech he made on Monday when inaugurating his new Shakespeare School at Stratford: 'I know,' he confessed, 'that if I tried to drag my children here, they would say they didn't want to come, that it would be boring, that they'd far rather play with their computer games.'

The heart bleeds. A picture materialises, does it not, of our deeply caring monarch-in-waiting, tilter at carbuncles, sworn opponent of all he deems to be meretricious, ephemeral, or just plain tacky, leaning on a lectern at the corner of the Highgrove nursery and attempting to interest Prince William in the fact that he, too, will one day be given the latchkey of this earth of majesty, this seat of Mars, this other Eden, demi-paradise, this fortress built by Nature for herself against infection and the hand of war, but is William listening? Is Henry? Are they hell, their eyes are glued to two enormous screens, their fingers are twinkling across two keyboards with all the unsettling dexterity of the contemporary young, they are hermetically absorbed in the pressing business of getting out of the dungeon and across the drawbridge before the Terminators climb out of the moat and eat them, they do not give a damn for their old man's fervent declamation of England's top iambs, they like things that go tink-tink-tink and bleep-bleep-bleep.

Very well, then. That is why, this morning, I offer my liege lord my sworn service. I have the answer, and I have it after a mere two hours' fiddling with my Macintosh software, for that is all the time that was required to devise *Hamlet: Prince of Nintendo*. Now, press this key: see, a rudimentary oblong battlement has materialised, with a little Lego-like bloke standing on it. He is called Bernardo. He squeaks, 'Who's there?' A multiple choice now appears: *(a) Postman Pat, (b) Francisco, (c) A Ninja Turtle*. Press the key again; if you have got the right answer, Francisco, Horatio and Marcellus appear. They are all scuttling about and squeaking like mad. What have they seen? *(a) Tyrannosaurus Rex, (b) Gazza, (c) A ghost*. If you select Gazza, Horatio explodes, preventing the game from continuing.

The choices, of course, become progressively trickier, particularly if you have selected correctly from *(a) Walked under a bus, (b) Martian fell on him, (c) Got murdered by someone pouring poison in his ear,* because you have now qualified to enter Part Two of the game, which concerns what Hamlet is going to do about it. If, for example, you select *(b) Put on a cape and run Claudius over in the Batmobile,* you will have to start again from the beginning, whereas should you choose correctly, you will arrive at the interesting teaser that neither you nor Hamlet knows what he is going to do about it, at which point the little Lego-like figure in the black outfit will ask you what you would do in his position, thus moving the game into its interactive phase, where you will be able to do anything you want, provided, of course, that everybody ends up exploding, as Shakespeare intended.

This, then, is what I am offering to HRH. He can only say 'I know thee not, old man: fall to thy prayers', but he is a sensitive cove, he surely wouldn't want to see a Prince of Wales make the same mistake twice.

63

Doom'd For a Certain Term to Walk the Night

The woman at the all-night unisex sauna in East Finchley was really very nice. Heart of gold. 'Yes,' she said, 'there *used* to be an all-night chemist in this parade, but it shuts at nine o'clock now.'

I liked 'parade'. I hadn't heard the word in a long time. It took me back. There were a lot of parades about when I was young. There were also a lot of all-night chemists.

'Sorry to barge in on you,' I said, 'it's just that your light was on. I drove down here because Golders Green police station said they thought there was an all-night chemist, but I couldn't see anywhere else open.'

'There's only us and the Iranian grocer,' said the sauneuse. 'Funny they didn't direct you to Warman-Freed in Golders Green Road. I think they're open all night. Shall I look up their number?'

'That's all right, thanks,' I said, 'I know where you mean.'

It was two a.m. when I got to Warman-Freed. It was closed.

'Shuts at midnight,' said the man in the all-night pizza parlour opposite. He was very nice, too. He turned from the coffee machine and said, loudly: 'Anyone knows where there's an all-night chemist?'

The half-dozen customers glanced up from their iridescent wedges. Five shook their heads, but a man in a herringbone overcoat said: 'You want bliss.'

Who, I thought, doesn't? Since, however, I also wanted the bottle of Distalgesic and the course of Amoxyl for which their prescription and I had been trawling the streets since half-past twelve, I took the chance that the herringbone overcoat housed more than a peckish evangelist doom'd for a certain term to walk the night, and repeated: 'Bliss?'

'All-night chemist, corner of Walm Lane and Kilburn High Road.'

I stood looking at the dark windows of Bliss for a bit, until the man from the all-night minicabbery across the road strolled over and said, 'All night? *All night?* They haven't been open all night for what, got to be three years, could be four, we've been here, what . . . ?'

So I asked him, because it was the sort of thing a mini-cabbie ought to know, and he said: 'No problem, John Bell & Croyden, get anything there, any time, Wigmore Street, on the left, just past that wossname, that all-night video place, what's it called, it'll come to me in a minute . . .'

It took me twenty, and I came to it because when I came to John Bell & Croyden, though the outside lamplight winked cheerily off scalpel sets and sphygmomanometers and stethoscopes and curious prostheses and tiny aluminium baths for this unfathomable purpose and that, no light at all shone from within.

'You're going back a bit,' said the proprietor of 24-Hour Video Rental. 'They stopped their all-night service donkey's years ago.'

'Only place I know,' said a customer, piling four dubious cassettes beside the till, 'is Boots at Piccadilly Circus.'

'He probably meant Boots at Marble Arch,' said the man behind the till at the all-night souvenir shop opposite Boots at Piccadilly Circus, where two young Japanese were trying on policemen's helmets, but if he did, he was wrong there, too, as anyone who has stood outside the Boots at Marble Arch at 3.30 a.m. will tell you.

So I went into an all-night coffee shop at the top of Edgware Road, and I had a large espresso, and I asked them if I could use their phone, and I rang the Royal Free Hospital because it was on what was going to be my way home, now, and I told them about how I had this prescription for my daughter who had this extremely painful ear infection, and could they possibly supply the medication, and they said not unless I brought the ear in and they diagnosed it first, and I said that was impossible but was there an all-night chemist's anywhere between Land's End and John O'Groats, and they said not that they knew of.

So I came home, and my wife said it was okay. Victoria was asleep now and it could wait till morning, and I pointed out that it *was* bloody morning, and I was going upstairs to write this piece about the greatest metropolis in the world and how you could get everything you wanted any hour of the day or night, saunas, pizzas, videos, minicabs, policemen's helmets, you name it – remember how it was when you were a kid, you couldn't get anything after midnight, except medicine.

64

Garden Pests

We physicists know a thing or two about the relationship between heat and friction. The thing I know is that there is a relationship. Had I not given up physics at 14, I should probably have found out what the other thing was, but there you are, you cannot be everywhere at once.

Anyhow, if God had wanted us to know everything, he would not have given us the British educational system. Free will is the Almighty's way, and who am I to argue with that? Especially since I gave up divinity the same term. Offered the choices, I shrewdly guessed that my life would be better served by an ability to decline *amo* and list the principal exports of the Gold Coast, and I have not been proved wrong.

This does not prevent me from taking as today's text the observation that heat produces friction. I have of course heard that there is a body of opinion which holds the opposite view, but that is no more than you would expect from mere theorists. They ought to get out and about a bit. And what they ought to get out and about to is more lunchtime drinks parties, now that the ozone has, as I understand it, gone through the greenhouse layer, and there's more to come, say the weathermen.

For we have suddenly become a race which drinks *al fresco*. We have people over at noon, and we usher them towards

363

lawn and flagstone, and we fill their right hands, and they amble about among shrub and tub, and the sun thrums down upon them, and they chat and chortle happily enough, and all is more or less as it was in the blissful days before it was 82° and still rising. And then the friction enters the soul.

Do not get ahead of me: I am not about to address that homicidal irritability which comes to lesser breeds when the mercury goes up. These are civilized folk of whom I speak – should the sun-kissed talk turn to, say, Heseltine or Latvia or the Booker Prize, they do not take swings at one another, they do not fumble beneath the sweated seersucker for Colt and life-preserver, they do not roll amid the petunias, their hands locked around one another's throats.

All that happens when the hot weather strikes is that they say things outside which they would never dream of saying inside. The only part, indeed, which the heat plays is to put them where they can do the saying. In the old, cold days of yore, you had people over for summer drinks, and they stared out at the drizzle for a bit, and then they got on with the sluicing and the small talk. What they never, ever, did was criticize their surroundings. They did not say: 'Did you realize your carpet has got moth?' Or: 'I know a bit about furniture, and that chiffonier is unquestionably fake.' Or: 'It's time you had that rising damp seen to.' Or: 'I've sat on a few uncomfortable sofas in my time, but this one takes the bloody biscuit!'

So why should it be that the simple act of shepherding them out into the sunshine should have the effect of stripping from them all pretence of civility? Why, as you are topping up his glass, should a guest nod downward towards his feet and observe: 'Yes, well, you realize of course that the only way to get rid of all this couch-grass is to dig the whole thing up and start again?', the man on his right chuckle and say: 'Never mind couch-grass, as far as I am aware couch-grass doesn't fall on you, have you taken a look at that chimney of his, I give it six months, tops' and the man on his left chip in with 'Yes, I noticed the chimney when I was looking at his guttering, you ought to have that guttering seen to, half the brackets have rusted off'?

Why do their wives then join you so that one can point out that if you don't do something about the leaf-curl on your eucryphia it'll be dead by tea-time, and another shriek 'First things first, have you seen the thrips on his gladdies, you'd think he'd never heard of Malathion!' while the third inquires icily whether you have something to bang her heel back on with, and her husband smirks and says, 'I warned you about that path of his, didn't I?'

Forgive me, I only observe this, I cannot explain it. To me, psychology is an even more closed book than physics.

65

Time for a Quick One?

Here's something you didn't know. Georges Simenon never had woodworm. The great Walloon was never infested. Do you still maintain that this little corner shop of mine trades only in frivolities?

Were I further to point out not only that his waste-disposal never had a spoon down it, but also that he knew a Chubb 3R35 deadlock nightlatch when he saw one, this would probably be too much hard fact for you to absorb all at once, you would almost certainly have to go and lie down, so I shall hold back for a bit. But be warned: the big stuff is on the way. When it comes to critical theory, I do not spar. I can go 15 rounds with the best.

Interim, the scene now shifts to Monday morning, to find me curled up with Patrick Marnham's new biography, *The Man Who Wasn't Maigret: A Portrait of Georges Simenon*. I read a lot of literary biography, you have to if you aspire to be a novelist, it is the best way of discovering what you need to do in order to write the sort of books you wish to emulate. I first committed myself to this 35 years ago, when I read William Faulkner (people did, then), only to discover that he had jotted his early masterpieces while working as a trawlerman, coal-heaver, oil-rigger, steeplejack and various other callings not readily on tap in the London suburbs, even if you could have fitted the Archangel run and refurbishing Salisbury spire into the A-level timetable, so I gave up on being Faulkner and went on to being Hemingway, until I found out that I would have to run through Pamplona doing the thing with the bulls that can give you a wound down there, so then I moved on to being Scott Fitzgerald, because all you had to do was drink, but it did not help me to write *Gatsby*, it just helped me to walk into the furniture, and that is pretty much the way things went with my fictional ambitions over the next three decades, you would be amazed what novelists have to go through, need I remind you that Trollope had to invent the pillarbox in order to fire up his muse?

But then came Monday. I had always admired Simenon – a hundred novels was it? – but I had never known how he had managed it until I read Marnham's book and discovered that Simenon had bedded 10,000 women, even though his wife claimed it was only 1,200 (did they sit down nightly with ready-reckoners and compare lists, did she cry, 'I see where you've gone wrong, Georges, you've got that big Irish readhead down twice'?), but it was still enough to get the novels going, and I thought to myself, that's not so difficult, I could do that, especially when I discovered that Georges would often knock off four women in the same afternoon by going up to them in the street, palpating their breasts, and then finding a doorway, it couldn't take that long, you would be back at the typewriter by teatime.

So I put down the book and I ran upstairs to choose a seductive tie, and I splashed on this terrific aftershave I have, and I was just going through the front door when Mr Elias came out of the kitchen I may have told you we are having rebuilt, and he said look at this, and it was a floorboard with a million titchy holes in, and I said what is it, and he said it is woodworm, you are infested, you will have to get Rentokil over, so I had to fix that up and wait in for on-site inspection and early estimate when I could have been out palpating, and that was Monday shot, but I made an early start on Tuesday and nearly got to the garage before Mr Elias caught up and said he could fit the new side door if I went down to Danico and got him a Chubb 3R35 deadlock nightlatch, so I drove to Swiss Cottage and I passed some really fantastic-looking women on the way, many of them conveniently near doorways, but when I got home again Mr Elias said that is the wrong lock, so I drove back to Danico, and I exchanged locks, by which time it was noon, but there was still half a day until Mr Elias said there was a spoon stuck down the waste disposal, and I said can't you do it, and he said do you want this new door in or not, and by the time I had dismantled the waste disposal it was half past two, and I had to write this piece for *The Times*, without even one palpation to inspire me.

Which is how I know that Simenon never had woodworm.

66

The Leaving of Cricklewood

Forgive me. I hate to be the bearer of double whammies but I have, this morning, no option: all I can pray is that you will somehow find the fortitude to bear what I bear to you. Provided, of course, that the first whammy has not already left you supine in some darkened room, gaunt and listless beneath your saline drip and waiting for a council carer to come in and massage your feet; in which event, you must not read one further word of this.

That first whammy – for those of you still standing, albeit still reeling – was borne by last weekend's *Sunday Times*, which, quite properly, gave over much of its front page to the shattering global news that Martin Amis was quitting the UK for New York, to escape media scrutiny and public preoccupation with his advances, his partner, and his teeth, to flee the new politics for which he so recently voted but with which he is now disappointed (he confesson himself nostalgic for Baroness Thatcher), to shed the 'middle-class boredom', of Britain and – since 'I have only got one big London book left to write – emigrate to where the history of the next century is already being written'.

What an extraordinary and culturally devastating coincidence! For I, too, have been suffering those self-same torments and, having come to those self-same conclusions, am determined to leave Cricklewood for good. I have only one big Cricklewood column left to write – it will address man's eternal quest to discover why, four years ago, a Barnet council workman bothered to draw a red ring around the pothole outside my house, when it remains a pothole to this day — and, as soon as it is written, I shall be off.

I have had more than enough of media scrutiny (the *Ham & High* rings up every summer to ask which paperback I am taking on holiday) and as for the public's preoccupation with my advances, every time I bring a book out someone asks me what I got for it and then nods and says he'd always wondered why I was forced to do so much daytime television, doesn't your wife work? Whereupon, my having replied that she is a doctor, he immediately rolls his trousers up and asks her to have a look at his knee, so if Martin thinks society is obsessed with his partner, let me ask him how often the radiant Isabel has been required to feel a wonky patella during her soup course while simultaneously trying to avoid the eye of the woman opposite who has clearly been stitched up, every which way, by a dodgy plastic surgeon and now, alerted by the exposed joint, wants to know whom to sue?

As for my teeth, preoccupation with these is reaching hysteria: I have this year alone had six reminders from my dentist to come in for a check-up, each more threatening than the last. Any day now I expect to hear the unmistakable noise of a man towing a drill up a garden path, so the sooner I change addresses the better.

And yes, like Martin, I am disillusioned with new Tony. It's been weeks now, and nobody in Cricklewood seems better educated, healthier, richer or more caring. All that has happened is that The Cricklewood Arms, our only middle-class pub, has changed its name to The Ferret & Firkin, which seems, so far, to have done little to lift the boredom for which it has been a byword throughout the 25 years I have been going in, having a quick pint, and going out again, without anyone looking up from the *Daily Mail* crossword.

There used, mind, to be a fairly interesting greengrocer opposite, he had once played in goal for Cyprus, but his wife left him last year and he went back to Nicosia.

So I have concluded, like Martin, that enough is enough (and here I must apologise to the Editor, who was desperate to run the story as a front-page lead until I told him that, if he did, my only column idea was this pothole with a red ring around it) and it is time to pack my traps and quit Cricklewood.

I am going where the history of the next century is already being written. I have often sat in its shimmering gridlock, day and night, rapt with envy at the radiant hypermarkets and bustling fast-food outlets and teeming wine bars of the city that never sleeps. And I, too, am nostalgic for Lady Thatcher. I shall emigrate to Finchley.

67

Lo, Yonder Waves the Fruitful Palm!

It is a soft March morning in 1871, and on the drive outside a sturdy London villa, the gravel crunches. Inside, a woman starts, looks up from her davenport, and drops her pen. A sudden vibration shakes her bodice. She knows that crunch. It is three long years since it crunched away, but hardly a day has gone by without her ear's being cocked for its crunching back. She runs to the door, and flings it wide.

'Lawks-a-mercy!' she cries, for popular fiction has been her only consolation during those lonely months, 'Mr Forster!'

'Good morning, Mrs Forster,' replies her husband, 'I am home!'

He enters, removes his topee, bends his sunbleached sideburns to her joyful peck, and places upon their hall table the subject of this chapter.

'And was your expedition fruitful?' enquires Mrs Forster, as her bosom settles.

'Not only fruitful, dearest,' he replies, 'but seedful, flowerful, and, yes, cormful, too!' (for as well as being a great botanist, he is also a great wag), 'and see, I bring you the most illustrious of my trophies!'

Her adoring gaze turns for the first time from his face, towards the hall table. 'What is it?' she says.

'It is a potted palm,' replies her husband. 'Henceforth, no seaside string quartet will ever be the same. It is found only

372

on Lord Howe Island in the Pacific, and since it was found only by me, it is called Howea Forsteriana. Even now, a clipperload is pulling into Tilbury, for the greater glory of English botany. I intend knocking them out at five bob a time, including earthenware tub and watering instructions.'

And now, as Mrs Forster swoons, the scene dissolves to another sturdy London villa, another soft March morning, exactly 120 years later, and another great botanist. On this occasion, his is the trembling bosom. He is staring at a polythene cloche tantalizingly fogged by condensation. He is, in apt concord with everything round him, rooted to the spot. Why is he not budging?

To find out, we must, having teleported ourselves this far, now go back six months, to an evening in September when the great botanist went to fill his dustbin, and found his Howea Forsteriana standing beside it. His wife had thrown it out, on the grounds that it was dead. The great botanist brought it back inside, on the grounds that one green frond was still hanging on, and observed to his wife that you wouldn't bin a canary with 90 per cent moult. You would attempt to revive it.

His wife said it was horrible to look at. The botanist, while forced to agree that the item could no longer be classed as decor, maintained that this was no reason to murder it. He had enjoyed a happily symbiotic relationship with the plant for ten years; when he breathed out, it breathed in, and vice-versa. They were mates. If you will not have it in the house, said the botanist, I shall stick it in the garden. At this, his wife selected a sharp snort from her professional repertoire, and pointed out that his moribund friend was a sensitive tropical soul who would not last five minutes out there.

The botanist glared at her for a bit, and slunk off to phone Kew. No chance, Kew corroborated, and went on to tell him more about William Forster than he thought he'd ever need,

373

but there you are, journalism is full of surprises, you never know your luck. Most to the point, they said that Lord Howe Island did not know the meaning of the word frost.

But the great botanist did not know the meaning of the word defeat. In a sheltered southern corner of his garden, he either planted or buried the palm, depending on whether he or his wife was telling it. He then put a polythene cloche over it, leaned a sheet of plate glass against it, and, in due course, watched the snow fall on it.

That is why, this March morning, he cannot budge. He dares not. Could be a corpse underneath. But he is not the great Forster's heir for nothing. He girds his loin; moves the glass; lifts the cloche.

There is a palm-tree there. It has new green stalks, and new green leaves. It has not merely survived the winter, it has thrived on it. This is the Tropic of Cricklewood. The great botanist does not, however, pause to preen. He runs to the dustbin.

They had a mango last night, and some fool threw away the pip.

68

Fabric Conditioning

I sat next to Peter Palumbo a year or so ago, at one of those nominally informal bunfights where 'Just a Few Close Friends' is hand-scribbled on the embossed paste board, and when you get there two liveried footmen shuck you from your Pakamac and the third shouts your name into a room containing most of the *Almanack de Gotha*, half the cabinet, and a shoal of tycoons not yet on remand, and you immediately begin asking yourself what your host thinks it is you've got that one of his other guests wants, because you were not born yesterday.

Anyway, Palumbo was an agreeable enough cove, he didn't spill anything on me or try that trick with the cutlery where you bang the spoon and the fork does a somersault, and I was therefore not surprised to learn, a few months later, that he had been made chairman of the Arts Council; if you keep going to informal dinners with Just a Few Friends night after night, and don't knock over the potted palms, you have only yourself to blame when the scrap of paper that unexpectedly falls out of your hat in the homegoing Roller turns out to have a black spot on it.

Especially if you cannot forbear from banging on publicly about the Cultural Fabric of the Nation: it is the one phrase of his I recall from that night's exchanges, and each time he loosed it, I rose snapping to the fly, ticking off the threat to that fabric, i.e., to theatre, film, music, books, painting – and, by Stilton time, to glove-puppetry and synchronized origami – from the Philistine hordes yomping behind a Delilah whose manic shears were cutting everything in sight. Palumbo's eyes would glaze excitedly at each new convoluted metaphor, oddly like those of a man attempting to remember a previous engagement, but whether my shafts were scoring it was not only impossible to say, it did not really matter, since I had no idea, then, that he would ever be in a position to do anything about them.

Indeed, the meeting lay forgotten until I opened last Friday's *Times*, where, lurking at the foot of page 5, was the phrase 'the Arts Council's plan to restore the cultural fabric of the nation by the year 2000'. Hallo, I thought, its new Akela cleaves unswerving to his mission, there will be a bob or two in this for hack and mummer, might I not be of even further assistance than last time? I phoned the Arts Council.

'This cultural fabric,' I said, 'what, precisely, does it . . .'

'To quote the chairman,' said the Arts Council, 'cathedrals are the greatest cultural glory of this country. He plans to refurbish their fabric by means of a full partnership between the public and private sectors. Other major public buildings, too, of course . . .'

I put the phone down. Bloody buildings. The man had not listened to a word I'd shrieked. He was a literalist: to him, fabric was no metaphor. New conks for gargoyles was what he was after, and a bit of Brasso on the weathercock. Naturally, the private sector would cough up for that: there is nothing iffy about a cathedral, shareholders will not leap up at AGMs and complain about chucking a million at York Minister. On the contrary, it is no bad thing for a board to be seen as God's benefactors, it is a corking plea in mitigation should their hands get trapped in the till, it has a thick edge over backing unframed paintings or unrhymed verse or unknighted actors.

And what irks me almost as much is that, even for the literalist, cathedrals should top the list when our cultural fabric is under charitable review. Someone will always look after cathedrals. Had I identified, that night, the true bee in Palumbo's bonnet, I should have turned myself into the Spirit of Cultural Fabric Yet to Come, dragged him down to Cricklewood, made him cringe at butchered conversion and greenfield encroachment, at junkfood facia and bunkered parking, at jerrycobbled estate and polystyrene precinct; I should have cocked his ear to the curfew tolling the knell of parting suburbia.

Bit late now. The window of opportunity has slammed, and one of the very few shortcomings of mock-mullioned double-glazing in snugfit cedarette surround is you can't hear anyone shouting through it.

69

Numbers Racket

Y ou will, of course, remember the opening sequence of *A Matter of Life and Death*. How could you not? It was a seminal moment in the history of tele-communications. No one who cares about phones could ever forget it. I wonder sometimes whether even Powell and Pressburger realized the magnitude of what they had stumbled upon: they probably thought they were just making a film about life and death.

The credits fade to reveal David Niven, piloting his bomber back from Germany. Things are not good. The Germans have taken exception to being assaulted by an actor in a cardboard Lancaster, and set fire to it. Furthermore, Niven has suffered a nasty head wound, as the result of heavy ketchup over the Ruhr. He is not going to make it back. We know this from his smile. It is the smile of a man whose director has just suggested that he should appear to have met with Triumph and Disaster and to be treating those two impostors just the same, though not for much longer.

It is at this point that he begins to trawl the ether, seeking some sympathetic voice to say pip-pip to. But nothing negotiates the RT save static – until, suddenly, a girl's voice crackles. It is Kim Hunter, a toothsome American wireless operator: as they chat, her bee-stung mouth trembles, her velvet eyes brim, and, even though the skipper has never seen her and can have no inkling that Miss Hunter is a little stunner, they fall in love. It is her voice which enraptures him. It is the last thing he hears as he goes into his terminal plummet.

What follows is two hours of fey tosh, with Niven dangling in limbo while supernal advocates dispute whether he is alive or dead, until he is duly redeemed by the love of the operator and allowed to resurrect. But none of that mattered. I knew this even at the age of 10, when I tottered, blinking, from the Southgate Odeon. What mattered was the core-truth; which was that you never knew who you might run into at the telephone exchange.

For four decades, that notion of limitless possibility sustained me. Nor − which has not always been the case with other dreams − did disillusion lie in wait for it with a sockful of sand. I have had some delightful natters, oft in the stilly night, with operators; many a chat, flirtatious, comical, subversive, has warmed the wires between us. Could be directory enquiries, who, as their wet thumb flicked the pages, would rabbit revealingly of this and that; could be some reverse-chargehand answering with a mouthful of pork pie, and before you knew it you were into an engaging exchange about nocturnal indulgence; could be just one of those who happened to be giggling as they connected, and you said what's the joke, and she said we're having a bit of a laugh down here, Denise is getting married Wednesday to this bloke with a peculiar walk, and from there it was but a short step to intimate conspiracies.

It's all over now. There is not a human being left at the nation's switchboards, save the handful required to press the buttons which activate BT's androids. Any enquiry is answered by a computerized thing. The thing says 'sorry, the number you want is ex-directory', or 'sorry, the number you want is unobtainable', or 'the cellphone subscriber you have dialled is away from his instrument at this time'. Last evening, after a thing gave me a number, I dialled it, and another thing said:

'You have been answered by a fax-link. Please fax now, or hold for a telephone connection.' It then played most of *Eine Kleine Nachtmusik* before putting me through to a third thing which said: 'Sorry, the number has been changed to . . .'

This is a bad business. In the Next Lot, when I am limping home with the tailplane shot away and my chute in tatters, what shall I hear when I punch the plaintive button? 'Sorry, this number has been changed to a fax-link and the subscriber is away from the instrument at this time, but if you would care to leave your name and code and number after the *Toccata and Fugue*, we shall try to get back to you as soon as . . .'

70

Eight Legs Worse

The other evening, I found myself looking at what appeared to be a tiny broken bagpipe. It was leaking. It was, furthermore, leaking something black, and, furthermost, lying in what it was leaking. None of this would have mattered much had I found myself looking at it in, say, a gutter or hospital pedal-bin. I should merely have shuddered and walked on, but what I found myself looking at it in was a dish. The dish was on a table in front of me, flanked by knives, forks, and spoons; in short, all the accoutrements required if what you were going to do with a tiny broken bagpipe was not shudder and walk on, but eat it. Not that there was any if about it. I was a guest. The tiny bagpipe had been cooked by my hostess.

All the other guests had one, too, and they were uniformly thrilled by them.

'Oh, wow,' they cried, 'squid!'

'*Stuffed* squid,' they elaborated, 'oh, wow!'

'In its own ink!'

'Oh, wow!'

I looked at mine. I gave it a little prod with my fork. Ink ran out of it. Though not a household name where marine biologists foregather, I know why the squid has ink in it. It is so that it can squirt it out to put off predators attempting to eat it.

It works.

Not, mind, that it seemed to bother the others. They could not wait to tuck in. They sliced off the tentacles, they sectioned the body, they spooned up the ink, to choral yumming and oohing punctuated by brief autobiographical solos about how they'd always wanted to cook squid, it looked so *wonderfully* marbled, but they'd never dared, were they alive when you bought them, how did you kill them, how did you clean them, how did you stuff them, how did you find out how to . . .

My points exactly, as a matter of fact; though not, with me, uttered ecstatically, just brooded on internally. As, indeed, they had been with the first course, *shorba*, when everyone had shrilled, oh wow, isn't this that fantastic Yemeni marrowbone soup, yes it is, oh what's it called . . .

But I had managed to get that down all right. I had succeeded in persuading myself that wherever the marrow had been extruded, it was unlikely to have been from camel bones. I didn't think you could buy camel bones in Barnes. I would have heard. There were little fibrous lumps floating about in it, mind, that could have been goat, possibly hare (I looked up the recipe when I got home), but I managed to corral them under my reversed spoon, and I don't think anyone noticed.

Now, do not misinterpret all this gustatory whingeing: I am no culinary philistine, I have tied on the bib at many an ethnic bistro and not shrunk from having a cockshy at the arcane, even when I have not had the slightest idea what *yukyuk* or *bugatti* were and the patron lacked the bilingualism to convey. I have probably eaten wild toad in a wart sauce and held up my plate for more. I may even have been asked on the drive home whether I liked the stuffed nostril and not stopped the car to throw up. It is not a question of squeamishness over this exotic dish or that, only one of suspicion and unease when faced with the ambitions of the amateur. For while it is one thing to order tiger stew from an Ulan Bator restaurateur with three rosettes in the Mongolian Michelin, it is quite another to have it ladled out before you in Stoke Newington by an English ophthalmologist whose hobby is deciphering oriental cookbooks.

And there is a lot of that about, these days. The British – released from esculent restraint by both the Elizabeth David watershed and the immigration of countless entrepreneurs carrying woks, pasta-makers, clay ovens, *bains marie*, fondue sets, spice-mills, and all the rest, and bent under sacks of enigmatic herbs, vats of curious oils and liquors and yoghurts, and unfathomable lengths of dried animal – have become the acolytes of a hundred different cuisines, eager not merely to patronise the myriad professional establishments but, God help us, to emulate them to the best of their domestic ability.

A best which is not always good enough. While I applaud the ambition to cobble a *yasaino nimono* or a *cocida madrileno*, I have to say that admiration has too often wilted at the first forkful to leave me with anything but doubt concerning the frenzied competitiveness which currently holds the middle-class dinner-party circuit in thrall. I used to motor forth of a Saturday night thinking, good-oh, she's bound to kick off with that terrific salmon mousse of hers, hit us with a roast saddle of lamb to follow, and bring up the rear with a bread-and-butter pudding that would have Anton Mosimann putting the Sabatier to the wrist, but I do not think that any longer; these days I think, oh hell, she was talking abut Uzbek cooking when we met at that dinner party where I had to spit the bits of birds' nest into my napkin, I bet she's going to give us stuffed head of something after the larch-leaf purée, and he never stops going on about being something of a fromoisseur, ha-ha-ha, he's probably found this amazing dog's cheese which you have to wash down with emulsified arak, I shall no doubt be on my back in Bart's tomorrow with a 'nothing by mouth' placard gummed to my drip.

It isn't just the cooking, either; it is the trust one is required to have in what went on before they got to the cooking, which is why, when that other evening someone asked how you cleaned a squid, I had a long pull of the Meursault and tried to think about something else. God knows what there is inside a squid. I remembered once watching *poulpeurs* preparing to market their catch on the Marseilles waterfront: they killed the squid by sticking their thumbs in the beaks and turning the bodies inside out, whereupon they chucked the entrails back in the sea, because there were poison sacs inside. Had my Barnes hostess known enough to do that?

I wasn't sure. So I just ate the tentacles. 'Phew,' I said, when the plates came to be collected and an eyebrow raised itself over my little legless bagpipe, 'That was one big squid! Do you know, I couldn't manage another bite.'

71

Do Dilly-Dally on the Way

You will groan (and who could blame you?) to recall my obsessive search, *passim*, for a Cricklewood hero. So let me lift your spirits: the search is over. After today, you will hear no more of it. Even if other local prodigies turn up as unexpectedly as this one, they shall not test your patience. I am satisfied, now, to let the matter rest, along with the blessed remains of a paragon whose ineffable *rightness* for me and Cricklewood sets her immovably above any putative contender.

Heroine, then. And those remains lie not 200 yards from my very gate, though I didn't know this until yesterday, despite having passed them umpteen times on as many short cuts through the cemetery at the top of the road. But yesterday's was a long cut: as I negotiated the wonky crosses, February suddenly did what February suddenly does, so, lacking an umbrella, I shot under a maple tree to wait for it to stop doing it. I was not alone, for that is the way it is in graveyards, but I did not immediately spot who was beside me, because the moss lay thick in the chisellings. It was only when I thought I saw what I subsequently knew I had that I ran my finger down the grooves to ream them out, and read: 'In loving memory of Marie Lloyd, born February 12, 1870, died October 7, 1922.'

Even then, and even as the fingers trembled, I couldn't be

sure it was her – *that* her, I mean. And then I read the mottled verse beneath.

> Tired she was, and she wouldn't show it.
> Suffering she was, and hoped we didn't know it.
> But He who loved her knew, and, understanding all.
> Prescribed long rest, and gave the final call.

Who else could it be? You could hear her singing that first couplet, and anyone who knew anything about Marie Lloyd knew the significance of the second, because she died in the middle of her act at the Edmonton Empire, in the middle, indeed, of 'One of the Ruins that Cromwell Knocked About a Bit'. Furthermore, she died because she had been knocked about more than a bit by her swine of a third husband, jockey Bernard Dillon, and (since, even with all that, irony remained unsatisfied) she died staggering as if drunk, but because the song required her to stagger as if drunk, the audience laughed and cheered while she terminally tottered. I do not know if He, understanding all, fixed it so that the last sound she heard was of an enraptured music hall, you would have to ask a believer, but there have been worse ways to go.

When the shower eased, I walked across to the cemetery office, and Cliff Green, who runs it, took down the book for 1922, and showed me an entry no less apt in its macabre comedy than the final call itself, in that Matilda Alice Victoria Dillon, known as Marie Lloyd, had been interred 12 ft down, for £52 2s 0d, and that her mother Matilda Wood had been interred above her (9 ft) in 1931, and her father above *her* (7 ft) in 1940, and her sister above *him* (4 ft) in 1968, and just as I had seemed to hear her sing before, now I seemed to hear her laugh, and I knew that laugh, I had heard it countless times on the wheezy old 78 I replay whenever I need a little of what I fancy to do me good, and Mr Green said there was one more thing I might like to know, which is that both gates of Fortune Green Cemetery had been opened only once, and that was on October 12, 1922.

It was the biggest funeral they had ever had, and they had been compelled to close those same gates an hour before the burial, because all three local police stations couldn't provide enough constables to control the weeping mob, and it was no good drafting in volunteers because, as you know, you can't trust a special like the old-time coppers.

Marie Lloyd, however, despite the dilly-dallying of the cortège from her house in Woodstock Road as the result of so many wreaths being flung at the cars by grieving bystanders that the half-mile journey took almost an hour, did, at last, find her way home, and I rejoice that it's just a step across the road from mine. Tonight I shall put on 'A Little of What You Fancy', turn up the volume, and open the windows for her to hear.

And if you remind me I'm not a believer, I shall, like Marie, just wink the other eye.

72

On a Wing and a Prayer

We were just leaving Westley Waterless when it happened. We were just leaving Westley Waterless for the third time in an hour. But, lest a picture may have come into your mind of a man and a woman unable to get Westley Waterless out of their system, tearing themselves away from it only to hear it calling them back, it should quickly be said that what we were in fact attempting to do was get our system out of Westley Waterless.

The system had been carefully worked out, last Sunday afternoon, in a little orchard in the mid-Suffolk village of Stansfield, which is six miles from Westley Waterless as the crow flies, or 27 if the crow's wife is using the *Collins Road Atlas*. Let us, however, not rush to blame either the crow's wife or the *Collins Road Atlas*, partly because those who have tried this will know that it does not get them anywhere, but also because the Suffolk signposts have their own ideas about where anything is, and these only occasionally correspond with *Collins's* opinion.

It may, of course, be that mid-Suffolk's mid-folk belong to the Ridleyite Tendency, and creep out at night to turn their signposts round to confuse Waffenbundesbank paratroops landing in Stansfield with a view to striking at the soft underbelly of Westley Waterless. Indeed, the hereinabove-mentioned system had not a little to do with such thoughts:

388

Sunday was not only a hot afternoon, it was the fiftieth anniversary of another hot afternoon, and, lying on one's back in an East Anglian orchard, you did not have to be a former secretary for trade and industry to imagine the cerulean welkin embroidered, once again, with vapour trails. In such a mood, and in, moreover, an open tourer, what more apt a homeward system than via the meandering network of unchanged Suffolk back roads which thread redly across the *Collins* pages like the veins on a drunkard's conk?

So that is why we were here, nostalgically belting between the high hedgerows, when it happened. It, too, was belting between the high hedgerows, but it was belting transversely, from one hedgerow to another. A susceptible cove, your Johnny synapse, especially if its brain has been thinking about the Last Lot: in the nanosecond before the thing struck, I could have sworn it was an Me109. Then it hit the offside wing and somersaulted over our heads, and I saw, after I had braked and looked back, that it was a pheasant. I got out, slowly, with that grisly admixture of chagrin and dread one cannot but feel at the hurt of a fellow creature, but it was all right, there wasn't a mark on her, the no-claims bonus was safe. The bird, however, was stone dead.

I know little of the countryside, and less of its juridical arcana. While I know that you cannot kill pheasants in July, I do not know what happens to those who do. Nor do I know if different laws obtain regarding pheasants wild and raised; did this corpse belong to a bloke who had lovingly hand-reared it so that he could lovingly plug it next October, and if so, might I not owe him something? The road was deserted, which was one answer to all such questions. I opened the boot; I put the pheasant in. After all, just to leave it there would have made its death meaningless; as links in the food chain went, it was one of the plumper.

'I'm not pulling its stuff off,' said my wife. 'Or out.'

'Just read the map,' I said. 'We don't wish to hang around Westley Waterless, now.'

'We never did,' said my wife, 'but that didn't stop us.'

We were, however, luckier this time. We found the way to Stump Cross, which is where you halt in order to have a row about whether to take the B184 or the M11. And, after a bit, to say hang on, what's that peculiar noise in the boot?

That little I know about the countryside does not embrace the habitat of pheasants. Is Essex all right for Suffolk ones? Not that I could have done anything about it if it wasn't; when I opened the lid, the corpse shot by me like a clay pigeon. Who knows, maybe it will find its way back to Westley Waterless? If, that is, it has the sense to ignore the signposts.

73

And Did Those Feet?

We didn't get corn circles in Cricklewood. You need corn. This left us marginalised from the great summer debate, and glum. For urban life is short on magic, and even mystery is brief: you usually conclude, after a bit, that it wasn't the fairies who nicked your milk, nor a warlock's curse that flattened your battery. Likewise, few midnight knocks betoken a time-warped Saracen or a basketful of royal foundlings; it is generally a minicabbie looking for Fulham.

What envy, then, we felt, down here, for lucky rural folk! We, too, wanted to squat in moonlit fields, craning to catch Titania treading a measure in the cereal, or listening out for a tinny voice to cry: 'We mean you no harm, Earthlings, see we bring Venusian toffees, and humorous T-shirts for your emir!' Even a hoaxer would have left a welcome hiccup on the flat oscillograph of our lives: what fun to have sprung out on Jeremy Beadle, just as he finished rolling his bogus circumference, and thrashed him to within an inch of his life!

But it was not to be. The corn got cut, the winter came, the country people snuggled happily beneath their thatch to dream of next season's yet weirder phenomena, and, down here, we ground our jealous teeth and reconciled ourselves to puzzling out, instead, the mystery of the single currency. It may not have come from Pluto or Cloud-cuckoo-land, but it was as close as we were ever going to get.

Until this morning. This morning, I looked out from an upper window on to a lawn thick with hoar-frost. Pretty enough, but that was not what made the heart lurch: for there, etched into the twinkling rime, was a huge circle, so impeccable as to suggest a 10ft set of compasses. No tracks led to it, nor any away; though shortly, as you may imagine, mine did both. I was on the lawn in a trice.

They were the footprints of a gigantic hound! Was this the fabled corn circle of the Baskervilles? Alas no; I peered closer, freezing a knee: these could not belong to any dog. No dog has a heel and five toes. Then again, no human being has a foot two inches long. And then even more again, what beast, be it canine or human, can materialise in the middle of a large lawn, leaving no trace of its passage thither, impress a perfect circle, and vanish as trackless as it came?

I ran back into the house, and up to the attic. You know the kind of box: it always has *The Coral Island* in it, and *Kennedy's Shortbread Eating Primer*, a few dead bees, and right at the bottom, *Tracking Made Easy*, which some dumb uncle bought you 40 years ago because he thought you might need to identify spoor left in your parent's fifth-floor flat, could be an okapi, funny place, Cockfosters.

So I took it outside, and I knelt again, with the book open at British mammals, and you would not believe the variety of feet that walk upon England's mountains green, but when it came to what had walked upon Cricklewood's garden white, nothing. As far as Capt. John Wills-Bourne, late of the Selous Scouts, was concerned, this footprint did not exist.

So I telephoned the Natural History Museum.

'It is most probably,' said the NHM woman, in that gentle but firm voice so often employed when talking to the deranged, 'a hedgehog circle. This is how they feed.'

'It is not a hedgehog's print,' I said, 'and even if it were, the hedgehog would be the size of a bulldog. Anyway, how could it leave no track but the circle?'

'It might,' said the woman, 'be a stoat or similar dropped by an owl. If it was hurt, it might have run in a circle until the owl retrieved it.'

I consulted *Tracking Made Bloody Impossible* again, to be certain.

'It is not a stoat,' I insisted, 'nor similar. And whatever it is, an owl could not have picked it up. A condor possibly, but this is Cricklewood.'

'If you fax us a photo,' sighed the woman, 'we'll try to identify it.'

So I went upstairs for the camera, and the sun was now streaming through the landing window; which I thought no more about, until I was back on the lawn. The frost had gone. The circle with it.

Theories c/o *The Times* on a postcard please. And country folk need not apply. They've had their turn.

74

Nothing But The Truth

If a man spends 30 years banging a key for money, it must follow that not everything he writes will come up to impeccable snuff.

There will be up days and down days, there will be up markets and down markets, but if hot meals are to be set upon tables and carpets laid upon floorboards, if pipes are to be professionally plumbed and cats professionally wormed, and if children are not to be dispatched barefoot to school (perhaps for no better reason than to escape the spectacle of their mother taking in washing at the back door even as the bailiffs at the front are distraining upon their father's chattels), then, willy-nilly, the loin must be girt and, though the *mots* may not always be *justes*, the quota filled.

Yet if those three decades have therefore spewed much of which I was not proud, they had not, until yesterday, delivered anything of which I was actually ashamed. But when I recall yesterday's *oeuvre*, it pumps the blood into the cheeks, even as the pump itself plummets to the bottom of the boots. Worse, yesterday I put my name to a piece of writing which could settle my professional hash for good.

Its plot was generated some nights earlier, when the next-door burglar alarm sounded. This did not greatly agitate me since it is a capriciously sensitive item and had doubtless responded to a raindrop or a coughing dog, but I went into the front garden to check – one of my dahlias might have fallen over – whereupon the lamp-light revealed a man paused at my neighbour's gate. Had this passer-by spotted something? I ran back, phoned the police, and ran out again with the idea of asking the man what he had seen.

It now dawned on me that what he had seen was the inside of the house, because he was disappearing up the road at a clip too nimble to be innocent. I clipped after, but before I could close upon him he darted into the unlit playing-fields opposite, and there is an age beyond which you do not follow the unknown into the invisible. Fortunately, even as my *amour propre* seeped, a police car hurtled around the corner, flung open its rear door at my wave, and we plunged together in a pursuit which happily ended at the quarry's collar.

As the result of which, I was of course required to make a statement. That I was not required to make it immediately was, I felt, all to the good: recollecting emotion in tranquillity means you can marshal a few smart adjectives and get the semi-colons right. Accordingly, when the CID amanuensis fronted up yesterday, I was ready. He opened his pad, I my mouth, and we set off together towards the Booker Prize.

I had never dictated a story before. Habituated to pecking syllables off a keyboard in between staring out of the window, I had not realized how wonderfully the mind was concentrated by sitting opposite a bloke with a big fat pad and an urgent ballpoint. The stuff poured out.

It was pretty good: true, there was a nod to Wilkie Collins, a whiff of Chandler, but it was in the main my own, and it rattled along a treat. As the policeman scribbled, I thought, this is a watershed, I could do trilogies, I wonder if he'd like to earn a bob or two on his day off?

We finished, and he passed the pad across. Was it, he enquired, a true record of the facts, would I sign it to this effect, would I attend court?

I read it. I said yes. It came out as a croak. For, though every fact was true, every embellishment had gone. The copper was as remarkable an editor as I had ever met. As he wrote, he subbed: it is a great art, though that is not what it produces. It produces *Janet and John*.

Soon, I shall be in court. Defence counsel rises. His client is alleged to have been caught bang to rights. His only course is to discredit the witness. He settles his gold pince-nez. He reads. 'I saw a man. The man was at the gate. The man had a brown jacket. He ran up the road. I ran after him. I got quite close. The man had little ears. The man ran across the road. I ran . . .'

Defence counsel tosses the sheaf aside, and takes off his pince-nez. 'Mr Coren, you have described yourself to this court, under oath, as a writer . . .'

The Last Decade
2000–2007

STEPHEN FRY

Introduction

'Lana' was my putrid anagrammatical camp name for him. 'Thank you for not making it Anal,' he said.

Alan Coren was fixed in my mind from an early age as the kind of person I wanted to be. It was always his wit on the radio that stuck in the mind more than anyone else's. Some time in the late 1970s he was on a quiz show involving quotations.

'What were Queen Anne's last words?'

'Alas, with me dies a whole period in table legs?' he ventured. Very Coren because clever without being clever-clever; funny, very funny without being modish or mean-spirited; and very Coren because it makes you go: 'Grrr. I wish my synapses could fire like that.'

In interview I heard him asked if he ever saved up bons mots either for the dinner table or for articles. 'No,' he said, 'if it can't come when bidden then I'll retire. I'm a hack not an artist.' Hack is a tough word, but he was a professional certainly, like Wodehouse or Coward. It is easier to admire and to like a pro than most artists, I have found. Artists are always feeling sorry for themselves, pros can't afford feelings of self-pity.

E.M. Forster once delivered a cruel but devastating two-word blow to *Punch*: 'suburban sniggers'.

During his masterful editorship of that magazine and the years following it, Alan slowly developed a full persona, that of Cricklewood Man: angry, exasperated, contemptuous and yet somehow never merely bilious or inelegantly splenetic. And certainly no sniggerer. He lifted *Punch* out of its self-satisfaction and introduced, not before time, the comedy of the fractured self. He owed much to Perelman, Thurber and Leacock, but that is no more than to say that P.G. Wodehouse owed a lot to George and Weedon Grossmith, W.S. Gilbert and Jerome K. Jerome: the pupil often matches, and sometimes outstrips, the master.

Bill Davies, Alan's predecessor at *Punch*, came into the office one day proudly bearing a dummy issue of the new magazine he was editing: British Airways' *High Life,* the first of a new generation of ultra-glossy airline magazines. Davies had got many of his *Punch* freelancers to contribute and he was anxious to know Coren's opinion.

Alan looked carefully through it. 'Congratulations, Bill,' he said, 'British Airways will be the first airline where you read the sick-bag and throw up into the in-flight magazine.'

Yes, Alan could be cruel. Cruel is funny when it is applied to those who can take it. No one who is truly funny will entirely avoid the jugular or the groin. Alan, so far as I am aware, only ever chose one of his own weight when it came to a no-holds-barred wit fight; he never bullied. He never lost either, you can bet that.

How he managed to be angry, alive, contemporary and complete as a humorist without ever revealing his real political, cultural, social, sexual, psychological self is a mystery to me. I wish I could have mastered that particular art. But I wish I could have mastered much of what Alan was. He lacked self-consciousness; that I admire, too. He had, as it happens, a fertile and perceptive brain outside the unrepentantly middle-class arena of his humour. Fortunately, the censoring membrane of wit never allowed him to become pompous about the genuine intellect within. Something else I could still learn from him . . .

He was kind to me personally on the achingly few occasions we met, but it was the kindness of his lifelong work as a humorist that mattered. He stimulated, fondled and rewarded parts of my brain that no one else has ever been able to reach.

75

Radio Fun

Today is a really big day. That is why I have just finished servicing and polishing my father's old Ferguson. See how it gleams! Savour how it smells!

Hear how it thunders when I start it up!

I haven't given my old man's Ferguson such a seeing to in the 15 years since he died, when I took it from his place and brought it to mine. I should say here (since it has just occurred to me that unlikely pictures may be forming in your mind's eye), that it is not an old Ferguson tractor, it is an old Ferguson wireless. It was given to my parents as a wedding present in 1935, and a very snazzy present it was; I stress this only because younger readers may think of a wireless, if they even know the word, as a titchy plastic box you clip onto your belt for jogging. They may never have seen a walnut and rosewood number the size and simulacrum of a Sheraton sideboard, standing on four sturdy cabriole legs, with six brass knobs on the front to fine-tune three enormous dials that glow in three different colours to let you know they're in business, we are Long, Short and Medium, sir, begging your pardon, sir, and we are here to serve you, we await your pleasure, sir, you have only to twiddle. It is a wireless worth getting married for.

And, culturally speaking (which it did), it brought me up. For the first dozen years of my life, much of what I learned and most of what I enjoyed came to me through this huge speaker cunningly fretworked into, for some reason, a spray of roses. Even after 1950, when my old man bought a TV set as big as a wardrobe (whose giant oak doors nevertheless revealed a screen as big as a fag-packet), thereby so filling our little front room with electronic carpentry that only two people could ever watch or listen at a time, the third having to stand in the hall, it was the radio that did the business. Not only did it teach me more of this and that (though not, in those Reithian times, the other) than any schoolteacher ever did, it also entertained me better than anyone I ever knew: it seamlessly graduated me from *Uncle Mac* and *Toytown* and *Just William* and *Norman and Henry Bones* – subtitled *The Boy Detectives*, despite the fact that Norman was queenie old Charles Hawtrey and Henry was matronly old Marjorie Westbury, a weekly *Radio Times* revelation that not only never bothered me at all, but probably did much to explain the infinitely elastic unbigotry for which I am a byword today – to *Take It From Here* and *The Goon Show* and *Ray's A Laugh* and *Hancock's Half-Hour* and all the myriad other comic masterpieces from the Golden Age of Ears.

I look at the Ferguson now, and I hear it then. See these three dials? Clock not only all the poignantly yesteryear Anglophone stations, Hilversum and Daventry, Allouis and Athlone, and, yes, Valetta and Cairo – there is a map of the world on the back of the set, faded now but still half pink where once it was half red – but also Oslo and Ankara and Prague and Paris and Breslau and many a polyglottal dozen more. Oft in the stilly night, I used to creep past the door rattling in concert with my old man's nostrils, and pad downstairs, and switch the Ferguson on, and wait while the dials began slowly to glow and the valves to hum and the speaker to whistle as I spun the dial in search of microphones a thousand crackling miles across the night. I learnt a lot of

French that way, and doubtless no small smattering, now sadly lost, of Lapp and Urdu.

It was, of course, only mine exclusively in the wee small hours: in the huge large ones, it served all three of us. Sometimes in pairs: since it took two people to move it so that my mother would have room to put up the ironing-board, I would occasionally hang around to listen to Mrs Dale's Diary; tricky for her, because, though she enjoyed having me there, the script would from time to time daringly offer a mildly gynaecological moment, and my mother dreaded questions. Care for another pairing? Me sitting with my old man as the football results came in and he checked his pools coupon, not because I chose to but because my mother knew if I was there he wouldn't swear.

But the proper pairing for today is one I didn't join. It was just them. You know why today is a really big day? Because it is Neville Chamberlain's birthday. If he were alive today he'd be 134, and people would pay good money to look at him, but when he was 70, what people did was listen to him. And it was on this Ferguson that he told my parents that no such undertaking had been received and in consequence this country was at war. Which is why I have fettled it. I rather fear it is time to switch it on again.

76

Not My Bag

Had you, last week, been taking a sundown stroll through the rolling Bucks verdure, you might have spotted a strange misshapen silhouette blemishing the evening horizon, rooted to a hummock. A stunted oak? A Saxon rood? An extravagant horse-dropping, piled and eroded by the summer wind? Or even, perhaps, a statue of Charles Laughton, raised by the Gerrards Cross Victor Hugo Society? That fearsome hump, those twisted legs, the shoulder dropping to the wonky knee as the agonised head wrenches unnaturally upward, poking its pitiful eye at the uncaring heavens – what could it be but the great hunchback himself, frozen forever by the sculptor's art?

It could be a wag practising his golf-swing, is what. That the figure displayed not a tremor of movement is explained by its having been swinging for three hours and finally come to a paralysed halt. Had some Samaritan not karted by, I might have been there yet, a topographical conundrum fit to rank with Stonehenge and the White Horse of Uffington. For the world would not know that the reason I was there was only because a malign joker had bought me, for my birthday, golf lessons. And I had just learnt them all.

Here is the first: if God had wanted man to play golf, He would have given him an elbowless left arm, short asymmetrical legs with side-hinged knees, and a trapezoid rib-cage from which diagonally jutted a two-foot neck topped by a three-eyed head. Here is the second: since the game can be played only by grotesquely distorting the body God did give us, golf was patently invented by manufacturers. For the natural way to play golf would be to throw the ball down the fairway, walk after it, pick it up and throw it again, and, having reached the green, throw it down the hole. However, in some distant eon, a chippie of fortuitous ineptitude whittled a cabriole leg a foot longer than the rest and, rather than write it off as a tax loss, decided to concoct a use for it. He then drew up a list of things you could not do, such as throw the ball, and an industry was born, with the game as a sideline, where the profit was limitless, provided you made the game constantly trickier. That is why 17 more holes were added, all so different as to require the industry to sell you as many different clubs, and when even these yielded inadequate profits, go out with shovels and dig bunkers, which led to a whole new species of club, and even more painful and humiliating contortion. No surprise that Hitler committed suicide in one.

With all these clubs and a body misshapen by their demands, man was clearly in no state to drag the stuff around, allowing a caring industry to ply him not only with bags, trolleys and karts, but with special shoes to tether him to the ground while swinging his ruins about, and special gloves to stop the clubs blistering his hands, and distinctively garish trousers to offset (inadequately) the risk of other golfers felling him, and 189 books called *Improve Your Swing*, which don't, because the industry wants you to buy the 190th.

Yet, having worked all this out as I stood rooted on my very first round, it struck me that I could have got it all wrong. Might God have wanted man to play golf, after all? Did He, sitting back on the seventh day, say: I'll call it Sunday, and I'll give them golf. They will all start imperfect, and I shall send them out with their imperfections, and I shall give them all manner of hazards along the way, and if improving touches them with pride, I shall make them worse; they will have days of joy, and days of despair, and each will test them after its own fashion, and from time to time I shall people the earth with saints like Hogan and Nicklaus and Woods, to set examples and to point the way of Truth, and the authorised version of My laws shall be constantly revised, to keep them on the hop, so that Man, and Woman that is born of Man, shall trudge the courses of the earth in fair weather and in foul, and be tested at every tree and rough and bog and bit that lies a foot outside the railings, and − just when things are looking up − dumb caddies shall poke an illegal 15th club into their bags to drive them nuts, and though they can never be perfect, it is in their striving that they shall become good.

More yet: even as Mrs Coren lowered me into the tub that night and went off giggling to broach the liniment, it occurred to me that perhaps Elysium might be nothing but a wondrous golf course, where the eternal day was free alike of hail or crosswind, and where we shall all be reborn with short rubber legs and straight left arms and all the other boons divinely withheld from us on Earth, and our swings shall all be perfect and all our putts plumb-straight. Either that, or you won't stand an earthly, or rather, a heavenly, of getting in if you're anything less than scratch; and, even then, you'll have to know Somebody. In which case, I may have left it a bit late, on both counts.

77

Queening It

Since today is HM the Queen's unofficial birthday, I know that you will want me not only to wish her many happy unofficial returns on all our behalfs, but also to take this opportunity to reply to those countless thousands of you who wrote to me regarding the recent Buckingham Palace statement that the Queen was exempt, 'by reason of her special position', from the law requiring her subjects to wear a rear seatbelt. Were there, you clamoured to learn, any other special dispensations which Her Majesty alone enjoyed?

The reason that I have not replied earlier is because, not surprisingly, there turned out to be a huge amount of painstaking research involved; but I'm delighted to tell you that I am now, at last, in a position to publish in the national interest what I hope with all my heart is a usefully informative – if by no means comprehensive – list.

When not travelling by car, for example, Her Majesty is uniquely entitled to stand upstairs on buses. Should she spit, however, she is liable to the same fine as anyone else, although she would, of course, be given time to pay. On trains, she is allowed to smoke in the lavatories, but not cigars or pipes. She may also lean out of the window without penalty, except on InterCity routes. On the London Underground, she may not go up a down escalator, or vice versa, but she is allowed to jump over the barrier if she hears her Tube train coming, provided she has a valid ticket for the journey. When flying, she is not permitted to get up before the plane has come to a complete halt, but she does not have to take care when opening the overhead lockers. She is, of course, allowed to lean her bicycle against shop windows.

Sport, as you might expect, is a somewhat more complex juridical area for Her Majesty. When bowling, she is permitted to deliver more than one bouncer per over – except in one-day matches – but she is nevertheless required to observe current ECB dress codes and not wear a headscarf when batting or fielding. She can be given out lbw, but never stumped, and in the unfortunate event of a run out, it is her partner who must surrender his wicket, irrespective of fault. As to football, the Queen is allowed, when playing in goal, to move before a penalty is struck, and would not normally be sent off for bad language, unless violence were involved. In rugger, she does not need to call for a mark or leave the field when bleeding, and in tennis she may abuse her racket as much as she likes. In athletic competition, she is allowed four attempts at the high jump and, when throwing the hammer, to put one foot, but not both, outside the circle. The Queen is also uniquely permitted to carry a spare baton in the 4 x 400 relay, in case she drops one. In snooker, she is permitted to pot the six remaining colours in any order she chooses. Should her opponent go down during a boxing match, Her Majesty is not required to walk to a neutral corner.

She is allowed to busk on her highway, but not in public houses which do not have a music licence. In zoos (with the exception of Whipsnade), Her Majesty is permitted to feed the animals.

When it comes to shopping, the Queen is allowed to go through the checkout marked '6 items or less' with 7 items or more, but no special dispensation applies in regard to taking the trolley from the premises. In Post Offices, staff may not ask her to go to the next counter, and in petrol stations she does not have to switch off the engine while filling up, though she must take the cigarette out of her mouth. She is allowed to bring her dog into foodshops, but if it widdles against anything, she is not exempt from prosecution, provided a notice to that effect is prominently displayed.

Should, however, a notice be prominently displayed in any public place stating that bill stickers will be prosecuted, Her Majesty may safely ignore this, just as she may with impunity disregard any injunction to leave these premises as she would wish to find them. She is not, mind, exempt from the law in the matter of spraying graffiti, and if told to use the footbath before entering a public swimming pool, she is legally obliged to comply. She is allowed to drop litter only in the royal parks, but may walk on the grass wherever she takes a fancy to do so.

And finally, when driving – in addition to the seatbelt dispensation with which we began all this – Her Majesty is also allowed to hoot after 11 pm, and overtake in the Blackwall Tunnel. If she were to park on a double-yellow line, however, her car would be liable to be towed away, but only by a peer of the realm, with a silken rope.

78

Domestic Drama

In common with all who figured (or rather, didn't) in last week's news about plummeting audiences, I don't go to the theatre much, these days. I cannot handle it as once I could. Theatre drains me, now. Theatregoers will maintain that that is precisely what it is supposed to do, it is why man first put on a crude bark mask, painted his feet blue, and began hitting himself on the head with a pig's bladder to the atonal accompaniment of a three-holed bullrush; and I have no argument with that. It is simply that, as I grow older, I find that the emotional sturdiness of my earlier years daily grows feebler. An evening of theatre leaves me wrecked.

Especially when it is a long evening of theatre, like the one I recently experienced. Major, in every sense: an eight-hour performance of such extraordinary dramatic breadth, variety, and intensity that the dreamt recollection of it, several days on, can still hinge me upright on my midnight mattress, sweating and jabbering.

The performance began at 6 p.m., with a bourgeois *bonne-bouche* of an opening scene that had a touch of Coward about it, a smidgeon of Rattigan, a whiff of Ayckbourn. Set in a London bedroom, it features a woman who cannot find her other earring and a man who cannot find his other cufflink shouting increasingly barbed questions at one another about state of clothes, choice of restaurant, means of transport, location of tickets, future of marriage, and so on. They are about to phone lawyers when the doorbell rings. It is an Estonian asylum-seeker with a clapped-out Vauxhall, saying he was booked to take them to the Garlic Theatre in Leicester, he has looked in map, is long way, everyone must go quick quick. The husband explains, not without hand signals, about the Garrick Theatre off Leicester Square and the Estonian trudges off to sit in the Vauxhall for an hour, swearing. The next scene, which owes much to Beckett, is set in what seems to be a skip. It is in fact a Vauxhall, stuck in a contraflow outside Lewisham. The three occupants are screaming at one another. None of them knows why they are outside Lewisham. After a while, an old man bearing an uncanny resemblance to Harold Pinter punches out the windscreen, pokes his head through, and gives them complex instructions about how to get from Lewisham to Leicester Square

Act II opens in the foyer of the Garrick Theatre, half an hour after the opening of *Feelgood*, with the couple trying to discover the secret of why people take £32 a seat off you and will not allow you to take the seat itself just because you have been in Lewisham, stuck in a play that has been going on while the play you have come to see has already started. The answer seems to be that Tom Stoppard has a lot to answer for, although there is some question about whether the question was Michael Frayn's. The husband goes to the stalls bar at this point and shouts at a lot of staff who aren't there. Eventually someone turns up and sells him two large whiskies for a sum which would have allowed him, in the days when he started going to the theatre, to buy his own pub.

We next see the couple (in an engaging little *trompe de théâtre* which invites comparison with Jean Cocteau) passing from the stage of their play into the auditorium to watch *Feelgood*, a piece in which a lot of actors shout at one another to scant purpose, as far as the husband can see an hour later, when he re-emerges into the foyer, carrying his wife, who always falls asleep. Both are starving, but (qv. Act I) neither has booked anywhere, because each had, of course, assumed that the other had done it. The wife says never mind, The Ivy is just around the corner.

Act III opens outside The Ivy. It might have opened inside, but for the fact that the next free table is on 3 March 2004, provided there is a cancellation. Since they cannot wait that long, the couple spend the next hour wandering through theatreland in a scene offering more than a passing nod to Edward Bond, looking no longer for a restaurant but for an all-night chemist to deal with the sprain of the husband's ankle caused by being shoved off the pavement by a mob of several hundred theatregoers with tattoos and stapled noses. Eventually they find a chemist, but it is so full of theatregoers waiting for midnight to transform their prescriptions into something to stuff into their stapled noses that the couple decide to hail a cab home.

But there is, of course, nothing to hail; so, poignantly redolent both of *Father Courage and his Swollen Bloody Ankle* and *Long Day's Journey Into North West London*, the play ends with the couple limping home at 2 a.m. to wonder aloud whether they should go to the theatre much, these days.

79

Road Rage

Last night, at the Camden Odeon, bang in the middle of *Bridget Jones's Diary*, I got my old trouble back. I hadn't had my old trouble for nearly 40 years. I last got it at the Swiss Cottage Odeon, bang in the middle of *Dr No*. You will say, aha, his old trouble clearly has something to do with Ursula Andress wriggling out of her rubber bikini, that would explain why it came back last night, it was on account of Renée Zellweger wriggling out of her rubber knickers, I rather think we have the measure of Mr Coren's old trouble, do we not – but you are wrong. While it is true that my old trouble is about cinema distraction, when some minor feature suddenly lurches the mind away from the major feature and strands it in an obsessional limbo while the major feature spools on unnoticed, it has nothing to do with snappy latex, or even snappy women. What it has everything to do with is snappy cars.

Now, quiz most filmgoers about James Bond's motor and they will begin rabbiting on about the Aston Martin which could deploy greater firepower than Nato while catapulting undesirable hitch-hikers through its roof. That is because they have forgotten 007's first car. It was a Sunbeam Alpine. I have not forgotten, because I had one, too. I had driven to *Dr No* in it in 1962, but it was getting on for 1963 by the time I got there, because the Swiss Cottage Odeon was at the top of Belsize Road, a 1 in 45 gradient, and the Alpine was the slowest sports car in the world. Which was why, a scant few minutes into the film, my old trouble came on: when Bond got into his Alpine, I did not see the exemplar of butch chic which product placement wanted me to see. I saw a gullible dork who had recently driven out of his local Rootes showroom leaving cackling salesmen rolling about on the floor. Things grew worse when, a little later, Bond effortlessly eluded the doctor's thugs in a highspeed car chase: an Alpinist myself, I knew that, had the arch-villain been not Dr No but United Dairies, their milk-float would have caught Bond within 50 yards. This was a bogus film, with a bogus hero, and, for the remainder of it, I could concentrate on nothing else: when Ursula Andress splashed out of the surf, it might as well have been Thora Hird.

I flogged my doddering Alpine soon after that to some Bondabee sucker, and bought an Austin-Healey 3000. A true sports car: had weedy Bond got in and turned the engine on, he would probably have fainted at the thunder. And every film it appeared in got the casting right: it was always driven by a raffish cove with wrists of steel and a bulldog briar. Never a twinge of my old trouble there. Offscreen, I drove mine with joy until 1969, when I sold it with grief, and bought the car which, last night, did bring on the old trouble again. I had to do that because in 1969 Mrs Coren gave birth to a *Times* columnist, and when I went to collect the pair of them from Queen Charlotte's Hospital, we could squeeze *The Times* columnist's carrycot into the little slot behind the seats only by shoving the seats so far forward that our knees covered our ears. Nor, when it began to rain at Shepherds Bush, could we shut the roof because *The Times* columnist was in the way, so he got wet. It didn't bother him, because he knew he would get at least three paragraphs out of it some day, but it bothered us.

The next day I chopped the Healey in for a secondhand Mercedes 220SEb cabriolet. It was not only the biggest convertible in the world, it was the safest: conceived out of postwar nostalgia for the Tiger tank, it was two tons of iron and walnut, with a three-ply reinforced hood able to protect *The Times* columnist from anything the heavens could chuck at him. For Jerry, it was a snook cocked at the shade of Bomber Harris, but for me it was a rite of passage: I was a family man now, tasked not to boy-race, but to trundle and protect. And that is why, last night, the old trouble came back.

In *Bridget Jones's Diary*, Hugh Grant plays a cad. We do not know he is a cad, though, until he takes the cuddly eponym off for a lively weekend; and the egregious signifier of his caddishness is his car. An autobuff's veteran one-off that gives the finger to the common Ferrari or Porsche, it is patently a Flash Harry's car; for that is what 30 years have done to the Mercedes 220SEb cabriolet. It irritated me no end; it ruined the film; it left the second half unnoticed. I just sat there thinking: this car was not put on earth so that smirking jerks could pull dippy women, it was given to us so that solid men could poddle invulnerably through the traffic with *The Times* columnist and his sister the *Observer* poker correspondent on the back seat, punching one another and shouting: 'Dad, Dad, are we there yet, Dad?'

80

Southern Discomfort

Most *Times* readers, I suspect, will not have been nearly as excited as I to spot a tiddly paragraph tucked away in a page 11 cranny of the newspaper's Monday edition. That is because most *Times* readers spend fruitful lives in worthwhile employment, instead of frittering away their brief span staring out of a window and wondering whether they will ever write a blockbuster novel. I, on the other hand, have spent 40 years busting my block in the effort to do exactly that, to no good end: because I cannot come up with a novel, in either sense, plot. On those infrequent occasions when I think I have thought of one, second thoughts serve only to make me think of who thought of it first. Bloody Tolstoy, I think, bloody Smollett.

Or, rather, used to think. Because, since Monday, I have been unable to think of anything but. I am thicker with plots than a Cabinet sauna, thanks to Ms Alice Randall. Here is that paragraph in full: 'The estate of Margaret Mitchell is seeking to block publication of a novel that tells *Gone With The Wind* from a slave's perspective. Alice Randall said that her novel *The Wind Done Gone* is an antidote to a text that has hurt generations of Afro-Americans.' The woman is a genius: though I do not know whether that genius extends to her writing – the book may be full of scenes showing mobs of enthusiastic spectators high-fiving one another and shouting

'Yo!' as Atlanta burns to a frazzle, or Rhett Butler being floored by an expertly swung banjo – frankly, my dears, I don't give a damn. For Alice's true genius lies in the invention of the obverse plot: everything that has hitherto been written can henceforth be rewritten from the other side.

My only problem now is selection. Patently, revisionism will, these days, have to go hand in hand with political rectitude – no publisher would touch *Sophie's Choice* written from Himmler's point of view – but, if anything, that casts my net even wider. Should I take a crack at *Lady Chatterley's Husband*, in which Mellors falls for the bloke in the wheelchair? Or *Ahab the Fishmonger*, written by a tragic hero ('Call me Moby') threatened with extinction at the hands of the catsmeat industry, a bestselling blubber from start to finish? What about *Robinson's Jam*, in which the cannibals, gamely refusing to chuck in the sponge and give up their time-honoured ethnic cuisine, not only barbecue Man Friday but also imaginatively extend their diet to include white meat? Then again, could there ever have been a minor fictional figure more constantly abused, and therefore more deserving of his own 15 minutes, or perhaps seconds, of retributive fame than the eponymous hero of *Portnoy's* ★★★★?

I was juggling all these options and more – having somewhat regretfully rejected *The Chumps of the Light Brigade*, metrically recounted from the point of view of a Russian gun-crew laughing fit to bust, on the ground, that poetry was not my bag – when a little lightbulb suddenly appeared in a bubble above my head, to be replaced an instant later by the dustjacket of *Snow White and the Seven Winners For Whom Stature Is No Impediment*. Not the catchiest of titles perhaps, but if you're looking for mega-sales nothing beats a book that does what it says on the tin, and here we have a community of dedicated but impoverished titchy mineworkers, living, through no fault of their own, a celibate life in a hole in the ground, who suddenly stumble upon a terrific-looking brunette, take her back to their pitiful premises, show her more caring concern than she would ever get from men twice their height, but – shrewdly thinking ahead – never lay a finger on her. And what is their reward for this impressive combination of kindness and restraint? She takes off with the first tall handsome horse-borne toff who catches her eye. Do the little guys take this lying down (admittedly not perceptibly different from their taking it standing up)? Not this time around, because they have figured it all out first. They have observed the loving couple for some time, disguised as shrubs (a boon of smallness), and they have photographs, they have tapes, they have tabloid contacts, they are sitting, wise to the irony, on a goldmine. They get to be as rich as Bernie Ecclestone or Paul Daniels. They live happily ever after.

Should I start typing it right now? Possibly, if I can just get this idea for a smash-hit play out of my head. I once saw something called, I think, *Rosencrantz and Guildenstern are Dead*. Might have been *Deaf*, but anyway, they were these two assassins, and I thought at the time how much better it would have been if the play had focused on their victim instead; so I might well take a crack at that first. Am I spoilt for choice, or what?

81

Poles Apart

There are some 12 million married couples in Britain, and I am confident that Mrs Coren and I speak for all of them when I say we are flabbergasted at the hysterical adulation currently being lavished on Mr and Mrs Thornewill. We are flummoxed; we are gobsmacked; we are stumped; and, yes, we are not a little gutted. We cannot for the life of us understand what all the fuss is about. Why are Mr and Mrs Thornewill being lionised and feted, simply for becoming the first married couple to walk to the North Pole?

What kind of achievement is that? To walk to the North Pole, you point the compass at the horizon and put one foot after the other. There being neither roads nor car, one spouse does not have to read the map while the other spouse drives; there is no risk of yelling, grabbing, chucking maps out of windows while swerving dangerously, or turning this bloody thing round right now and going straight home, it wasn't my idea to come in the first place. Nor, as night falls, is anybody sitting in the middle of nowhere interrogated as to why they didn't have the sense to fill up when they had the chance, or invited to explain in words of one syllable why they won't stop and ask someone the way, since there is no one to ask, unless you speak bear. As for finding mutually satisfactory overnight accommodation, transarctic spouses do not have to run in and out of a dozen hotels to find a room one of them neglected to book in advance, or end up sleeping foetally on the back seat while drunks widdle on their bumpers; transarctic spouses have a folding nylon hotel on their little sled, and when they are tucked up snugly inside it and fancy dinner, they do not go nuts trying to catch the waiter's eye or ringing a room-service voicemail that never rings back, they simply pop a bubble-pack and chomp on a nourishing pellet that tastes of nothing requiring comment. Neither of them orders a second bottle when they know what it does to them, your father was the same, nor do they engage in stand-up rows about toenails in the bidet or hairs on the soap.

Upon arrival at the North Pole, no married couple will suffer recriminatory disappointment. Of course it is not finished. It is not even started. There is no lying ratbag of a manager to wave a brochure at, there are no rooms better than the one they thought they'd booked, and the swimming pool is a reproachless umpteen miles across, albeit solid. Neither spouse will find the place infuriatingly classier or tackier than the other had led them to believe: the clothes they stand up in will be absolutely perfect, because, if they try to change into anything else, they will not be standing up for much longer, they will turn blue, topple, and snap.

Polar couples do not bicker about what to do during the day, either: shopping, scuba-diving, sightseeing, paragliding, gambling, visiting the doll museum, lying by the pool staring at that woman, I wasn't staring, and so forth, are unavailable for marital dispute. What polar couples do during the day is walk. They do not even have the option of standing still. If one of them stands still for more than a few seconds, he or she becomes a permanent topographical feature. Nor are they required to argue nightly about whose turn it is to get up at the crack of dawn and bag a lounger: any territorial claims that German couples might have entertained about the Arctic Riviera have so far proved to be atypically muted, and while there must always be a chance that, some day, Herr und Frau Jerry will be sprinting out six months before sun-up to begin oiling one another at minus 60 degrees, it was not, as I understand it, a problem for the Thornewills.

But did this first mould-breaking couple run, as so many of Britain's other 12 million have run, the risk of holiday boredom? Unlikely: while there are, admittedly, precious few topics of Arctic conversation, all of them white, no couple can manage more than two seconds of speech before tugging their balaclavas back up, lest their lips go solid and chip off. Since most duologue therefore consists of waving mittens about, the likelihood of vacational chat occasioning marital ennui is remote; unless, of course, one of the Thornewills was a semaphore freak.

In short, their chilly stroll was a doddle from start to finish. I was not in the least surprised when Fiona hugged Mike and confided to the phalanx of goggling hacks that 'the trip has brought us much closer together. I really want to encourage other couples so that they too can achieve their lifetime's dreams.' Bang on the money, Mrs Thornewill: look for me and Mrs Coren this very weekend, and you will find us shopping at Sleds 'R' Us.

82

All Quiet On The Charity Front

*A*s you know, many supermarkets, local authorities, and even some branches of the Royal British Legion have stopped issuing pins with poppies this year, lest people not merely prick their fingers, but also claim compensation for wounds. Understandable, given these poignant memoirs of one veteran Poppy Day survivor, which I make no excuse, on this special day, for quoting:

There was three of us up there that morning, in the thick of it as per usual, me, Chalky White and Nobby Clarke. The rain was coming down stair-rods, the wind went through you like a wossname, knife, but the mud was the worst. Slip off the pavement and you was done for; the lads do not call white vans whizz-bangs for nothing, you never hear the one that gets you.

Anyway, we was all keeping our heads down, because there was poppy-sellers all over; they'd moved up in the night and now they was in position everywhere, but you couldn't hardly see most of them, they are crafty buggers, you got to give them that, you see an empty doorway, you reckon you're all right, and suddenly they spring out from nowhere, they are on you before you know it. That is how they got Chalky that morning: we was creeping along, staying close to the wall, we was all but at the pub, we could hear blokes getting 'em in, we could smell roll-ups, and then Chalky only goes and sticks his head over the top for a shufti, and suddenly me and Nobby hears that terrible rattle what is like nothing else on God's earth, and poor old Chalky finds hisself looking down the wrong end of a collecting tin.

Course, me and Nobby stood up as well, it is one for all and all for one in our mob, and we marched out, heads up, bags of swank, and Chalky shouts: 'Wiffel ist es, Kamerad?' because he has always been a bit of a wag, he does not let things get him down, nil carborundum, and this woman takes his ten pee and she gives him one of them looks they have, they are not like us, never will be, and hands him a poppy and a pin, and he says, 'Aren't you going to pin it on for me, Fraulein?' and she says, 'You want a lot for ten pee,' so I say, 'Leave it out, Chalky, it is not worth it, I'll do it, come here,' and I hold the poppy against his lapel and I take the pin and Chalky says, 'Is this the Big Push they're always going on about?' and I laugh so much that the pin goes and sticks right in my finger.

Blood gushed out. I must have lost very nearly a blob. 'Stone me!' yells Nobby. 'That is a Blighty one and no mistake. You will have to go straight home and put an Elastoplast on it.' Chalky looks at the woman. 'This is the bravest man I know,' he says. 'He has got his knees brown, he has done his bit, but that does not mean he likes the taste of cold steel up him. Look at that finger of his. It will not grow old as we that are left grow old. It may very well end up with a little scar on it. It might even turn sceptic and drop off into some corner of a foreign wossname, he will never be able to find it. So gimme my ten pee back.'

At this, despite the agony and spots before the eyes, I wade in, too; do not call me a hero, mind, I was just doing what any man would do in the circumstances, you would do the same. 'As soon I get this finger seen to,' I inform her, 'I shall be using it to dial my brief!'

At this, she lets out a shriek, chucks the ten pee at us, and runs off. Typical or what? They do not have no bottle, poppy-sellers: oh, sure, they may look hot as mustard quartered safe behind their lines, parading up and down outside Harrods in their spotless Barbours and their cashmere twinsets, with the sun winking off of their diamand brooches, and all smelling of Channel 4, but it is a very different matter up the sharp end in Lewisham, there is more to poppying out here than bull and bloody blanco. Me and Nobby and Chalky watched her skedaddle, and we gave a bit of a cheer, and then Nobby took my feet and Chalky held me under the arms, and they carried me past a number of material witnesses into the Rat and Cockle, and Chalky went off to get them in, and Nobby lit a fag and put it in my mouth, and he said: 'Could have been worse, mate – suppose it had been her what had stuck it in Chalky? He would have been pushing up daisies by now.'

'She might have got both of you,' I said. Nobby shook his head. 'No chance. One of 'em tried once, caught me off guard, took a quid off of me and before I could stop her she had shoved a pin straight through my lapel. It might have done me serious mischief if it wasn't for the Bible I always keep in my breast-pocket. I found it in a hotel bedroom, you know.'

'Bloody lucky,' I said. 'It could so easily have been a towel.'

'Or a rubber shower-mat,' said Chalky, setting down the drinks.

'A man needs a bit of luck,' said Nobby, 'out here.'

83

Ah, Yes, I Remember It Well!

We had been watching happily for the best part of a bottle when my wife said: 'Oh, blast, I think a dog's going to come round the corner in a minute.'
In a minute, a dog came round the corner.

'Well, that's it, then,' she said. 'We've seen it before.'

'I thought we might have done,' I said, 'half an hour ago. When they pulled the body out of the water with the boathook.'

'Why didn't you say anything?' she said.

'I wasn't sure,' I said. 'They're always pulling bodies out of the water with boathooks. I might have been remembering an old *Morse*, or an old *Wexford*, or an old *Bergerac.*'

'Or an old *Taggart.*'

'Or an old *Taggart*,' I said. 'Exactly.'

'Instead of an old *Frost*,' she said.

I looked back at the old *Frost*. 'We could carry on watching,' I said. 'After all, it's only a boathook and a dog, we don't know how it ends. We don't know who dunnit.'

'We might remember,' she said. 'There's another hour to go. We might suddenly remember after 45 minutes. I think there's a bit, later on, where he argues with his Superintendent. It might jog our memory. It might all come back.'

'They all argue with their Superintendents,' I said. 'It didn't jog our memory in that *Midsomer Murders* we watched last week.'

'No, it didn't,' she said. 'What jogged our memories in that was the nurse on the bicycle.'

'It didn't jog mine,' I said. 'I was enjoying it. You could've kept quiet about it. You could've just carried on watching.'

'No, I couldn't. As soon as I saw the nurse on the bike, I remembered, and then I remembered there were two slit throats coming up, and then I remembered the killer was the twerp in the blazer. I couldn't have just sat there after that could I?'

'He was only pretending to be a twerp,' I said.

She looked at me.

'Hang on,' she said, 'if you remembered as well, what was the point in either of us watching?'

'I didn't remember then,' I said. 'I've only just remembered now.'

'You might have remembered then,' she said. 'We might have both carried on watching, with just me knowing we'd seen it after the bike bit, until something else happened half an hour later which jogged your memory, and I'd have been watching for half an hour for nothing.'

'It's called marriage,' I said. 'It is fraught with that kind of thing. I might have not had my memory jogged at all, and then at least one of us would've been happy.'

'Happy,' she said, 'is putting it a bit strong. I didn't even think much of this one . . .' she waved her glass at the screen '. . . when we saw it the first time.'

'You didn't say that while we were watching it this time,' I said, 'for the hour before the dog came round the corner.'

'It wasn't the hour I didn't think much of the first time,' she said. 'Now I know it was the one with the dog, I can remember not thinking much of the whole thing, after it had finished the first time.'

I reached for the remote, and switched off. 'Don't you want to know who dunnit?' she said.

'Not enough to sit through it for 45 minutes – until he

has the row with his Superintendent,' I said. 'Even if it doesn't jog my memory, it might jog yours, and I wouldn't want to carry on sitting through it knowing you knew who dunnit and just weren't saying.'

'But we're not even certain this is the one where he's going to have the row,' she said. 'It might be the one where his dim but lovable sergeant asks for a transfer to traffic division because his wife is pregnant again and wants him back home at a reasonable hour. If it is that one, the car blows up.'

'No, I remember the one where the car blows up, and it didn't have a boathook or a dog that came round the corner. Anyway, it wasn't his car. Frost's car has never blown up. You're thinking of Dalgleish's car.'

'The Triumph roadster with the dickie seat?'

'No,' I said. 'That is Bergerac's car.'

'There's one *Morse* we've seen three times,' she said. 'It was cars that reminded me. Morse's nice old red Jag got dented. You winced.'

'I could only have winced the first time,' I said. 'I wouldn't have forgotten a thing like that.'

'Who are you kidding?' she said.

I picked up the programme guide, and peered at it. 'God, I hate the summer,' I said, after a bit. 'Would we have seen *Have I Got Old News For You*, with Eddie Izzard? Before it had the Old in it, I mean?'

'Is there anything left in that bottle?' she said.

84

I Blame the Dealers

The report in yesterday's *Times* that Pietro Forquet, Italy's most venerated bridge master, had, during Friday's national championships, been tested for drugs, will have stunned players the world over. Not because, as non-players might jump to conclude, bridge is the very last game in which drugs could play a significant part, but because, as every player knows, it is the very first.

What point was there in testing Signor Forquet for substances so integral to the game since the dawn of bidding that, without them, it can never properly be played at all?

Let us illustrate this with a hand played in the opening match of last weekend's Cricklewood Championships. North, South (Mrs North), East, and West (Mrs East) have begun the evening with their narcotics of choice, large dry martinis, straight up, no twist, and have now sat down at the card table – East somewhat heavily, with the result that the table lurches, spilling their pencils on to the carpet. North, South and West glance sharply at East, who declares that the table must have a wobbly leg. West responds that it is not the table that has wobbly legs. North and South say nothing, but exchange a glance, noticeably irritating East, who suspects some tacit coded message. Each player now bends to retrieve his pencil but North, in straightening up, bangs his head on the corner of the table, to which South says Oh God, not you, too, North's response being What do you mean not me, too, at which East intervenes with Yes, what do you mean, not him, too, and West counters with You know what she means not him, too. North in emollient reply refills everyone's glass, deals, and opens one spade.

East passes, and South replies with I seem to have 14 cards. West says I have 11, North swears and says It's these cards, they're sticky, it must be the gin, and East says it's the gin all right, and now exchanges his own tacit coded message with West. After the reshuffle, North deals, again, goes white, and, before speaking, lights a cigarette. East says those are my fags, I thought you'd given up, which South answers with, yes he has, he is nervous, he has obviously got an amazing hand. North shouts Thank you, partner, shall I just tell them what I'm holding, has a coughing fit, and opens two clubs, indicating slam potential. East passes, and South responds with You're sweating, have you had your pill? West says What does he take, is it a beta-blocker, I didn't think they mixed with alcohol, whereupon East replies, They don't, it affects your judgement, he probably doesn't have a two-club opener at all, I bid two diamonds, to which North shouts that he can't do that, he has already passed, but East argues that he can, because South hasn't bid yet. North now brings his fist down on the table with such force that South's drink topples into her lap. She rushes out for a cloth, dropping her cards, face up, on to the table, thereby revealing more than enough points to have made the grand slam her partner invited.

While South is away, West pours herself another large one, and, grown consequently maudlin, stares at South's cards until the tears begin rolling down her cheeks. East says What is it now? and West sobs I never get cards like that, I never ever get good cards, to which West responds It wouldn't matter much if you did, and West howls What is that supposed to mean? and runs out, just as South returns, in a blouse and slacks, saying It may interest you to know that I have had to chuck that dress in the bin, it is ruined, whose deal is it, where the hell is West? In response, there is a thud and assorted tinkles from beyond the room, and, after some time, West shuffles unsteadily in. She is covered in earth and petals, and opens with You ought to do something about that rug, to which North responds What rug? encouraging the reply You know what bloody rug, the one that slides and could kill people, evoking South's intervention of How can it slide, it has that big Edwardian pedestal jardinière standing on it, the one my mother left me. West says Pass. South asks East what she means by Pass, is this some convention I haven't come across, and East responds you have now, it means there isn't a jardinière standing on it any more, look at the state of her.

It is at this point that the distraught West gropes frantically inside her handbag, leading North, South and East to conclude that she is looking for a mirror and make-up, but West is actually engaged in a sly finesse, since what she is really after is her Valium. Before anyone can intervene, she has popped four pills, washed them down with the remaining contents of the jug, and slumped face down on the table. East deals.

85

The Long Goodbye

If I shove up the sash of my loft window tonight, for the last time, and I risk my neck with fraying sashcord, for the last time, by poking my head out, for the last time, an ear to the nocturnal hum of Cricklewood, shall I hear, above that hum, the cheery song of a cockney ghost? Why not? She is, after all, just a couple of hundred yards away, and tonight is her cue, if any night ever was, for song. True, she has been silent in her grave, in the cemetary at the corner of my road, since 1922, but what of that? I shall hear Marie Lloyd singing, even if nobody else does.

Because she will be telling me not to dilly-dally on the way. And she is right: I shall not dilly-dally long. Just long enough to tell you, who have dallied here with me over the long years, that, an hour or so ago, off went the van with my home packed in it. I, however, did not walk behind with my old cock linnet, I stayed behind with my old cock typewriter, because I wanted this empty house to echo, for the last time, to the skeletal rattle of the old Remington boneshaker which took down my first Cricklewood communique, 28 years ago. I shall not pass it to you from there, mind, because a lot has happened in 28 years and newspapers do not take typescript any more; I shall, in a bit, pocket it, and go off to my nice new house, and transcribe it onto a computer which will phone it to *The Times*. I am not, if you are reaching for the

432

Kleenex, doing this out of mawkishness; I am doing it because if I just went off and did it on my computer, I could not write about being in Cricklewood, since my computer is on the van, and when it gets out of the van, in an hour or so, it will not be in Cricklewood.

All right, pluck the Kleenex: I cannot fib to you, you know me too well, I am doing this partly out of mawkishness. Anyone leaving the house in which he has spent half his life will be a mawk. Do you, by the way, know what a mawk is? It is a maggot. At least, it was when Old Norsemen were naming things, but if you were pondering why this word should gradually have turned into what it means now, stop. Especially with Marie up the road, and with me feeling, tonight, a trifle mortal, too, and furthermore, sensing around me the ghosts – though sceptics among you are welcome to call them memories – of all those who have passed temporarily through this house during those 28 years, and have now passed permanently elsewhere.

If I look down into the garden from this open window, I can see them all on the lawn, drinking, talking, eating, laughing, sniffing the roses, plucking the raspberries, peering in the pond for fish, poking in the shrubbery for cricket balls, all that. It is, of course, pitch dark down there, so you wouldn't be able to see them, but I can. I can even see me, though it requires something of an effort to recognise him, because it is his first day in the garden: he is slim, he has hair, he has one child on his shoulders and one in his arms; a feat he would find a little tricky now, since, in a trice, both have become a mite more cumbersome.

I can hear the trees in the dark tonight, because there is a breeze. The slim hairy one garlanded with kids could not have heard them, not because there was no breeze, then, but because there were no trees, except for the giant acacia in the middle of the lawn, the focus of my eye-line for 28 years every time that, stumped, I looked up from the daily keyboard. Could be, what, a million times? Two million? A lot of stumping has gone on, up here. But all the other trees – the maple, the cedar, the cherry, the chestnut, the beech, the hawthorn, the fig, the crab apple, the eucalyptus, the thugia, the pear, the photinia – came to the garden in little tubs, and most of them are higher than this loft, now, which is why the breeze is having such sussurant fun in them. It is probably having so much fun that some of the leaves are falling, though I cannot see them, because what I can do is sniff autumn on that breeze, not the best of scents for mawkies. We should have sold the house in the spring, but the trees looked so good, and the lawn so lush, and the plants so buddie, that we thought, okay, house, one last summer.

There is only one song about Cricklewood. The wizards in the BBC archives found it for me a few years back, when I was, as so often, banging on about the place for Radio 4. Its opening couplet runs: 'Cricklewood, Cricklewood, you stole my life away / For I was young and beautiful, but now I'm old and gray.' Not much of a song, perhaps, hardly one for Marie, but it'll do for me, tonight. It is time to close the typewriter and slip away. Tomorrow to fresh woods and crickles new.